LIFE
WITHOUT
RESERVATIONS

Growing Up at the Famed
Ambassador Hotel 1921 to 1938

A MOTHER-DAUGHTER MEMOIR

CARLYN FRANK BENJAMIN
LISA BENJAMIN GILMOUR

CHRISTMAS LAKE PRESS

Published by Christmas Lake Press 2026
www.christmaslakepress.com
Copyright © 2026 by Lisa Benjamin Gilmour
ISBN 978-1-960865-41-0

Cover: Carlyn Frank, age 14, Los Angeles.

Half-title page: Carlyn Frank (at head of table) and friends at the Cocoanut Grove on Christmas Eve. Ambassador Hotel, Los Angeles, 1934. (Photo by Dick Whittington, courtesy of Marc Wanamaker/Bison Archives)

LIFE
WITHOUT
RESERVATIONS

Dedication

Dear Mom,

I'm so proud of the book you have written and grateful to have finished it in your honor.

What an amazing journey this has been. I wish you were here to read it with me.

Love,
Lisa

ACKNOWLEDGMENTS

It is with deep appreciation and gratitude that I acknowledge the many people who supported me on the road to completing my mother's memoir.

I know with all my heart if I had not met Martin Turnbull, the wonderful author of many popular novels about the golden age of Hollywood, you might not be reading this page today. For the past four years, Martin has been my coach, my sounding board, my cheerleader, my shrink, and my inspiration. He believed in me when I was sure I was never going to stop editing and doubted whether anyone would read my book. Martin assured me that it was absolutely normal for an author, especially a new one, to feel that way. Martin, you are the North star that helped me keep my promise to my mother to finish what she began.

To the two dearest people in my life: my wonderful, supportive, and loving husband, Mark, who read chapters of the manuscript out loud so I could hear where the bumps were, and my son, Jamison, who told me nearly every day how proud Grandma would be and how proud he is of me. You both kept me anchored and steady, especially during those very tough months in 2023.

To two of my best friends, Elizabeth Kahn and Sharon Rich. Thank you for being my unofficial beta readers, reading countless versions of my manuscript and giving me super-helpful, honest feedback. Thank you for your keen eyes, editing expertise, consistent encouragement, and your loving friendship.

Thank you to my official beta readers: Penny Billings, Penny Collins, Adelaide Kahn-Fowler, Debra Shinn, and Laurie Woodrow, who were one hundred percent committed to the task at hand, providing insightful and thoughtful feedback that helped me immensely in the early stages of the manuscript.

With over one hundred images in the book, I have several librarians and archivists to thank who helped me with my many requests for images, permissions, copyright attributions, etc. What an education they gave me. Christine Adolph, Librarian, Photo Collection, Los Angeles Public Library; Madeline Northcote-Smith, Reader Services Coordinator, The Huntington; Genevieve Maxwell, Reference Services Librarian, The Huntington; Marlene Moser, Reference Archivist at Architecture & Design Collection, UCSB; Chris Nichols, Senior Editor, *Los Angeles Magazine*; Yuriy Shcherbina, Digital Manager at USC Libraries; Ben Shepard of Wrights Media; Paul R. Spitzzeri, Museum Director, Workman and Temple Family Homestead Museum; and Marc Wanamaker of Bison Archives for bringing me his rich treasure trove of Ambassador Hotel images.

A special thank you to Sibylle Allgaier of Heliphoto; Harry Drake, Principal of the architectural firm Practice, for his generous help in educating me on the preservation and reconstruction challenges the firm faced when building the Robert F. Kennedy Community School that sits on the former 24-acre site of the Ambassador Hotel; and Matt Morseth of Practice, for helping me understand the lay of the land of the massive school campus in relation to where iconic elements of the Ambassador used to stand.

I want to thank other friends and family who were always interested in my progress and provided encouragement and love over the nearly six years it took to get Life *Without Reservations* over the finish line:

Laurie Yeates Adams, Ben Benjamin, Lyn Benjamin, Rachael Benjamin, Bruce Cathcart and Jaime Ullman, Annabelle Collinson, Dana and Mark Collinson, Emily Collinson, Mary Erickson, Carla Fantozzi, Cedering Fox, Jen and Larry Good, Ayn Grinstein, Pam and Pete Kennedy, Nancy Krichen, Michael Leventhal, Paul Lichenberg, Kirsten Luebkemann, Carla Malden, Kristen Reynolds, Nancy Rubin, Doug and Joanne Schwartz, Melanie Wainwright.

Christine Wolf, my official memoir coach—I knew it was a match made in heaven from our first Zoom meeting. Thank you for preparing me so thoroughly to find a publisher who would love the book. Your expertise, encouragement and friendship played a huge role in getting *Life Without Reservations* published. And speaking of which—thank you Thomas Fiffer and Julia Bobkoff of Christmas Lake Press, for your invaluable guidance, unending support, and your over-the-moon enthusiasm about my mother's story. We did it!

To Erika Rundle, my expert copyeditor, Daiana Marchesi for her meticulous typesetting, and Aaron Davis for the compelling front and back cover design of the book.

Aunt Jackie, what a gift you gave me before you passed in 2025. You helped fill in the blanks in Mom's manuscript. You challenged with humor some of the ways Mom remembered things. You were the younger sister of six years, so that may have factored into things! You called me often to tell me how much you loved what I was doing and loved how the book was coming along. Thank you to my cousin, Doug, your wonderful son, who sat at your bedside reading chapter after chapter and noting your comments in the margins. And to my cousin Dana—your amazing daughter, whom I consider my sister—thank you for believing in me and for the joy you took in seeing how much your mom loved being a part of my memoir writing journey.

And my Cookie girl. My sweet golden who was by my side for many years while I typed away.

CONTENTS

The Retelling: A Daughter's Loving Reflections

"I'd like a small bowl of oatmeal, one pancake, and crisp—very crisp—bacon. Oh, and a glass of orange juice and toasted buttered rye bread. Yes, thank you, please hurry. I need to leave for school."

This is how I always pictured my mother, Carlyn Frank Benjamin, as a young girl ordering her breakfast from room service during the nearly two decades she and her family lived at the legendary Ambassador Hotel in Los Angeles.

Around the time I was in elementary school, I can remember my mother sharing stories about how she never grew tired of exploring every nook and cranny of the hotel, especially all the fabulous shops. Enjoying lively birthday parties, lunching in the hotel's coffee shop while sitting next to famous people like Bing Crosby (who had late-night performances at the Cocoanut Grove, a premier jazz club located in the hotel), watching Olympic diving medalists and hopefuls practice in the pool, meeting Charles Lindbergh after his famous transatlantic flight, and on and on. It was truly a magical place to grow up.

Rincon Bungalow, on the grounds of the Ambassador, had been my mother's unique and beautiful family home since 1921, when my grandfather and great-grandfather were hired to manage what would become one of the most successful and iconic hotels in the world. And, for the first seventeen years of my mother's life, the magic never stopped—until one fateful morning when she learned that the family had to pack up and leave.

The year was 1938.

Although my grandparents never disclosed any details about why my grandfather's "services were no longer needed," it was in *that* moment that my mother's life would shift traumatically from one of extraordinary privilege to one that was ordinary.

Throughout my life, my mother told and retold the same stories about growing up at the Ambassador, what an enviable and sophisticated life she had led there, and the utter heartbreak of having to leave that rarefied world. By the time I entered junior high, I could easily complete the stories in my head before she finished retelling them. Her repeated reflections became irritating to me. Had I been a more mature and supportive listener, I would have been able to hear the deeper story she was telling about her life, and the anguish she endured being forced to leave the only home she knew. Still, knowing all this, it took me decades to appreciate the significance of it all. Although Mom never explicitly said the words, "My life ended at seventeen," I knew that was how she felt—her new life never seemed to count as much. And, as her only daughter, I know she had a remarkable and beautiful post-Ambassador adult life.

When sharing happy stories about her childhood and adolescence, Mom was transported right back to the first-class resort hotel that was her whole world. Located at 3400 Wilshire Boulevard in Los Angeles, between downtown and the beach, the Ambassador came to exemplify the much sought-after, enchanting, and seductive southern California lifestyle so perfectly marketed in magazines and newspapers, particularly during the 1920s and '30s.

Mom delighted in being the center of attention. As the daughter and granddaughter of the hotel management, she was adored and treated like royalty by the staff. She had the run of the place, much like the storybook character Eloise of the famed New York Plaza Hotel.

In the fall of 2004, Mom invited me to join her for what would become her last visit to her childhood home. (The Ambassador was fully demolished less than two years later, in January 2006.) I didn't think much of it but wanted Mom to have company for this emotional visit. Shuttered since 1989, it was no longer much of a home—or a hotel. The Ambassador was fenced off, with large *NO TRESPASSING* signs replacing the glowing neon marquees of years past. This stately and glamorous resort, an icon of Los Angeles history, faced a steady decline after the horrific assassination of Robert F. Kennedy in June 1968. This, coupled with the slow deterioration of the surrounding neighborhood due to drugs and crime, created the perfect storm that finally led to the Ambassador's demolition—though not without a herculean, nearly two-decade effort by the Los Angeles Conservancy and other advocates to save it.

"We're on a mission," Mom confided to me on our drive to the hotel property. Always dressed to the nines, she was wearing one of her signature St. John knit suits, navy blue with white trim and gold buttons. A look of determination shone in her eyes.

"What's our mission?" I asked.

"We're going to Rincon, the name of the bungalow where my family and I lived until I was seventeen—you remember me telling you all about it, don't you? We are going to get the sign that bears its name. I'm not going to let them destroy that, too." That sign would become the last remnant of my mother's childhood home. We drove down Wilshire Boulevard, and as we approached the demolition site, I heard her breath catch. Mom had seen it many times before, but it never failed to reopen the old wound and elicit the same gasp of despair. "I can't believe," she exclaimed, "something once so synonymous with the city couldn't be protected, not to mention the end of my childhood home."

"I know, I know, Mom. So much iconic architecture—just torn down. And what replaced it? Office buildings, parking lots, strip malls. . . It's just awful."

Mom sighed. "That's because no one values the past. And what it represents."

Mom turned into the lot and parked in front of a small kiosk where the hotel's security guard sat. Though there was little left to steal, this grumpy man—who looked straight out of central casting—seemed determined to keep this broken-down facade protected from the curious, die-hard Ambassador aficionados, who would have given anything to check in one last time. We had often seen them standing in front of the fading hotel, in utter disbelief that this treasure of Los Angeles history would soon be served up to the wrecking ball.

Although Mom had received prior permission from the head of hotel security to access the property, when we arrived, the guard would not let us in.

"Your names aren't on the list," he barked.

"I never needed to be on a list. I *lived* here," Mom declared, with her requisite sniff. And she proceeded to regale him with the story of her life at the Ambassador, hitting all the same notes she did with me as a child. His eyes widened at certain details only she could tell. "Bing Crosby and I swore by those turkey sandwiches served by Todd—the fountain guy—in the coffee shop. And did you know there was a full-blown zoo on the property? Bears! A lioness! Even an anteater—oh gosh, he was my favorite. And let's not forget the underground tunnel connecting the hotel to the bungalows. You know how celebrities are—William Randolph Hearst, F. Scott Fitzgerald, and Charlie Chaplin needed their privacy."

"Well lady, after all that, how can I say no? I guess you really did live here. You must have had an incredible life." We both chuckled at Mom's persuasive ways as he unceremoniously unlocked the gate and ushered us onto the hotel grounds. As we walked down the once-grand driveway, now bordered by dead grass, Mom said, "This used to be the most beautiful green lawn, perfectly landscaped, and over there"—she pointed toward the bungalows—"was a gigantic, round flowerbed with hundreds and hundreds of flowers. I could see it from my bedroom window." At that moment, I realized she was pointing to the very bungalow where she once lived. It was now a dilapidated shell. We walked off the driveway onto a cement path that ran under the remains of the trellised porte cochere. Its columns, once graced by vibrant flowering vines, were now wrapped in brittle leaves. The roof that had provided shade to guests was now a nesting place for birds and spiders, and a playground for scampering squirrels. Mom picked up the pace. She was on a mission. She was leading me back into the past, in the direction of the structure she once called home.

Carlyn Frank Benjamin in front of the family's Rincon Bungalow at the Ambassador Hotel. Los Angeles, 2003. (Still image captured by Steven Hankins Photography from video produced by Robert Clampett, Jr.)

Mom came to an abrupt stop. We now faced the last remnant of her childhood, an unremarkable wooden plaque bearing the name of the family bungalow. It was fastened halfway up the wall between two second-story balconies hovering above us. The individual capital letters, in black, were secured against a beige background, much like the color of the room-service oatmeal delivered to Mom's bungalow most mornings. Somehow, we had to abscond with that sign! But how could we get it off the building? And how could we leave with the sign undercover? Though Mom had charmed the security guard into letting us in, I suspected it would take more than charm for him to let us walk out with a piece of the hotel. We had no idea how any of this would unfold, but what an adventure this excursion had turned out to be!

As we stared at the sign, wondering how we would get it off the wall, we heard footsteps approaching. And then a voice. "Mrs. Benjamin? Is that you?"

"Mom?" I whispered. "Who is that?"

"That's Ray. He's a lovely man. I believe he's the head honcho for something to do with the property. I don't really remember. We've become friends over the years, since I joined the campaign to save the hotel. I'm sure Ray will help us today."

Mom turned to Ray. "It's so good to see you again."

He opened his arms for a hug. "What brings you here today and how did you get in?"

"It's a long story, but I can be very persuasive." Then, in her most persuasive voice she explained, "That sign defined my life for seventeen years. We're here to take it back with us." Without comment, Ray pulled a tool off his belt, grabbed a nearby stepladder, and unbolted the sign from where it had resided for decades. When Ray handed Mom the sign, it gave me such joy to see how happy she was, wrapping her arms around such a meaningful piece of her childhood. The next day, my husband fastened the Rincon sign to a wooden beam running the length of my mother's back porch, overlooking the lush Kenter Canyon in the Brentwood section of Los Angeles. Today, the sign proudly sits on a window ledge in my kitchen, and every day as I look out, it reminds me of the time Mom and I were partners in crime.

The Rincon sign from Carlyn's family bungalow at the Ambassador Hotel. Los Angeles. (Gilmour Family Collection)

Once Mom's precious treasure was securely in our possession, she gave me a tour of Rincon. Given the stained and torn carpet on the entrance stairwell alone, I knew it was going to be a shocking sight. What was once, as Mom described, a beautiful, light-filled home with seven rooms and three bathrooms, with room service just a call away, was now entirely unrecognizable. Upon entering the bungalow, we were met by a mess of peeling paint, water-stained wallpaper, and that rancid mildew smell that comes from years of neglect. Vines were growing through cracks in the broken glass windows, doors were hanging off their hinges, and chunks of ceiling plaster littered the floor like crude walking stones. It felt like the set for a *Twilight Zone* episode—starring my mom—in which she was transported into the future to see what would become of the beloved world she had been forced to abandon.

I stopped, froze, and grabbed Mom's hand when I noticed bullet holes riddling the carpet and walls. It was clear that what we had been told about the Los Angeles Police Department was true: For years, once the hotel closed, they had used it for SWAT team practice. In addition, movie crews used much of the interior and exterior as sets, tramping around and adding further to the hotel's deterioration. Amidst such decay, I began to listen—*really* listen for the first time—to my mother talking about what living at the hotel had been like back in its prime.

Carlyn Frank Benjamin walking up the stairs to the Rincon Bungalow. Los Angeles, 2003. (Still image captured by Steven Hankins Photography from video produced by Robert Clampett, Jr.)

The Rincon Bungalow living room. Los Angeles, 2003.
(Still image captured by Steven Hankins Photography from video produced
by Robert Clampett, Jr.)

As we wandered through each room, Mom tried to bring back a vision of what Rincon once looked like: the comfort, the beautiful furnishings, the tasteful décor and the double-hung windows framing the view of the gorgeous, expansive landscaping as far as the eye could see. Mom had a front-row seat to it all—until the show came to a sudden end. She had been back to the hotel a number of times since it had closed. In 2003, a video team followed her around while she shared stories about growing up at the Ambassador; at the time, I had paid about as much attention to this videotaped mini-memoir as I had to her stories. On another visit she was accompanied by her sweet granddaughter, Rachael. But this visit with me was proving to be the most emotional. Here we were, standing among the debris—which was soon to be rubble. She looked at me and said with such deep sadness in her voice, "My childhood is gone."

"Mom, I'm so sorry," I said, wrapping her in a hug.

She proceeded to give me a tour of each room, explaining what it had looked like and the things that had happened there.

"This is the corner where our Christmas tree caught fire," Mom said, pointing. "It had lit candles on it. If the paint was still on the wall you'd see the burn marks. My father grabbed an afghan off the couch, ran to the bathroom and quickly soaked it under the shower, and then put out the fire!"

As we continued our journey through the hotel grounds, Mom told me about her visit in 1990, a year after the hotel officially closed. Her seven-year-old granddaughter, Rachael, had asked to see "the five-hundred-room house" where her grandmother grew up. Mom was more than eager to take Rachael on a tour. Because the hotel was closed and off limits to the public, she had been given permission to walk the property, yet when they arrived, there was a problem similar to the one we ourselves experienced. The guard told Mom they had to be escorted everywhere. This annoyed her to no end. "As if I could get lost after living here!" she said under her breath. Once again, my mother's persuasiveness and persistence paid off, and she got the escort mandate waived. They spent the next few hours walking the grounds with Mom pointing out everything about her childhood and teen years, including the Rincon bungalow.

Mom recalled that Rachael, clearly stunned by the bungalow's deterioration, asked in her seven-year-old way, "How could you have lived like this? Did you sleep on the floor? Where's the bathroom? And the refrigerator?" Rachael's big brown eyes widened as Mom explained how her home had originally looked in its elegance, and why it had fallen into such a sad mess.

I can't remember when Mom began to write her memoir; she never dated her versions. But some years after our Rincon sign caper, Mom mentioned she had sent her memoir to a publisher, who had rejected it. They said that unless she could write salacious and gossipy tales about the comings and goings at the hotel, no one would consider it. The only salacious thing Mom could write (and I doubt it qualified) was her recollection of an up-and-coming starlet, Lupe Vélez, known as the "Mexican Spitfire"—and also for not wearing underwear. This lack of underclothing was apparently evident when she wore a tight-fitting, light-colored gown to an event at the Cocoanut Grove. Mom had stationed herself in the hotel lobby, waiting to see Ms. Vélez saunter by so she could confirm whether the rumors were true. And—according to Mom—they were!

I couldn't believe Mom's story would only have appeal as an exercise in name-dropping. I immediately asked for a copy of her manuscript. "You know you have one," she said in a rather disappointed tone, and then I realized she had given me a draft years before, which I hadn't bothered to read and sadly knew I wouldn't be able to find. So I sheepishly asked for a replacement.

It turned out that Mom had written over 200 double-spaced pages. She wanted to share her memories with the many people obsessed with the hotel and its storied past, and fascinated with Los Angeles history and old Hollywood, as well as with those who had fought so tirelessly for the Ambassador's survival. Naturally, Mom also wanted the book to preserve our family history. She knew there would be great public interest, regardless of one publisher's opinion, so she explored the self-publishing route. She wanted to finish her memoir and see it as a book. However, I think that initial criticism hampered her ability to push the manuscript over the finish line, and she was starting to show signs of aging and forgetfulness.

In the fall of 2016, a few months before my mother passed, she brought up the topic of her unfinished manuscript. I could tell how disappointed she felt. Up to this point, I hadn't considered offering to help her move the book forward. In fact, I hadn't done more than glance at the replacement copy. At that moment, I surprised myself and asked her if I could finish it. To my utter delight, she surprised me with a heartfelt yes. Preserving the legacy would now be up to me.

Mom had always been fiercely independent, insisting on doing everything herself. Advice, no matter how well-intentioned, was rarely welcomed. She needed to control people and situations to create a reliable and safe outcome. Although I don't know for certain what in her early childhood may have triggered that need, I do believe that losing control over her life at seventeen deeply shaped her as an adult. Her willingness to entrust me with her manuscript was nothing short of remarkable. It was a rare moment of surrender, a quiet acknowledgment that some things must be released. On January 9, 2017, five months shy of her ninety-sixth birthday, Mom died from complications due to dementia.

In 2019, my husband, Mark, and I decided to sell Mom's Brentwood house, which was also my childhood home, located about fifteen miles from the Ambassador. One day, while sorting, packing, and otherwise donating ninety-five years of Mom's life, I opened the bottom drawer of her desk, and there it was, snugly bound in a faded red report cover: the original. Holding her manuscript, with the title missing from the front cover and faded blue Post-its still stuck to the pages, I stood in grateful silence. Mom had worked so hard to preserve the stories—not only of her opulent childhood, but also of those who tried so diligently to save the Ambassador and its history.

Carlyn's original Life Without Reservations manuscript, discovered in her Brentwood (Los Angeles), California home in 2019. (Gilmour Family Collection)

I sat for a while at her desk in my old bedroom—still painted yellow, with one section covered in bright wallpaper saturated with beautiful spring flowers—with tears in my eyes. For the very first time, I began reading this rough draft of Mom's early life. I missed her so much. We were packing up the home she had lived in for over fifty-five years, and the home I had lived in from the time I was seven until I left for college. To say the least, it was one hell of an emotional day. And there I was, reading her story and realizing I had a daunting responsibility ahead of me. I closed the worn manuscript and packed it away until the pandemic gave me the opportunity to find the box in my hall closet and get started.

To be clear, Mom remembered things in her own unique way. I've discovered that some of the dates and events she recorded don't always align with those found in other sources. Still, I preserved the dates as she remembered them in her manuscript, honoring her personal sense of chronology and the way she experienced her life.

When I promised my mom I would finish her book, I hadn't thought about including my own observations in the story.

However, the more I became engaged with the manuscript, the more I felt compelled to write about my own feelings and experiences in response to Mom's narrative—both my childhood memories and my reactions to discovering many things about my mother that I hadn't known. Even though I hadn't always listened, Mom's early life—growing up like a princess and suddenly having to transition from "royal" to "ordinary"—informed nearly every aspect of her post-Ambassador life and unavoidably permeated mine. It also felt important to add context and expand on the historical aspects of both the hotel and Los Angeles in the 1920s and '30s. I've included these observations and connections in a "Dear Mom" letter at the end of each of her chapters as a way to "collaborate" with her, and to share how her life and memories influenced mine.

In addition, my work on the manuscript reminded me that Mom's life was one spent fighting for important causes, a life of philanthropy, a life with notable friends, a life with a loving family and a marriage to an extraordinary man. That she felt her post-Ambassador life never fully measured up is a mystery I will never solve. To commemorate the fullness of her life, I've included several additional chapters to share some of the beautiful stories she left untold in her original manuscript. Keeping my promise, it's an honor to bring my mother's memoir forward.

And now, I offer *Life Without Reservations.* I hope you find it historically compelling, emotionally engaging, and maybe a tiny bit salacious.

Lisa Benjamin Gilmour
Los Angeles, California

BOOK I

MY MOTHER'S STORY

1

AN UNFORGIVING
SENSE OF LOSS

My name is Carlyn. I was never told the full story about the day my world was upended. But it changed my life in ways I could never have imagined. The year was 1938. I was seventeen years old.

My eleven-year-old sister, Jackie, and I were playing a card game on the floor of my bedroom when our mother walked in. She asked us to come sit on the bed with her. She sat stoically and bravely and told us we had to pack up and move out of Rincon, our lovely bungalow on the grounds of the iconic Los Angeles hotel, the Ambassador. This had been the home my parents and I shared for seventeen years, starting for me in 1921 and for my sister in 1927. At the time, at least to me, it felt like we had to move immediately. Mother went on to say that the new bondholders who had taken over the hotel had brought in their own management team and that our father's services were no longer needed.

I could tell how painful the situation was for Mother to share with us. After all, during the twenties and thirties my father and grandfather had created and maintained the Ambassador Hotel as one of the most sought-after luxury resort hotel experiences in the country, and now, out of the blue, our father was "no longer needed" (my grandfather had passed in September 1932).

Mother didn't use the word "fired," but she also didn't say he had resigned, even though, thankfully, that is how newspaper accounts referred to my father's "departure." In fact, the articles quoted my father as saying he left the hotel to pursue other opportunities, which was not true. There were no other opportunities, because his exit from the hotel was completely unplanned. As a highly respected, nationally recognized hotel man, he had to save face among his peers, family, friends, and the hotel staff, who were fiercely loyal to him.

Some time after we'd left the hotel, a relative found an article in the *B'nai B'rith Messenger* that reported, although unsubstantiated, that perhaps the new management was "unfriendly to the Jewish people." The article went on to say that Mr. L. C. Reed, the new executive vice president, had supported the Jewish community all his life. However, Mr. Reed may have been pressured by the bondholders to relieve my father of his duties.

Given the climate of anti-Semitism during that time, it is conceivable that my father's religious beliefs could have overshadowed his exemplary hospitality skills and his eye for creating a highly lauded, one-of-a-kind guest experience. But as a teenager, I didn't concern myself as to why my father was no longer needed. I was too caught up about *my* having to leave my home and my privileged life and worried what my friends would think.

My father and grandfather had been employed at the Ambassador since it opened in 1921. My father started out as the purchasing manager and my grandfather as vice president and general manager. When my grandfather passed, my father took over my grandfather's position, filling his very successful role. But now, during the height of the Depression, with my father unemployed, my mother must have been terrified about our financial future. Even worse, the new management and bondholders would charge my father $500 a day if we continued to live in our bungalow.

Jackie and I have different memories as to how the conversation with our mother went that day. Mine says we left bag and baggage the next night and moved in with a family member who lived nearby until our mother could find a suitable and affordable home to rent. My sister recalls our move taking a week or more. She also said we didn't move in with a family member, but that we moved into a rented home on South Highland Avenue in Los Angeles. She remembers the move being somewhat stressful, but she did not experience the anxiety-inducing dread that became my new identity. Regardless of our differing emotions, my version of the events is what I felt to be true at the time—and still do.

Jackie was only eleven, which might explain why moving away from the hotel didn't leave the same mark on her as it did me. I, however, have carried an unforgiving sense of loss my entire life.

Whether we fled like refugees in the night, or drove quietly away in the daylight, it doesn't really matter to my aging memory, because what I *do* deeply remember is the darkness, fright, and shame I experienced. I could not grasp how this could be happening to me. How was everything I'd ever known being taken away? How could I move away from the only home I'd lived in almost since birth, and lose all the fanciful accoutrements and the status that came along with living in a hotel such as the Ambassador? Absorbed with my own loss, it was not until much later in life that I realized the hell that my parents also must have gone through.

Dear Mom,

Reading this chapter is always hard for me, but not as hard as it must have been for you to live. I can't imagine how you managed this seismic shift in your life—losing your home, your security, and your identity, overnight—all without fully understanding why it happened in the first place. You tell the story from the distance of memory, but I can feel the full force of what you experienced and the depth of the loss that you carried with you forever after.

Though we'll never know for sure, it does seem plausible that the new bondholders could have decided they didn't want a Jewish person running the hotel, no matter how successful your father had been. I know Aunt Jackie believes it was bigotry that led to their decision. That is such a sickening possibility, but to me it feels like the only thing that makes sense, given your father's incredible success in creating such an outstanding resort hotel loved by people all over the world. I know you found out years later that, leading up to his "departure," your father had continual dreams about snakes because the bondholders were making things very difficult for him ahead of the axe falling.

I get why your parents kept the details of that day tucked deep inside their pride. But I wish they'd told you the full story, as it surely would have helped you process your feelings, and helped our own family understand all that you and yours had experienced. But sometimes we don't get the answers we need at the time we need them. I also wish I knew how your parents managed this drastic upheaval of their life. What was it like to be around your father during this time of transition? What was it like going to sleep that last night knowing in the morning your life would be permanently altered? With all the stories you told me so many times, you never talked about that last night in the hotel. Why didn't you write about it in your memoir?

I don't believe you fully reconciled the despair you experienced at age seventeen, or the insecurities that developed during your lifetime as a result. Nevertheless, that experience—as painful as it was—shaped the generous life you lived. And for that, I am most grateful.

Love,
Lisa

2

ON THEIR WAY

Though my parents never let me in on the secrets surrounding our sudden departure from the Ambassador, they and my grandparents loved sharing family history. I learned that my parents and grandparents moved from Chicago to Los Angeles in 1920. My parents, Ben and Beatrice Frank, were newly married and travelled by car, and my grandparents, Abe and Anne Frank, travelled by rail. My parents were on their way to Los Angeles by way of a cross-country camping adventure that my father thought would be romantic. That was not the same sentiment felt by my proper, sophisticated mother. Mother was not keen on the camping idea from the get-go, which was made even more apparent on the first night when it rained so hard the tent shed its green dye all over her satin trousseau lingerie. It was at that moment she knew she should have protested more strongly and insisted they stay in a hotel.

It was therefore no surprise that this was my mother's first—and last—camping trip. However, all was forgiven, as I was told I was conceived in that tent during that summer night's rain in August 1920. The campsite, it turns out, was on the outskirts of Butte, Montana, where, unbeknownst to me, my ten-year-old future husband was living on Granite Street with his sister, Rosalie, and their parents, Arthur and Belle Benjamin.

Carlyn's parents, Bea and Ben Frank, on their wedding day.
Chicago, August 1920. (Gilmour Family Collection)

Traveling by rail on the Santa Fe line was very special to my grandparents, but especially to my grandfather. At the age of 21, in 1892, he had become general manager of the Fred Harvey Company restaurant and hotel franchise. During his employment, my grandfather developed the concept for what would become the Fred Harvey dining car service on railroads, which later expanded to the Harvey House brand of restaurants along the famous Atchison, Topeka, and Santa Fe Railroad station stops. A large, ornate sterling silver loving cup—"Presented to A. Frank by Santa Fe Dining Car Employees, December 31, 1902"—graces my mother's baby grand piano at my sister

Jackie's home today. For those of you unfamiliar with a "loving cup," it is a large bowl, traditionally made of silver, with a handle on each side. They were used back in the day as shared drinking cups at weddings and other ceremonial events. They were also used to symbolize friendship and unity.

My grandparents moved to Los Angeles because my grandfather had been hired as the vice president of the Ambassador Hotels System and would serve as the new manager of the Hotel Alexandria in downtown Los Angeles on Fifth and Spring Streets, where my grandparents also lived for a time. When the Los Angeles Ambassador Hotel opened in 1921, my grandfather was brought in to be the vice president and general manager there, as well. He served in management roles at both the Alexandria and Ambassador for several years, commuting regularly from downtown Los Angeles out to the "country"—the now mid-Wilshire Boulevard site of the Ambassador.

My parents moved to Los Angeles because my father had been hired as the purchasing manager for the Ambassador Hotel and was waiting for it to open. Prior to their arrival, both my father and grandfather had extensive restaurant and hotel management experience in the Midwest, which had brought them much acclaim for their business acumen. Abe Frank was part owner of the famous Sherman House in Chicago, and it was he who conceived of the idea for the College Inn restaurant (located inside the hotel), which later became a highly notable jazz venue during the 1910s and '20s. And both my father and grandfather, for a time, were managing owners of the historic Oliver Hotel in South Bend, Indiana.

Uncle Lester, my father's younger brother, came from Chicago to Los Angeles in 1922 and was hired at the Ambassador as an assistant manager in charge of overseeing guest reservations and entertainment. A few years later, he opened the men's haberdashery on the Casino floor of the hotel. The haberdashery—along with more than thirty other "smart shops," as they were called in those days—was one of the key attractions for gentlemen guests.

When my father and grandfather were working together at the Ambassador, my father reported up to his father and they became an unstoppable team, setting the bar for excellence in hotel management. Elegance, charm, and sophistication were always the order of the day and night. They graciously catered to the whims of their guests, from the simple to the outrageous. They were both truly remarkable and brilliant businessmen.

The Ambassador was *the* place to see and be seen. From everyday vacationers to the most famous, celebrated, regal, and admired people of the time, the resort offered everything anyone needed and was home to guests for a few days or a few months, and sometimes longer. And who could blame them? It was twenty-four acres of meticulously landscaped grounds, luxury accommodations, the finest entertainment, and first-class service. Why would anyone ever need to leave?

Before moving to the Ambassador, my mother said we lived in a very small, elegant apartment on the corner of Eighth and Alvarado Streets just two blocks from Westlake Park. I was born on May 11, 1921, and my temporary nursery was a bassinet that was stationed behind the door to their apartment. A few months later, our home on the Ambassador Hotel grounds was finally completed and the Rincon bungalow became our residence for the next seventeen years. However, before I go any further in telling you the full story about my life growing up at the Ambassador, you need to know how the hotel came to be. It is quite a fascinating and historic tale.

Dear Mom,

Wow. Why did I not know *any* of this?

Your parents and grandparents seem like fascinating people who led adventurous lives. I wish I'd heard a lot more about them when I was growing up, so I could have asked you questions.

For instance, how many people can say their parents told them they were conceived on their honeymoon, and how many people can say that their future husband, a preteen at the time, lived somewhere nearby with *his* parents?

How fun that you and the hotel were both "born" in the same year, and just a few months apart! I wonder how your mom handled the stress of moving from Chicago to Los Angeles, being newly married, with a husband starting a new job, and caring for a new baby?

It was interesting to learn that my great-grandfather, Abe, created a jazz club. Is this why I have always been a lover of jazz music?

I thought you'd like to know that during a recent visit with Aunt Jackie, we found the loving cup the Fred Harvey staff gave to your grandfather, stashed away in a cupboard in her house. I'm adding sterling silver polish to my shopping list!

Love,
Lisa

3

BREAKING GROUND

Growing up at the Ambassador, I never *gave a second thought to the history behind this truly magnificent hotel, with its expansive and beautiful grounds.*
It was just there, and it was home. So for my memoir, I did some digging into the story of how the Ambassador came to be. My research revealed things I hadn't known. In 1869, twenty-five years before Wilshire Boulevard became Wilshire Boulevard, and fifty-two years before the Ambassador Hotel opened, Gottfried Schmidt purchased a 160-acre parcel of land from the Public Land Survey System for $1.25 an acre. Here, the Schmidt family ran an impressive and expansive dairy and chicken farm. Imagine that! Where the glorious Ambassador hotel stood, there were once chicken coops and cow pastures.

While maintaining the farm, the Schmidt family took notice of the growth of Los Angeles as a major developing city. Following the lead of some of his neighbors, Schmidt and his sons began to sell off parts of their acreage to residential developers starting in 1890. In 1919, the Ambassador Hotels System made an offer the Schmidt family could not refuse. Construction of the hotel, surrounded by barley fields and dirt roads, began immediately. (I have a vague memory from when I was about seven or eight: There were still agricultural fields, and dirt roads along Wilshire, but closer to the

La Brea Tar Pits, a few miles from the hotel.) Two years later the original property had been transformed into the Ambassador Hotel, designed by the famous architect Myron Hunt, who also designed such iconic structures as the Hollywood Bowl, the California Institute of Technology (Caltech), Mount Wilson Observatory, and the Rose Bowl—all of which, I might add, are still standing, unlike the Ambassador! Several years after we left the hotel, renovations were made by the renowned architect Paul R. Williams, a trailblazer whose elegant architectural style helped shape much of Los Angeles in the early 1920s and '30s.

The Ambassador Hotel under construction. Los Angeles, 1920.
(archHunta, Box 1. Myron Hunt Collection, 1912–2006 [bulk 1912–1914].
Hunt, Myron, 1868–1952, creator. The Huntington Library,
San Marino, California)

The building was shaped like a sprawling yet elegant capital H, consisting of two long parallel wings (north and south) that housed hundreds of guestrooms and suites, joined by the middle of the H as a central connecting bar. Hunt designed it this way to maximize cross-ventilation, natural light, and courtyard views. The unique design was considered to be extremely modern for the times. The "connecting bar" housed the lobby, Casino level shops, coffee shop, and the entry to the Cocoanut Grove.

Bird's-eye view of the Ambassador Hotel with the "H" clearly visible.

Standing in the lobby, you had access to the courtyards opening on either side: the formal gardens along Wilshire to the north, and the quieter south gardens with the pool and tennis courts. From these central rooms you could wander farther back to the great ballrooms—the Fiesta Ballroom, which later became the Embassy Ballroom, and, beyond it, the famed Cocoanut Grove. It was a building designed for movement, spectacle, and surprise—and for me, a young girl growing up inside the H, every bit of it felt like a promise of something magical waiting just around the corner.

The grounds of the hotel were expansive, bordered by Wilshire Boulevard on the north, Eighth Street at the south, Catalina Street to the east, and nearly all the way to Mariposa Avenue to the west. There was an empty lot on the corner of Mariposa, just off the hotel driveway, that at one time was the site of a golfer's practice driving range.

The number of acres the hotel occupied varies depending on which websites, vintage hotel brochures, newspapers, magazine articles, or books you read about the hotel's history. The reported acreage ranged anywhere from twenty-one to twenty-seven acres. For the purposes of my story, I am going to go with twenty-four acres, because that is what I remember.

The hotel became the catalyst for the development of Wilshire Boulevard, which was named for developer, publisher, and revolutionary Henry Gaylord Wilshire. Wilshire donated land to the City of Los Angeles for a boulevard stretching westward from Westlake Park (today's MacArthur Park) all the way to the ocean in Santa Monica.

According to a 1919 article from the *New York Times*, the Ambassador Hotel's original name was the California Hotel. I had never heard about the name change, so I set out to find more information. What I found was a photograph of the original hotel Block Plan from Myron Hunt's office, dated February 10, 1919. The name "California Hotel" was written on the lower right corner of the photograph. That was really something to find!

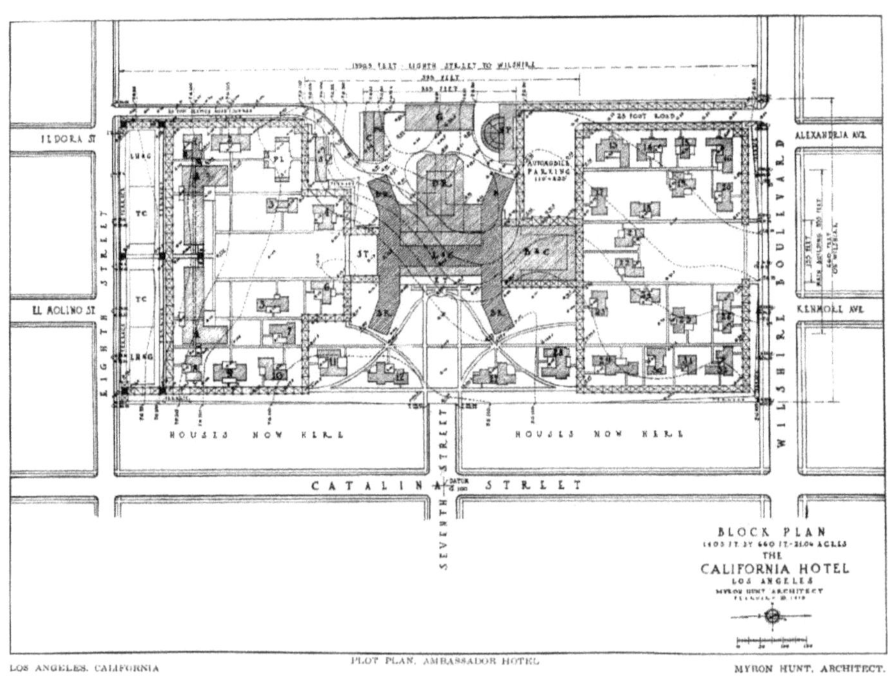

Architectural drawing of the block plan for the Ambassador Hotel. Los Angeles, 1919–1920. (The Building Review, November 1921, plate 63)

Detail from an architectural drawing of the block plan for the Ambassador Hotel. Los Angeles, 1919–1920. (The Building Review, November 1921, plate 63.)

I couldn't figure out exactly when the hotel name changed, but there are blueprints dated later in 1920 where the California Hotel property title was replaced with the Ambassador Hotel. So I did a little digging, and found an article dated December 1, 1919, from the *Los Angeles Evening Express* which explained that S. W. Straus & Co., an investment firm dealing with mortgage bonds, purchased five of the largest and most successful hotels owned by D. M. Linnard, who was regarded as "the greatest hotelman of his time."

The newly purchased hotels were the Hotel Alexandria, the under-construction California Hotel in Los Angeles, the Ambassador of Santa Barbara, the Ambassador in Atlantic City, and the Linnard Hotel in New York City. Mr. Linnard was apparently tired from all the east coast/west coast travel and agreed to sell his properties. As a result, the five hotels came under the umbrella of the Ambassador Hotels System. According to the article, it was S. W. Straus & Co. who changed the name of the California Hotel to the Ambassador, in order to match the names of the other two hotels named the Ambassador.

You might be wondering why a hotel of such grandeur as the Ambassador would be built literally in the middle of nowhere. In 1918, Charlie Chaplin and his brother Sydney established a movie studio in Hollywood where a great many people wanted—and needed—to be, because movies had become the major export of Los Angeles. However, downtown Los Angeles, east of Hollywood, was also seen as an important growth area for the city. The

Hollywood crowd and the downtown crowd were at odds with one another, but they both knew they had to be connected somehow if they were going to help Los Angeles become what the famous Mulhollands, Gettys, Culvers, and Chandlers sought to establish: "the greatest city in the world." To do this, they had to recognize and accept that the Wilshire district would link these two very different parts of the city. But even with all the marketing efforts to draw visitors to the southern California lifestyle with its alluring climate, the area still lacked the scale of accommodations needed to satisfy the ever-growing number of visitors seeking the California experience. Enter the Ambassador Hotel. Set in the heart of Wilshire Boulevard and connecting the east side and the west side, it became the big draw for tourists far and wide as Los Angeles was thriving financially and roaring culturally in the 1920s.

For most, the Ambassador Hotel was a beautiful vacation retreat, but for me, it was my *entire world*. Everything and anything I could ever want or need was there for me. It was as though I was a 24/7/365 days-a-year guest. But at the same time, I felt a little bit like I owned the place!

The Ambassador Hotel. Los Angeles. (archHunta, Box 2. Myron Hunt Collection, 1912–2006 [bulk 1912–1914]. Hunt, Myron, 1868–1952, creator. The Huntington Library, San Marino, California)

Dear Mom,

The more I work on your manuscript, the more I've come to appreciate the architectural style of Los Angeles in the 1920s and '30s and why you were such a staunch advocate for saving architecturally relevant buildings in your city. It is eclectic, bold, and intricate (just like you), with styles ranging from Mediterranean Revival (the Ambassador) to Art Deco to Craftsman and more. And I'm grateful for the thorough research and detective work you did. You painted a picture that will come alive for anyone who reads your memoir. I know it did for me.

I remember so many times being in the car with you, heading east on Wilshire Boulevard through Mid-City, driving past the Ambassador long after it had closed. You'd always shake your head in disbelief, as though you were seeing it in its shambled state for the first time. You often pointed out the history behind many of the buildings that were still standing, such as Bullocks Wilshire, the Talmadge Apartment building, and Wilshire Boulevard Temple, where you and Dad were married in 1944. You would become emotional while sharing what these buildings meant to you, lamenting how other iconic LA buildings had been replaced with an office building, a car wash, or a parking lot. And, although you were a passionate believer in education, especially for those living in underserved neighborhoods, you never got over the destruction of the Ambassador to make way for the Robert F. Kennedy, Jr. Community School, a 24-acre K–12 school on the grounds of the hotel. The impact on your heart may have been softened, if as promised, several of the most iconic elements of the hotel had been preserved (the Cocoanut Grove being one of the more important to you) and transformed into areas for students to learn and socialize. Instead those features were replicated or newly constructed after the demolition. Promises and hearts broken.

I'm sorry I wasn't more appreciative of your feelings when I was younger.

Love,
Lisa

4

WELCOME TO THE AMBASSADOR

Ambassador Hotel advertisement in The Chicago Tribune,
January 2, 1921.

The Ambassador had its official invitation-only opening at midnight on January 1, 1921, with the grand opening for the public on January 18, 1921. There is a very detailed accounting of what it took to open the hotel, and a lot of fun facts reported in the January 1 edition of the *Los Angeles Times.* Since the opening was five months prior to my birth, the following article will serve as "my memory" of that historic day. *Please note, the article below is verbatim from the Times and contains grammatical and punctuation errors.*

To prepare for the opening, three shifts of workmen toiled night and day for a week on the finishing touches with meals prepared and served to the men at the incomplete hotel. 500 employees were on hand when the hotel opened at midnight to receive guests. This army of servants is headed by Rudolph Frel, formerly chef for the Empress Eugenie and the Grand Duke Michael of Russia, came from Paris to preside over the cuisine of the Ambassador. The Ambassador, which represents an expenditure of $5 million, occupies 27 acres of terraced gardens on Wilshire Blvd. 600 guest rooms have been completed and work is underway on 400 more. Each is an outside room containing not less than two windows, as in designing the building, Myron Hunt, the architect, planned to flood the whole structure with an abundance of sunlight.

Not included in the article, but important to note: Grover Sholem, the interior designer for the hotel, is quoted as saying, "Sunlight is essential to the hotel as it is the embodiment of the spirit of California." He wanted the guest rooms to have the look and feel of southern California, with large windows not only for seeing the sights but also to allow for lots of sun to showcase the very California-style interiors of wood and wicker, soft colors on the walls, and beautiful fabrics on the beds. And they certainly did.

That same article in the *Los Angeles Times* describes, in exhaustive detail, the immense scope not only of the hotel structure, but also its luxuriously appointed interiors, where thought was given to every possible need and, it seems, no expense was spared:

> The hotel building has 13 acres of floor space and 1900 windows and 2200 doors, 30,000 yards of curtain material were used to drape the windows, and the floors are covered with 28,000 yards of carpet. Also 500,000 square yards of plastering was used in construction. The decorative scheme of the rooms include pastel tints in the furniture, delicate cretonne, attractive English prints and original paintings

on the walls. 10,000 chairs were needed to furnish the hotel. The dining rooms and grills are so constructed that 4000 diners can be accommodated at one time. 1200 persons alone can be seated in the main dining room which covers half an acre of floor space. Hanging window boxes and stately palms provide the decorative scheme. The music in the main dining room is to be provided by Adolph Tandler's orchestra at luncheon and dinner each day, and on Sunday nights Mr. Tandler will present a concert in the lobby. The Zinnia Grill was planned for less formal parties is a creation of black patent leather, red ochre and gold and the Zinnia colors interwoven throughout the design. The music and the grill is to be furnished by Max Fisher's dance orchestra every night. Other rooms for diners include the Palm Room and the Parrot Porch the last tinted in blue and orange. Fisher's orchestra will also play for dancing in these two rooms. In the ballroom 1000 couples can dance. The room is surrounded by loges. With a spacious stage at one end the room can be converted quickly into an auditorium. On the arcade floor of the hotel there are 40 fashionable shops including a bank. At the extreme end of the arcade is the Ambassador theater with a seating capacity of 600. The hotel is surrounded by lawns and a quarter of a million trees, plants and shrubs including many old palms. A few miles away on Pico Boulevard is the 18 hole golf links for the hotel, with the handsome clubhouse. The course was laid out by Herbert Fowler, English golf course architect. Other statistics concerning the big hotel furnished by Myron Hunt, follow: 30 miles of feed pipe, 60 miles of telephone conduit, one mile of flower boxes, 1 1/2 miles of drain tile, two garages. For the entertainment of the guests, the following features have been provided: a Symphony Orchestra, a dance orchestra and a string sextet and a riding academy.

Although the article claimed there were six-hundred guest rooms on twenty-seven acres, I know from later accounts that the number of guest rooms when the hotel opened was five hundred. I believe there were a lot of rooms for staff to use as their residences; I just don't know if there were one-hundred rooms set aside for them. However, it's also quite possible that the discrepancy in the room count was just a typo, as it seemed there were lots of typos in newspapers back in the day.

Entering the hotel upon arrival, guests were greeted by a grand and ornate lobby. Imagine walking into this stunning space with soaring ceilings and seeing an enormous Italian fireplace, gorgeous crystal chandeliers, handmade Oriental carpets, marble fountains, and luxurious draperies—and that was just within your first steps.

The Ambassador Hotel lobby. Los Angeles, 1929.
(Courtesy of Marc Wanamaker/Bison Archives)

When I didn't have a friend to enjoy the day with, the lobby was a fascinating place for me to spend my time. The hotel offered guests a funny type of golf game to play there. I loved to sneak around the large decorative pillars to spy on the "golfers."

Mr. Golderer, the Ambassador's Sports Director, introduces guests to indoor croquet golf in the hotel lobby. Los Angeles, circa 1929. (Courtesy of Marc Wanamaker/Bison Archives)

Honestly, it was more fun to just people watch and make up stories in my head about the kind of life they led. The bell captain's desk was in the lobby next to the front desk, and the bellhops were my best source of information about who was in-house and what they were doing. Behind the front desk was a machine called a Scripter. With a special pen, you could write a message from the lobby and send it to several locations throughout the hotel. I would stand by the machine and read the messages as they came up from various departments. Interesting information could also be obtained by chatting with the desk clerks standing behind the beautifully polished walnut front desk counter where hundreds and hundreds of mail slots made up the back wall. The slots held envelopes with messages for guests. Though I was tempted, I never snatched one and opened it. If I had, my father would have had something to say about it. Room keys were attached to a heavy large round brass medallion with the hotel logo in bas-relief. This design resulted in very few lost room keys.

The Ambassador Hotel's brass key fob (front).
(Gilmour Family Collection)

The Ambassador Hotel's brass key fob (back).
(Gilmour Family Collection)

A wild story repeated by my father and reported through the decades, is that Marion Davies, a Broadway and film actress, rode a horse through the lobby one night to impress Mr. Randolph Hearst, her lover. My father said when he asked Mr. Hearst if he was surprised by Miss Davies' actions, he replied, "Yes, because she hates horses!"

Visitors to the hotel arriving by automobile found their way up the long driveway from Wilshire to the carriage entrance leading to the Casino level where all the shops were located. The doormen, Casey and Huey, in their burgundy uniforms with gold buttons, greeted guests under the porte cochere. I really enjoyed talking to them. They both spoke with a thick Irish brogue. Sometimes I would overhear them playfully gossiping about guests. One day, Casey said to Huey, "Did you see the gams on that new starlet when she exited her car?" And Huey said, "No, I didn't, Casey, I was doing my job carrying her luggage into the lobby!" If my father or grandfather had heard their comments, no matter how innocent, they would have had a fit! It didn't bother me a bit, because they were always swell to me. They let me hang around watching famous movie stars and families checking in with kids. Seeing movie stars was exciting, but I always hoped there would be kids my age so we might play together while they were vacationing at the hotel. I loved going a few rounds in the revolving door that opened into the lobby. The glass sections of the doors were edged in a strip of rubber, and it made a keen sound as I went around and around, getting very dizzy. The bellmen were there to greet the guests and bring in their luggage. When that happened, I was asked to immediately stop playing in the revolving door. I always stopped, but only after one last spin around.

The "revolving door" of Hollywood elite coming in and out of the hotel was not a big deal for me like it was for the gobsmacked adults. I was probably six or seven when luminaries such as F. Scott Fitzgerald, Charlie Chaplin, and Tom Mix were hanging around. My father and Tom Mix were great pals and played a lot of practical jokes on one another. The Fitzgeralds were, along with others, called "permanents," because they lived full-time at the Ambassador. They were my neighbors.

As a teenage girl, my blasé attitude as a child turned to heart-pounding excitement over seeing handsome leading men such as John Barrymore and Buster Crabbe enter the hotel. It was *the* place to be. Hollywood journalist Adela Rogers St. Johns, quoted in Margaret Tante Burk's *Are The Stars Out Tonight? The Story of the Famous Ambassador and Cocoanut Grove*, "Hollywood's

Hotel" (1980) recalled the significance of the Ambassador in developing a strong film community:

> There was absolutely no other place to go . . . back then the film stars and producers didn't have the large and beautiful homes they have today . . . nor did they know how to entertain in the grand, elegant and aristocratic manner that the hotel could provide. So this is where we all came to meet one another, to be seen, to be coddled, amused and entertained.

Dear Mom,

I loved reading the detailed description of all the pieces and parts that came together through such tremendous effort to create this immense luxury resort. Explaining the unique layout and H-shaped design of the hotel helped me visualize it. I couldn't help but wonder if you had been born a decade or so earlier, how you would have described the excitement and anticipation of opening day. How fun it would have been to hear how you spent that first day, what you wore, and who you hobnobbed with!

The story about the revolving door from the front of the hotel into the lobby brought back memories of you and me turning and swirling in the revolving doors of department stores and hotels. We'd stand together in one of the glass sections of revolving doors, spinning and spinning, much to the chagrin of others who didn't know how to have fun!

I remember you telling me that Mr. Hearst was a regular guest at the hotel, and he and your dad became good friends over the years. I wish I knew more about their friendship. I would love to know what they talked about, what they laughed about. Did they drink and play cards together? Did they play practical jokes on one another as your father did with so many high profile guests who became friends? But what I would love to know most are the details about the many visits you said your dad made to Hearst Castle to attend Mr. Hearst's lavish parties and swim in that gorgeous outdoor Neptune swimming pool. I was over the moon thinking how amazing it must have been.

I wonder why your dad never included you, your sister, or your mom on his visits to Hearst Castle. Did he simply need a break from the rigor of hotel management? Or was there another reason? Or another someone who also attended the parties?

Love,
Lisa

5

RINCON 16

Looking back on my first seventeen years, before everything changed, I remember it all with a sense of great joy. It was truly a life without reservations. My life was carefree, and I soaked it all in with great panache. In the early years of writing this memoir, I realized my life at the Ambassador had been much like that of Eloise (from Kay Thompson's 1955 children's book *Eloise*), the happy-go-lucky fictional girl who spent her childhood in New York's high-rise Plaza Hotel. I, however, spent not only my childhood but also my teen years living an incredible life at one of the most famous hotels in the world. I knew every nook and cranny, every bell captain and desk clerk, hostess, hatcheck girl, chef, elevator operator, band leader, and the like. Looking back decades later, I think of myself as the "Horizontal Eloise." Just in case that moniker might conjure up a different image, I am referring to the horizontal orientation of the hotel with its six stories and long horizontal H-shaped structure.

The Ambassador Hotel. Los Angeles, 1921.
(Security Pacific National Bank Collection/Los Angeles Public Library)

Our home was Rincon Bungalow 16. (I don't recall why it was "16." It wasn't as if there were Rincon Bungalows 1 to 15!) Ours was one of four original bungalows on the east side of the property. The bungalows were named Rincon, Spanish for corner or nook, Reposa, for a rest or to lie down, Siesta, for an afternoon nap, and Huerta, for orchard or garden. At the time, the three other bungalows were reserved for visitors, famous and otherwise, who wanted an extended stay or privacy away from the main hotel.

The bungalows were basically miniatures built in the Mediterranean Revival-style architecture of the six-story main hotel building. This style was very popular in the 1920s and '30s in southern California, particularly in Los Angeles. For the bungalows, Myron Hunt featured many of the signature lines that identified that style: rectangular floor plans, symmetrical facades, stucco walls, a low-pitched, clay-barrel tile roof, and double-hung windows.

You could connect to each bungalow by walking beneath the lovely heavy wood pergolas, topped by thick layers of palm fronds. I could walk all around the grounds on rainy days without the dreaded galoshes and umbrella and stay perfectly dry. And I loved using the pergola's shelter to roller-skate on those days. There was even an underground tunnel that provided high-profile guests with a quick, under-the-radar escape route to and from their bungalows. The tunnel also provided the staff the means to quickly get from the hotel to the bungalows for room service and other guest needs.

The Rincon Bungalow at the Ambassador Hotel. Los Angeles, 1924.
(University of Southern California Libraries and California Historical Society)

According to Margaret Tante Burk, Hollywood stars would stay for extended periods in the bungalows—celebrities like Gloria Swanson, Tallulah Bankhead, John Barrymore, and others. I recall some of them, but they kept to themselves. Burk also noted that bungalow guest Albert Einstein witnessed Jack Dempsey, the famous boxer, push his wife out of a first-floor window after an argument. Cari Beauchamp, author of books about early Hollywood, wrote that men who had recently separated from their wives stayed so often that in gossip columns of the time, "he's checked into the Ambassador" became a euphemism for "the marriage is over."

F. Scott and Zelda Fitzgerald were bungalow neighbors of Rudolph Valentino and his lover, the silent film star Pola Negri. I vividly recall Negri using the walkway in front of Rincon to exercise her pet cheetah, who was attached to a leash. She was always wrapped in some glamorous fur. Negri was the original femme fatale and had romances with frequent Ambassador guests such as Charlie Chaplin, yet it was Valentino to whom she became engaged just prior to his passing. It was widely reported that upon hearing of his death, Negri collapsed outside Reposa Bungalow just in time for publicity photos to be shot. I was just five when all that took place, so I can only go by hotel lore.

Pola Negri leaving the Ambassador Hotel to attend Rudolph Valentino's funeral in Beverly Hills. Los Angeles, September 7, 1926. (Courtesy of Marc Wanamaker/Bison Archives)

Another interesting and widely reported celebrity incident between the Fitzgeralds caused quite a stir. In 1929, they were staying in one of the Ambassador bungalows while F. Scott wrote a movie script for United Artists film studio. During their stay, they had met Lois Moran, a seventeen-year-old aspiring actress, at a luncheon given for them by Douglas Fairbanks and Mary Pickford. F. Scott apparently was very taken by Miss Moran and as a result Zelda Fitzgerald, in a jealous rage, set fire to her own clothes in the bungalow bathtub and torched the bungalow furniture—along with all the hotel bills they had accumulated. Although there are no records of legal charges or financial penalties against her, I am sure my father and grandfather must have somehow recouped some of the expenses associated with the damage. Having such a high-profile celebrity creating such chaos must have been a huge public relations problem for my father and grandfather. I have no idea how things were handled, as I was only eight years old. What I do know is that it is a true story.

And poor Zelda, as documented, was eventually diagnosed with schizophrenia and spent her days in and out of psychiatric facilities. Ironically, she died in a fire at the Highland Hospital in Asheville, North Carolina in 1948.

My family faced another situation that involved people who needed to be institutionalized. On the southwest corner of Catalina Street and Wilshire Boulevard, located at 3350 Wilshire Boulevard, sat an absolutely gorgeous European-style mansion dating from 1909, with fancy wrought-iron grillwork and a pale blue-green tile roof built by Los Angeles entrepreneur and banker Marco Herman Hellman.

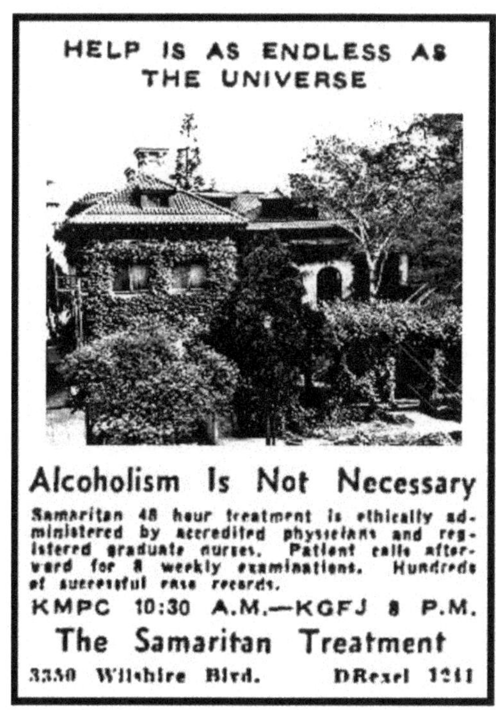

A 1935 Los Angeles Times advertisement for the Samaritan Treatment Center.

Sadly, due to some poor business dealings, in the early 1930s he had to sell his twenty-two-room mansion, which in 1935 became—of all things—an alcohol rehabilitation hospital, called the Samaritan Treatment Center. Like other institutions of its kind, it had facilities in cities across the country; and was said to have offered a forty-eight-hour cure.

The decision to open a facility such as this, literally right next door to the hotel, faced a vigorous protest from hotel management and the surrounding neighborhood. Unfortunately, the treatment center won out. Once the patients moved in, on quiet evenings my sister and I could clearly hear the residents screaming and moaning. The sounds of their pain wafted into our bungalow. I was fourteen and my sister was nine. We were very frightened by what sounded to us like people being tortured. The Samaritan Treatment Center remained in business until around 1943, when it was sold. I can't recall how long we had to endure the screams from the residents, but eventually they faded. My father must have figured out a kind way for us, and those guests occupying the other bungalows, to block out the harrowing cries.

Now, let's get back on track and get you up to Rincon. Back in the day, if you were to visit us, the first thing you'd see before walking up the fourteen steps to the entrance of our living quarters would be the door to a lovely guest room on the right side of the bottom floor entry. And on the left, there was a little utility room to the side of the stairs where the housekeepers kept their supplies, though one night it turned into a puppy nursery. This is where our dog—Inky Dink, a black Scottie—thought would be the perfect place to have her eight puppies. We all spent the night sitting up with her, watching her bring her pups into the world. It was a very special event in my life. I wish we could have kept one of the puppies, but my mother insisted that one dog was enough.

Continuing up the remaining thirteen steps to the top of the stairs, you would come upon the landing at our front door. Once inside, the first thing you'd notice would be my mother's baby grand piano draped in a gorgeous white silk Spanish shawl, hand-embroidered with colorful exotic flowers. That view filled one corner of the living room—or "parlor," as it was called in hotel-speak. A portrait of my mother dressed in a lovely silvery evening gown, wearing the same white silk shawl, was placed on the wall by the piano all the years we lived there. Each time Mother sat at the piano she practiced Franz Liszt's Hungarian Rhapsody No. 2. Sitting on top of the piano was an exciting new invention—a crystal radio, set in a beautiful, highly polished mahogany box given to my father as a grateful gift from one of the band leaders.

We had a couch and coffee table and two big chairs to complete our living room. There was a small dining room where we ate when meals were ordered from room service, instead of eating them down at the hotel. Funny to recall that it was I who mostly occupied the dining room with my math tutor for two excruciating sessions a week. There was also another small room just off the dining room where my parents would entertain guests and have drinks and caviar before having dinner at the Grove. For our family, room service was just the way people ate. It was not a big deal. However, at one point, mother grew tired of it and converted one of Rincon's bathrooms into a tiny kitchen.

My parents had their own private room away from my sister and me. I recall what a huge closet they had in their room, and how large all the bathrooms were. They had that wonderful hexagonal white porcelain tile so popular in the 1920s. In fact, I have the exact tile in two of my bathrooms in my own home, which was built in 1931. Every bathroom in the hotel and bungalows had a window. I was very thankful for that design detail, because when I was locked away in my bathroom learning how to smoke, my exhale was pointed right out the window! My bathroom was also my pomegranate-eating sanctuary. When I was younger, during pomegranate season, I would undress, sit in my empty tub, and enjoy the only sensible way to eat that delicious fruit: letting the juice dribble down my front and stain my hands. Then the evidence of my messy encounter was showered away.

Off my room was a lovely, covered porch with its canopied green canvas swing. When I was old enough to pay attention to such things, I appreciated the beauty of an enormous round flower bed with hundreds and hundreds of beautiful flowers that were planted and replanted all year round. I could see this display from the balcony of my room as I looked west toward the hotel. This circular garden was featured on many postcards and photos and in magazine articles written about the hotel.

Carlyn's bedroom in the Rincon Bungalow. Los Angeles, 2003.
(Still image captured by Steven Hankins Photography from video
produced by Robert Clampett, Jr.)

Our family had a mynah bird named Blackie, and his cage hung from the ceiling of my porch. He was a funny young bird who my father taught to speak like Mae West. The bird would call out to guests passing by under the pergola walkway, "Why don't you come up and see me sometime?" Depending on the recipient of the greeting, this brought either amused glances or angry stares from the walkway below. My father also taught Blackie to whistle in the exact way he would whistle to let my mother know he was walking back from the hotel to our bungalow at the end of the day. The only problem was that the bird would whistle when my father was not on his way home, much to my mother's utter frustration.

One summer, my parents asked Walter Winchell, the famous gossip columnist (who was a great friend of my father's) and Walter's wife, June (who was my mother's best friend) if they would keep Blackie for us when we were away for a few weeks. The Winchells were permanents. Unfortunately, they overfed Blackie and sadly he died . . . but on a stomach stuffed with the grapes he loved!

My room had twin beds so I could have sleepovers. And, best of all, when I was a teen, I got my very own phone. On weekends, Goldie, the head operator of the hotel, would hook me up with my girlfriends from junior high, and we'd have conference calls before anybody knew what a conference call was. Usually, it would be Muffet, Sis, Norma, and Linda from their homes in Hancock Park and Beverly Hills. We could all talk at the same time because Goldie would plug us all in together with the long dangly connecting cords of the hotel switchboard. We talked for hours about boys, clothes, parties, makeup, and everything in between.

When my sister, Jackie, came along in 1927, identical suite accommodations were there for her. Unlike my room, however, Jackie had another small bedroom that opened into her room, and depending on the year, a nursemaid—a Fräulein or a mademoiselle—would sleep in that bedroom. More about the live-in help in a bit.

There was also a charming den in our bungalow. My mother and I loved the den. It was small and sweet and you could sit and look out at the trees and the back of the Craftsman-style houses that lined Catalina Street. My father had bought one of those machines where you put a wide rubbery belt around your waist. You'd strap it on and the belt would allegedly jiggle your fat off. My father kept this modern contraption in the den, but I honestly never recall him using it! And if he did, it didn't make a lick of difference!

On the night of the Long Beach earthquake, March 10, 1933, my mother and sister and I were sitting in the hotel dining room about to order dinner. Then, just before 6:00 p.m., the windows rattled loudly, and things started to shake. It was terribly scary. The quake registered 6.4 on the Richter scale. Chaos ensued because most of the hotel guests had never experienced a quake, and they all scrambled down and assembled in the lobby—my mother, my sister, and I included. My father, with his wonderfully calm demeanor, quieted everyone down. Because the hotel suffered very minor damage, he was able to rally the troops and had a huge buffet dinner set up, free of charge. Guests ate while the house orchestra played through the night as the aftershocks rumbled on and on. Individuals and families from the neighborhood convened on the massive front lawn of the hotel and camped out overnight, some for days, too afraid to return to their apartments.

Another very human and caring gesture by my father, upon hearing that the area hospitals were overcrowded with people injured during the quake, was to set aside twenty-five hotel rooms for some of those patients. My mother told me that celebrities who were already staying at the hotel set up a charity bridge tournament in the lobby and the money raised was given to an earthquake relief fund.

Dear Mom,

This was such a fascinating chapter.

Years after the hotel had closed when we did our walk-through, you described in detail how your lovely home once looked and how much the memories of living there meant to you. Reading about Rincon in this chapter made it come to life again, and I felt as if I was once again standing next to you, with you telling me all the stories about your enchanted childhood. I loved how that made me feel.

How charming that your father signaled his return from the hotel to the bungalow with a signature whistle. These days, it's the ping of a text or buzz of a quick phone call—neither sound is as comforting and as familiar as that whistle must have been, except when Blackie was the whistler!

In the late 1960s, when I was in junior high, you agreed that I could have my own phone, just not my own phone number. I became the proud owner of a pink Princess telephone from the General Telephone Company. I was very surprised you agreed to it, but after reading this chapter I see why you did. You knew from experience how much fun it could be talking on the phone, girlfriend to girlfriend.

Reading about your dad and his kindness and generosity after the Long Beach earthquake so beautifully reflects his pay-it-forward spirit. He passed it to you, and you passed it to me.

Love,
Lisa

6

MY FIRST MEMORY

There's not much to report before my third birthday, which is pretty much my first memory of what was to become a most extraordinary childhood. On the morning of my birthday, Sunday, May 11, 1924, a crew of hotel housemen brought over an enormous (to my eyes) round table and chairs from the hotel and proceeded to set them up for my twelve guests.

The menu was creamed chicken in a patty shell (what we refer to today as a pastry shell), fresh green peas, mashed potatoes—and the best part: chocolate ice cream made from scratch in the hotel kitchen, and birthday cake, made by the hotel's award-winning pastry chef. This menu was the standard birthday party lunch served at the homes of my friends between our third and seventh birthdays. Later, when our tastes became more "sophisticated," hamburgers and root beer or Delaware Punch became lunch du jour. And even later, chicken à la king was standard on the hotel's dining room menu. It was the same creamed chicken without the patty shell but with the addition of a touch of red pimentos, which I detested, but they gave it an elevated taste for adults.

The guest list for my 1924 fete remains mostly a lost memory. It likely consisted of boys and girls of guests in the hotel, and those children whose parents were friends of my parents, as I was not in school yet so there were no school friends to invite. However, I do remember Albert Denmon, the house detective's son, who sat to my left at the big round table. Albert was an older boy, perhaps four or almost five, with beautiful brown curls and big blue eyes. I was crazy about him in my three-year-old way. We often played together on the hotel grounds—sometimes using the golf course sand traps as our own personal sandboxes. Sadly our "romance" ended when he blew out the candles on my birthday cake before I could even take a deep breath. His action, albeit mischievously innocent, made me so mad.

After lunch, while the waiters cleared the dishes to make way for the opening of presents, we ran around the grounds playing tag under the watchful eyes of mothers and nursemaids. Gifts opened, we rushed to play the usual party games followed by the "entertainment." Mother gave each of us a room service soup bowl filled with soapy water and a small white clay bubble pipe. Arranging ourselves on the steps leading to the walkway in front of our bungalow, the girls' party dresses and the boys' short flannel pants were protected from the dripping bubbles by large linen napkins from the hotel dining rooms. We blew bubbles for what seemed like hours. It was so much fun and such a sweet memory.

Then, a late arrival! Her name was Josephine. She was a little thing—much smaller than me. Her hair was very short and light brown. Dressed in a red satin skirt trimmed in gold braid and a red-and-gold pillbox hat tied under her chin, she walked on her hands up the path through the floating bubbles. She had a long tail. By now you've guessed that Josephine was . . . a monkey! She arrived with her guardian, Joe, the organ grinder. As Joe slowly turned the handle of the shoulder organ, playing the only tune it could produce, Josephine danced around at the end of her bedazzled leash, holding out her shiny little palm asking for pennies. Each of us had a small bag of bright new coins that Mother handed out for us to give to Josephine. She accepted every donation with squeaky cries of joy. Josephine was both a performer and a companion for Joe. She had the cutest little face and delighted all of us with her kind temperament. But when the pennies ran out, Josephine did, too—she hopped up on Joe's shoulder and off they went.

For many years Jo and Joe never missed one of my birthdays. Although, later, as a preteen, when the type of parties I had were more age appropriate, I realized Jo and Joe hadn't been around for a long time. And I missed them.

When I finally started school, the birthday parties of my school friends were held in homes—considered mansions at the time—that were developed in the 1920s by the Hancock family from profits earned from oil drilling in the former Rancho La Brea, a Mexican land grant consisting of over 4,400 acres. Even though my hotel life was never boring, I was a bit jealous of my friends who lived in those big houses.

The parties were always fun, although there were a few I didn't want to go to. Some houses and parents made me feel so shy and uncomfortable that when the time came for me to leave home, I would throw up in the flower beds on my way to meet my driver in the hotel garage. I don't remember anything specific about why I felt this way, I just remember that I did. Thankfully, by the time I arrived at the party I forgot about the anxiety that had caused my shyness and settled in for all the fun.

We played blindman's bluff, keep-away, and pin the tail on the donkey, but the big thrill was always musical chairs. Also, it was great for me to know that there would never be a guest named Josephine at any of my friends' parties. I secretly felt very special because Jo only came to mine.

Although the following photo is not from one of my birthday parties, I thought it was an enchanting image. It is a birthday party for six-year-old Gwynne Pickford in 1921 on the grounds of the hotel. Her mother, Lottie, was silent film star Mary Pickford's sister. Mary and her husband, Buddy Rogers, later adopted Gwynne after Lottie died in 1939 at age forty-three.

Gwynne Pickford and friends performing on the south lawn of the Ambassador Hotel. Los Angeles 1921. (Courtesy of Marc Wanamaker/Bison Archives)

Dear Mom,

Reading this chapter, I was inspired to figure out *my* earliest memory, and I have to say I struggled to come up with something before I was five or six. Of course, that doesn't mean you didn't do anything memorable with me. But after sitting with my thoughts, I started to remember one Christmas Eve lying in bed, trying so hard to get to sleep so Santa would come. To this day, I swear I heard bells jingling above my bedroom ceiling on the rooftop; you and Dad never let on about the bells. But even if you had told me it wasn't Santa, I knew it was.

And Josphine the monkey—boy did that bring back some memories. Not that I was there when Jo and Joe were your honored guests, but there was a similar Jo and Joe that I loved seeing whenever we had dinner at General Lee's restaurant in Chinatown on the east side of Los Angeles. There was a little monkey with the red pill box hat and red ruffled skirt. She and her organ grinder handler, who was a stout Italian-looking fellow, were always stationed in the plaza area outside the restaurant. I would have a penny in my hand, and the monkey would scamper up and snatch it away. I know this is going to sound bizarre, but what I remember the most is how creeped out I felt when her leathery hand and long nails grazed my palm. But it didn't stop me from giving her lots of pennies!

Love,
Lisa

7

THE GROUNDSKEEPER, THE PLAYHOUSE, AND THE NANNIES

In my sixth year, a three-room playhouse appeared behind our bungalow. It was the wonderful "Frisco" Mari, the hotel's original groundskeeper, who came up with the idea to have the hotel carpenter shop build the playhouse for me. I always felt as if Frisco and I were buddies because he wanted me to have a proper playhouse. But before I tell you about my wonderful playhouse, I must share the marvelous story of Frisco Mari.

Frisco was a kind, quiet, and hardworking man. There was always a little dirt under his manicured fingernails, and he wore a large hat to shade his head. He smelled of rich earth combined with the quiet scent of freshly cut flowers. He loved the reaction from easterners when they saw plants such as bird-of-paradise, hibiscus, and geraniums for the first time. He was the first in California to acquire a hibiscus plant from Hawaii. In a November 1971 feature article about Frisco Mari in the *Los Angeles Times*, it was reported that one of his favorite guests—a fellow flower lover—was Al Jolson. He would accompany Frisco around the gardens to talk and walk and admire the grounds.

The article celebrated Frisco's fifty years with the hotel. Obviously, my family and I had moved out of the hotel decades before that celebrated day; luckily, we hadn't lost touch, and I was able to congratulate Frisco on such a milestone. In the article, he talked about how he loved his job and how happy the guests were to be surrounded by such lush and gorgeous grounds.

Frisco Mari, the original groundskeeper at the Ambassador Hotel. Los Angeles, 1971. (Los Angeles Times Photographic Archive, UCLA Library Special Collections)

Frisco told the reporter that at one time he had 25 people on his staff. In particular, he had two full-time men cutting flowers and three full-time women creating flower baskets. Back in the day when guests traveled by trains rather than planes, upon their departure they were given baskets with fresh flowers to carry home. He went on to say that every year they raised between 3,500 and 4,000 lilies and poinsettias for baskets during the Easter and Christmas holidays. And over 30,000 carnations were used each year to be displayed in the guest rooms and the lobby. He noted that in 1970, over 92,000 flower baskets were made. Clearly, Frisco kept count of life not so much by days and years, but by flowers.

Frisco had a second life that most of the hotel staff knew nothing about. He and his family raised Arabian horses. In 1949 or so, Mr. H. H. Cotton was somehow financially connected to the Ambassador and owned the land that became San Clemente. He was also a thoroughbred horse owner. When Mr. Cotton and his wife visited an Arabian king, the king gave Mrs. Cotton his Arabian mare. The Cottons didn't know what to do with the mare and they offered it to Frisco Mari. For Frisco, this was a gift of kindness and appreciation for his beautiful groundskeeping work. This one beautiful horse launched a very successful Arabian horse business that Frisco's three daughters ran. Their ranch, Sol de Villa, started out in La Puente and then moved up to the Santa Ynez Valley in Santa Barbara County. At one point I believe they had over forty-five Arabians!

Roadside sign marking the entrance to Frisco Mari's Arabian Horse Ranch in the Santa Ynez Valley, California. (Photo by Kelly Elm)

Frisco was very fond of my father and grandfather, and vice versa. He always said they treated him like family. Frisco proved to be so talented that he was quickly promoted to head groundskeeper. His father was a landscape architect, which is why Frisco was so good at his craft. According to my father, Frisco designed the greens for the Rancho Golf Club, which opened in July 1921—though he was never given proper credit. It was originally owned by the Ambassador to provide a professional course for those guests who wanted something more challenging than the eighteen-hole pitch-and-putt that wound through the hotel grounds. (Rancho Golf Club became a municipal course in the mid-'40s and was renamed Rancho Park Golf Course.) Frisco's love of the Ambassador and the grounds—with its thousands of trees, plants, shrubs, and flowers—created a special oasis, a modern-day Eden, that was such a large part of the charm of the hotel.

My playhouse stood under the canopy of a large California pepper tree. I would pick the pink pepper berries and roll them around between my thumb and forefinger until the bright pink skins peeled off the brown centers. The wonderful spicy scent of berries remained with me all day. The playhouse had a peaked roof and a front porch and stood behind our Rincon bungalow—my home away from home.

I can see it all so perfectly in my mind's eye. The front door opened onto the living room and had a double-hung window. It was furnished with a little kid's piano and bench, and a child-sized chaise lounge. An open doorway led to the dining room with a table and four chairs. The kitchen had a sink under the window, with running water and an electrical outlet on the wall for a little stove that only got hot enough to make lukewarm cocoa. Cocoa and cookies were the main items on the menu, served on what became my favorite tea set. There was also a bedroom, but the bed was more for show than sleeping as it was too small for me. I think one wall had wallpaper with a floral print. As I write this, I realize how extraordinary my playhouse was, and how fortunate I was to have it. I don't know where the furnishings came from, or who paid for all of it, but my father was likely involved. He was aware of my budding taste for elegance, and he probably told Frisco to spare no expense. As with the hotel, my playhouse catered to the whims of its guest and had every comfort I could want.

In an earlier chapter, I mentioned the live-in help who used the extra little bedroom off my sister's room. They were an interesting bunch. There was Miss Otto, a nursemaid who wore starched white uniforms and looked as large as the capitol O of her name. She was as nice and jolly as could be. A staunch Catholic, she attended Mass every Sunday morning at St. Basil Catholic Church at 3611 Wilshire, two blocks from the hotel. Built in 1920, it looked like a medieval fortress with huge concrete towers. At my young age, its size was quite overwhelming. Sometimes Miss Otto would invite me to walk with her to Mass. I loved those early Sundays. I especially liked the ceremonies conducted by the priests in their white and gold robes: the little container that puffed out smoke and the passing of the baskets up and down the rows of pews for the contributions. I always had a dime or a quarter to invest. I never got to taste the wafers the priest handed out to most everyone. To my unknowing eyes, they seemed like cookies. And the sunlight streaming through the stained-glass windows was always my favorite part of the visit.

Then there was Fräulein Hilda, who loved to walk, and she thought I should want to walk as much as she did. Once, on her day off, we hoofed it all the way from the hotel to her friend's house in Hollywood. I don't remember how we got home that afternoon, but we must have taken a bus or a streetcar. I know we didn't walk! When I was a "naughty girl" I was made to stay in my walk-in closet, in the dark, until Fraulein decided I could come out. The closet was large enough for me to stretch out under the clothes hanging from the wooden pole while I cried in the blackness with my heart pounding. Although I can't remember trying to open the door, I am sure she locked it. She was just that awful.

The dreaded closet in Carlyn's bedroom at the Rincon Bungalow.
Los Angeles, 2003. (Still image captured by Steven Hankins Photography from video
produced by Robert Clampett, Jr.)

It was Fraulein who is responsible for my adult-onset claustrophobia, which I began to understand after many discussions with my therapist. It all stems from my need to control situations that feel out of my control. Elevators always give me the same heart-pounding feelings while I anxiously wait for the automatic doors to open, as if Fraulein was somehow in charge of their mechanism.

After Fraulein left (or perhaps was dismissed), came Mademoiselle Colette. Her idea of punishment—when I couldn't remember the days of the week in French—was to make me stand in the corner until *lundi, mardi, mercredi, jeudi, vendredi,* and *samedi* came into my brain. I think she let me forget about *dimanche*—Sunday—because it was her day off! I did manage to speak French *un peu,* all of which I totally forgot by the time I chose it for a language class at John Burroughs Junior High School.

Mademoiselle would often walk me up Wilshire to the elegant Talmadge Apartments at 3278 Wilshire Boulevard at the corner of South Berendo Street, where thankfully they still stand today. The building was named for Norma Talmadge, the glamorous screen star of the early '20s. When she married producer Joe Schenck, he built the apartment building as a gift for her—thus the name. I loved to play with my friend, Ruby, who lived at the Talmadge. Her family had a tiny garden behind the building. Mademoiselle enjoyed visiting with my friend's nursemaid, and I loved the beautiful brick building and the little garden, so different from the acres available to me at the hotel.

Across the street from the Talmadge, at 3300 Wilshire, is the Immanuel Presbyterian Church, built in 1929, located in what is now called Koreatown. I remember the incredible stained glass inside. And within a five-minute walk from there was the Wilshire United Methodist Church at 4350 Wilshire Boulevard. This is where, in 1945, at the age of seventeen, Shirley Temple married John Agar, a sergeant in the Army Air Corps during WWII who eventually became an actor. It was reported that over 12,000 of Shirley Temple's fans gathered in the street to catch a glimpse of the star and her bridegroom, bringing traffic to a halt for hours. It was also reported that in the early years, the church stirred up a big controversy by holding a jazz concert in the sanctuary.

For a short time, my sister and I were cared for by a tall, beautiful lady who came complete with uniforms, long blond hair, and a golden harp. I think her name was Miss Rose. The parlor at the Rincon became a music room with a harp and the baby grand piano. I guess Rose's harpist abilities were greater than her nanny qualities, because she and her instrument were not around for very long. I missed watching her plucking the strings with her long fingers and thought of her like a princess from a fairy tale.

Dear Mom,

I know I've said it before, but I can't stop thinking about what an enchanted life you led at the Ambassador! It just blows me away.

You always spoke so fondly of Frisco Mari. I remember when you and Dad went to visit him and his daughters at their ranch in Santa Ynez, probably back in the early '70s, and, among many other things, you reminisced about the playhouse built just for you.

If I close my eyes, I can picture you holding court in it, sitting with your friends in your doll-like living room in your soft-as-sateen dress, you and your guests excitedly waiting for the water to barely warm for the cocoa. You learned how to be the perfect hostess early in life. I can almost hear your voice in my head, "Oh, it's ready," you say, jumping up from your chair. "Who would like marshmallows?"

Did you choose that floral wallpaper for the bedroom walls? Did you clean up your cocoa mugs, or did you expect Housekeeping to do it? And could Frisco and the playhouse carpenter ever have fit inside if you invited them for a thank-you cup of cocoa? You had so much from an early age. And then to have it all taken away. Not just the playhouse, gardens, room service, shops galore, and parties. But also a lot of very special people. And though you had visits with some of them years later, it was never quite the same.

I am certain you never visited with Miss Otto, Mademoiselle, and Miss Rose. And it is so unfortunate you had to endure the wrath of Fräulein Hilda in particular, and her lasting impact on your life.

But, Mom, I wonder why your mom had to hire so many different people to look after you. Could it be that you were a tad difficult? Bossy?

Love,
Lisa

8

DEL VALLE DRIVE

I was twelve years old or so when my parents wanted to do some remodeling to our bungalow. This meant we needed to move out for a few months while the construction was taking place. We rented a house in a Los Angeles Mid-City neighborhood called Carthay Circle. It was great living in a real house . . . except there was no room service.

Our temporary home was a quintessential Los Angeles Spanish style house on the corner of Del Valle Drive and McCarthy Vista, two blocks south of Wilshire and Crescent Heights Boulevard. South of the house, and across San Vicente Boulevard, was the beautiful Carthay Circle Theatre. It had a tile roof and a tall bell tower, probably the architect's idea of a Spanish cathedral. A small park was at the intersection of McCarthy and San Vicente, and across from our house on the opposite corner stood a huge empty lot where, after the spring rains fell, tall weed-like grass that came above my knees sprouted up.

The house had three bedrooms and two baths. An enclosed patio opened from the living and dining rooms, which had beautiful wood-beam ceilings. There was a guesthouse/housekeeper room and bath that was separate from the house and could be accessed from the backyard.

My grandmother on my mother's side, Lena Barnett, moved in with us. Grandmother's home was at the Ambassador, but she didn't want to stay there if we were going to be away for too long. She was in her eighties, and she would sit with me at the card table by the fireplace and teach me how to play dominoes and Cassino, a fishing card game originating in eighteenth century England. I loved those times with her.

Grandma Barnett had excellent hearing for her age. She could be lying in bed with some ailment, true or imagined, and if someone from anywhere in the house mentioned going for a drive or visiting friends or relatives, Grandma was up and dressed and was waiting at the front door clutching her (never without) handbag. She was a handsome woman with hardly a gray strand in her beautiful "Titian" hair, which she usually wore in a chinois. (The term Titian was derived from the famous Italian painter who would often depict women with reddish-brown hair in his paintings. It's an absolutely gorgeous hair color.)

I don't remember if Mother's baby grand came with us from the hotel or if there was already one present, but a piano stood in the corner of the living room, with a metronome that tick-tocked away when my hated piano teacher arrived for my lessons. I much preferred playing records of popular tunes on the wind-up phonograph in the tall mahogany cabinet—Eddy Duchin's "Did You Ever See a Dream Walking?," Hal Kemp's "Shuffle Off to Buffalo," and Bing Crosby's "My Love"—to practicing piano scales to the relentless rhythm of the metronome.

For the first time in my life, I had neighborhood friends to play with. I loved playing softball with all the kids. We played in the street almost every afternoon. One day at bat I missed the ball. It came so fast that it hit me in the middle of my stomach. I fell to the ground with the wind knocked out of me. I was sure I was going to die as I lay there trying to get some air, but I also thought it was really something special to have that happen to me. It only lasted a minute or two but for a little while my friends, who looked like they thought they'd killed me, surrounded me on the street as I gasped for breath. In an odd way I loved the attention I got.

The Helms Bakery man, dressed in a beige suit with his tidy bow tie, arrived in the neighborhood each afternoon. His yellow truck with blue trim was surrounded by windows and musically offered the best jelly doughnuts anywhere! They were the kind where the bright sugary purple jelly oozed out all over your fingers and clothes the minute you bit into it. It was always exciting to see the Helms Bakery trucks around town, because in 1932 they became the official baker of the Summer Olympics held in Los Angeles, and they supplied all the bread for the games.

There was also an ice man who brought huge squares of ice in his truck for those in the neighborhood who had yet to own an electric refrigerator. He wore a rubber-like apron and would deliver the ice using giant tongs or hooks, resting the ice on his shoulder as he walked up to a customer's house. If we were lucky enough to catch it at the right time, meaning a piece of ice got broken off the block, the ice man would give us a nice hunk to chew on. And of course, the Good Humor ice cream truck sang its way down the street every day just in time to spoil our appetite for dinner. The Good Humor man was always spotlessly clean in his white jacket and slacks, bow tie, and hat.

A vegetable truck with fresh produce arrived twice a week with only the sound of a horn to let us know he had arrived. Trucks driving through our neighborhood carrying sweets, bread, ice, veggies, and ice cream always made me smile when I heard their tunes or honks. Having this neighborhood experience was so much fun for me. We didn't have these kinds of food trucks arriving in front of our bungalow at the hotel. I'm sure any delivery that came to the hotel arrived in huge trucks to accommodate the quantities needed to create thousands of meals a day.

The empty lot across the way was a wonderful playground. A boy whose name I can't remember, whose father worked at the hotel in some management capacity, lived not far away. We became fast friends. After a good rain we would head over to the empty lot and pull up the grass in great clumps and swing it over our heads like a cowboy swinging a lariat. This made for spectacular grass fights. We built forts and fought each other with our grassy weapons until we were so muddy and exhausted we had to call a truce.

There was a little section of shops about a fifteen-minute walk from my house. The Piggly Wiggly grocery store, a shoe repair business, an ice cream store, and a drugstore made the area seem almost like a small town. Important movie premieres were held at the Carthay Circle Theatre, which was built in 1926 at the height of movie palace obsession in Hollywood. Designed in the popular Spanish Colonial Revival style, it became known as the "Showplace of the Golden West." It was one of the most famous movie palaces of Hollywood's Golden Age.

Located at 6316 San Vicente Boulevard, the theater was demolished in 1969 to make way for office towers—another sad statement about the lack of respect shown for beautiful historic buildings in Los Angeles. The interior of the theater, which could seat over 1,000 patrons, was nearly circular, save for the open end that housed the orchestra. For movie premieres, the klieg lights would be trucked in during the afternoon and all the neighborhood kids would walk over and watch the men setting up for the evening. At dusk they would be turned on—three or four depending on the importance of the film—and start sweeping across the night sky. In those days, opening night for every movie had klieg lights, drawing the attention of people who would come from all over the city to watch the stars arrive.

Movie stars had to walk up a long, long path to the entrance of the theater. The crowd stood behind the ropes on either side to wave and holler hello as the stars walked quickly past. The interior of the theater was beautiful. The walls were painted with murals depicting scenes of early California life. The requisite fire curtain, made of fire-retardant asbestos-based materials to prevent or contain a stage fire spreading to the auditorium, showcased a painting depicting the Donner Party and their harrowing journey attempting to cross the Sierra Nevada mountains in 1846.

On Saturdays, my friends and I would go to the movies and head up to the balcony of the theater. I would sit there thinking how wonderful it would be to go to a movie premiere with all the movie stars rather than just standing and watching from the sidelines. At sixteen, my wish came true. My friend Michael Levee, who I'd known since we were both three years old, invited me to attend the opening of *The Life of Emile Zola,* starring

Paul Muni, with Michael's parents. (Michael's father, Michael Sr., was Mr. Muni's agent.) In the photo, you can see the name "ZOLA" hanging from the middle of the tower.

Premiere night for The Life of Emile Zola at the Carthay Circle Theatre.
Los Angeles, September 13, 1937. (Los Angeles Times Photographic Archive,
UCLA Library Special Collections)

With this invitation, a search for the proper dress began. Mother and I went to Bullocks Wilshire where we found the perfect dress—or should I say, it found me. However, it was $49.95, which was a lot of money to spend in 1937, particularly on a dress for a teenager. I had never had such an expensive dress. It was a heavy silk-slipper satin in a deep rust color with a full skirt, big puffy sleeves, and a tight bodice with square neck front and back. I felt like an absolute movie star in this stunning dress. It remains one of my most favorites. I don't have a photo of me in that dress from the premiere night, but here I am with friends waiting to head into the Cocoanut Grove, and I am wearing the dress! You'll notice that each of us girls was wearing the exact same shoes. Maybe they were the best shoes for dancing?

Carlyn Frank (second from right) and friends at the Ambassador Hotel on prom night, waiting to go into the Cocoanut Grove. Los Angeles, 1937.
(Gilmour Family Collection)

After years growing up watching movie stars from the sidelines at the hotel and on San Vicente Boulevard, here I was all dressed up walking along the path *with* the movie stars. After the theater, Michael's parents said it was time for supper and dancing at the Trocadero on the Sunset Strip. It was the most glamorous and exciting night for me! The Trocadero was an upscale nightclub that opened in 1934 and quickly became a place where stars went to be seen. And I felt like one of them!

Dear Mom,

Although I didn't have the number of the Del Valle house, based on your description of it, I'm sure Mark and I located it one afternoon on our way home from a Sunday brunch in West Hollywood. It was just as you described: a Spanish house with a tiny park across the street. Although I'm not sure it qualifies as a park, it was a small grassy area with a large shade tree. The more I continue to work on your memoir, the more I want to see everything you wrote about.

Since I never knew my great grandmother, Lena Barnett, it's lovely to read about how close you two were. And I loved the story of your grass fights with the neighborhood boy. Picturing you covered in mud and grass made me laugh, since I certainly never saw you look messy in any kind of way when I was growing up.

I remember when we lived in Westwood, the same food trucks came by our house each week. Hearing the Good Humor man approach set my feet running! It was the 50-50 bar that was my favorite, but in the summer, it was always the rainbow snow cone I loved. It inevitably dripped its sticky, staining food coloring on my clothes—kind of like you dripping pomegranate juice on yourself.

Your friendship with Michael continued to be special. You and Dad were such great friends with Michael and his wife, Margie. I wonder if you and Michael had crushes on one another when you were teens? I wish there was a photo of you in your beautiful satin dress attending the movie premiere. But the group photo with your buddies does show how lovely the dress was. I know in person you must have looked positively stunning in that rust color, set against your olive skin, dark brown eyes, and dark hair. You were so beautiful, Mom.

Love,
Lisa

9

THE MINIATURE CITY

I spent a lot of my spare time on the Ambassador's Casino level, with its array of marvelous shops that seemed as long as a city block. I don't know why they named it the "Casino" level, since there was no casino there. Regardless, I loved it because it had everything for everyone in one perfect location. The marketing brochures referred to it as a "Miniature City," and invited guests "to find a complete shopping and entertainment center where the finest merchandise of all kinds may be secured at prices which defy competition."

I remember almost all the shops and businesses, especially the psychic and the hair rejuvenator. Though mentioned in the brochure, I don't remember there being a surgeon's office, of all things. I don't recall how many shops lined the Casino floor when I was making my rounds, but I believe eventually there were nearly forty.

I. Magnin

When I. Magnin opened in the Ambassador in 1921 it was a beautiful store. When you walked in, there were two levels, with the millinery and accessories on a lower level, and up four steps to the couture room where all the expensive dresses were kept. A lot of local society women came there because it was convenient for them to shop at Magnin's and then enjoy lunch in one of the Ambassador's elegant dining rooms.

The I. Magnin store at the Ambassador Hotel. Los Angeles, 1921. (Courtesy of the California History Room, California State Library, Sacramento, California)

The "Boulevard Browsings" column in the June 1933 issue of *Vanities Magazine*, focused on Los Angeles nightlife, fashion, glamour, and entertainment culture, had the most elaborately detailed description of Magnin's store window at the Ambassador. Here is the copy, verbatim, typos and all:

Magnin's at the Ambassador Hotel, stresses cool shears for morning, noon and night. A tucked blue chiffon, studded with tiny white stars. And in traditionally collared and cuffed in white pique, takes one easily through till tea time. For that gracious hour, over the less formal dinner, there is a languidly lovely ensemble of pear-beige mascara crepe, in diagonal tucks even unto the pearl satin blouse of ravishingly textured satin. For evening, Magnin's goes triple shear, with a white organza concoction, liberally sprinkled with black coin dots.

Now that's a window description!

There's a story that Florence Holland, my grandfather's secretary, told me many years ago when my sister Jackie and I met with her at her retirement home in Seal Beach, California, to talk about the old days at the Ambassador. Florence spoke about a young woman who was looking in the I. Magnin store window at a beautiful dress. She said someone of "royalty level" came out of the elevator and saw the young woman standing there. Florence couldn't resist and eavesdropped on their conversation. The gentleman said, "Do you really like that dress?" The young woman said, "Oh, I just love it, but I can't afford it because I'm a working girl." He replied, "I'll buy it for you." Without hesitation he strode into the store and bought her the dress. I had never heard that story before, so it was a real treat knowing about it for the first time.

I was head over heels about a beautiful coat at I. Magnin's, for which I saved and saved. It was probably way over-the-top for a teen, but I always had sophisticated taste. Because of my "status" at the hotel, the store manager was nice enough to put the coat on layaway for me. I don't think she believed I would ever have enough money to buy it, but eventually I did. It was such a gorgeous coat, and in fact, it still is. I occasionally wear it out and to this day it makes a beautiful impression. It's a heavy slipper-satin coat, embroidered with black bugle beads sewn in to look like vines and flowers. It's very full and has great big sleeves. It looks like a judge's robe.

Years before Richard Blackwell became simply known as Mr. Blackwell, the eccentric and famous fashion designer, my husband and I were at a fundraising event in Los Angeles. It was probably in the early 1950s and I was wearing the coat. Mr. Blackwell saw me. He immediately walked over. "Where did you get that coat?" he asked. "It's remarkable. I'd like to do a knockoff." I can't recall what transpired after that conversation, except I know I never released the coat to him to borrow to make a pattern. Regardless, many years after buying the most expensive piece of clothing I'd ever owned at that time, the fact that Mr. Blackwell loved it validated my sound decision to make the purchase back in the thirties.

In 1939, a year after we left the Ambassador, I. Magnin opened a beautiful, big new landmark store designed by Myron Hunt, the architect of the hotel. The new store was located two blocks down Wilshire Boulevard from the hotel and, according to I. Magnin history, it was the first store to be operated entirely by electricity and to be completely air-conditioned.

Weaver-Jackson Beauty Parlor

Security First National Bank had a branch on the Casino floor. Some days I would deposit money from birthday gifts or from my allowance, but when my mother was having a finger wave at the Weaver-Jackson Beauty Parlor across the hall from the bank, I liked to stop in and chat with the tellers.

The Weaver-Jackson Hair Company started in Los Angeles in 1907 and by 1929 they were operating a system of ten salons, the most prominent of which was established in the Ambassador Hotel that same year. Weaver-Jackson invented the finger wave, which was designed to soften the appearance of the bobbed hairstyle. Stylists would shape or mold the wet hair into S-shaped undulations with their finger and comb. Once dry, the hair fell into a deep wave style. It was really the rage back in the twenties and many movie stars adopted it.

There was also a crazy permanent wave machine located in the back room of the beauty parlor, and it always intrigued me. The smell of the wave solution—a very unpleasant odor— announced it was in use. I always had to go back to see if anyone famous was connected to it. In those days the machine looked like a mechanical octopus, or a prop from a science fiction movie about a woman whose hair could generate electricity. Invented by a German hairdresser in the

A 1931 advertisement in the Los Angeles Times for the Ambassador Hotel's Weaver Jackson Beauty Shop.

early 1900s, the wave machine had twelve long, heavy electrical cords, each weighing about two pounds, which hung down in a circle from a round top, each cord ending with a clip that attached strands of hair to the rods on the head of the curl-seeking patron. I always hoped that I might have a perm, but my mother said my straight dark-brown hair was perfect the way it was.

If I continued walking along the Casino floor, past the drug store and the Fountain Room coffee shop, I would see the haberdashery that catered to men with expensive taste in clothes, and where my father had three or four suits or dinner jackets made to order each year. The haberdashery was owned and managed by my father's brother, Lester. Once past the haberdashery I would bounce up four steps to Robert Anstead's Remembrance Shop.

The Remembrance Shop

I really loved Bob Anstead, owner of a beautiful store filled with exquisite gifts. Bob let me walk around his shop and look at all the beautiful things anytime I wanted. One year, just before my parents' wedding anniversary, I wanted to buy them something pretty. I took my piggy bank to Bob's to pick out a gift. I especially liked a set of dessert dishes I had seen in the shop a few days before. I asked Bob to show me the plates with the pink borders and the flowers in the middle. I liked them because on the back of the plate there was a crest and a crown and it said "Bavaria," which sounded so glamorous to me.

Bavarian china dessert plate (front and back) from the Ambassador Hotel's Remembrance Shop. (Gilmour Family Collection)

I remember when I asked the price and Bob told me they were $80, I emptied my piggy bank out on the counter and found I was $67 short. As usual, my taste was well above my budget. I looked at Bob. "Oh gosh, I'm sorry. I guess I can't afford those little plates. I was going to give them to my parents as an anniversary gift." Bob didn't miss a beat and said, smiling, "We have a special price for you." I was thrilled. I'm sure the bill for the balance was sent upstairs to my father's office. He wrapped the dishes in a pretty box, and I took them back to my room to hide until the big day. When my mother passed in 1955, I inherited many of her beautiful dishes and crystal. I still have these plates in my home and use them often.

Bob was always a very special person in my young life. I remember going to his house with my parents for dinner a few times. He lived in the lovely Crenshaw/Wilshire neighborhood where one of the most famous houses on his street was the location site for Gloria Swanson's home in the film *Sunset Boulevard.* Sadly, the historic house was demolished in 1957 to make way for an ugly ten-story office building.

Ambassador Drug Company

A big attraction for me on the Casino floor was the drugstore; there I would find a seat on the bottom shelf of the news and magazine rack and look at all the magazines that mother said I shouldn't because they were *risqué*—a word I found intriguing. I would hide a *Whoopee* or *Capt. Billy's Whiz Bang* inside a *Photoplay* or *Modern Screen* (which were acceptable to Mother), and try to figure out the meaning of all the cartoons and stories. I also really liked the movie magazines because they always had pictures of the movie stars who came to dance at the Cocoanut Grove.

The shop owner, Mr. Franklin, was very nice to me and let me wander around as long as I wanted. At the rear of the store behind a red velvet curtain was temptation: a single slot machine. Sometimes I would try my luck with a nickel or two from my allowance and when nothing appeared in the little metal cup at the bottom, I would linger by the perfume counter to sample grownup perfumes like Shalimar, Arpège, and Chanel No. 5. The countertop contained open sample bottles with little glass stoppers that I could dab behind my ears before crossing the hall to the Fountain Room coffee shop for a chocolate soda at the lunch counter. I'm sure I carried a heavy fog of scent from my over-sampling as I hopped onto the stool.

Ambassador Fountain Room Coffee Shop

In 1930, I was nine and allowed to spend afternoons on my own. Every so often I would sit at the lunch counter in the Fountain Room coffee shop next to Bing Crosby while he ate breakfast. He seemed a bit hungover. I didn't know that word then, but he looked somewhat disheveled. He ate breakfast in the afternoon because he went to bed so late after singing in the Grove until one o'clock in the morning. I don't recall talking much to him. He seemed to want to be left alone. I might have asked him to pass the salt for my turkey sandwich. But honestly, I don't remember.

The Ambassador Hotel Fountain Room counter and Coffee Shop.
(Ambassador Hotel brochure, 1936)

Usually I would ask Todd Jones, the fountain manager, to make me an ice cream soda. Todd made the best soda, even better than Chapman's Fancy Ice Creams on Wilshire Boulevard near Western Avenue. Chapman's was an elite ice cream store because they said their ice cream was "fancy." And amazingly, the building was in the shape of an iceberg, so I guess icebergs were considered "fancy" back in the day.

Todd would plop heavy dark chocolate syrup into an ice cream soda glass, the kind with the shallow bulge below the rim. This glass design, which was there to protect the glass from breakage, was very important in the hotel business. The glasses were aptly called Nonik (no-nick) Glassware. Once the chocolate syrup settled in, Todd would dip into the ice cream container and scoop up a large ball of creamy vanilla for the base. He took a spoon with a very long handle and mixed the ice cream with the chocolate until it got all mushy. Just a dash of milk was mixed into that and then he asked, "Say, Carlyn, the usual?" I said, "Of course, you silly!" The soda came with two additional flavors of ice cream, and my usual was chocolate and coffee. After Todd added the two scoops came the part I liked best: He pulled the shiny black handle of the soda water dispenser with the white marble hand grip and the soda filled the tall glass to the edge. Then he slowly pushed the handle back, halfway, and made a beautiful chocolate foam that slid over the top of the glass and down the side. I never drank the liquid until I used the spoon to eat the foam off the top. It was like a cobweb of chocolate that disappeared in my mouth. Then I would finish all the ice cream and take two yellow paper straws and drink the soda down to the bottom of the glass when it made the most disgusting noise that caused grown-up diners at the counter to stare. Which thoroughly amused me—as well as Todd, though he knew better than to show it in front of the customers.

Ambassador Theater

Sometimes, after school, my friends and I would head to the movie theater at the other end of the Casino floor. I knew where to find the light switch and how to start the Wurlitzer organ. According to the Wurlitzer shipping manifest taped to the organ's back, it was delivered on October 6, 1929, after which it was used for musical accompaniment when silent movies were screened. My friends and I would pump away on the foot pedals and try to learn all the different keys to create the many musical instrument sounds. The stage lent itself to playacting, so we also spent many afternoons after school or on a rainy Saturday on the stage doing charades and singing and dancing for our own amusement.

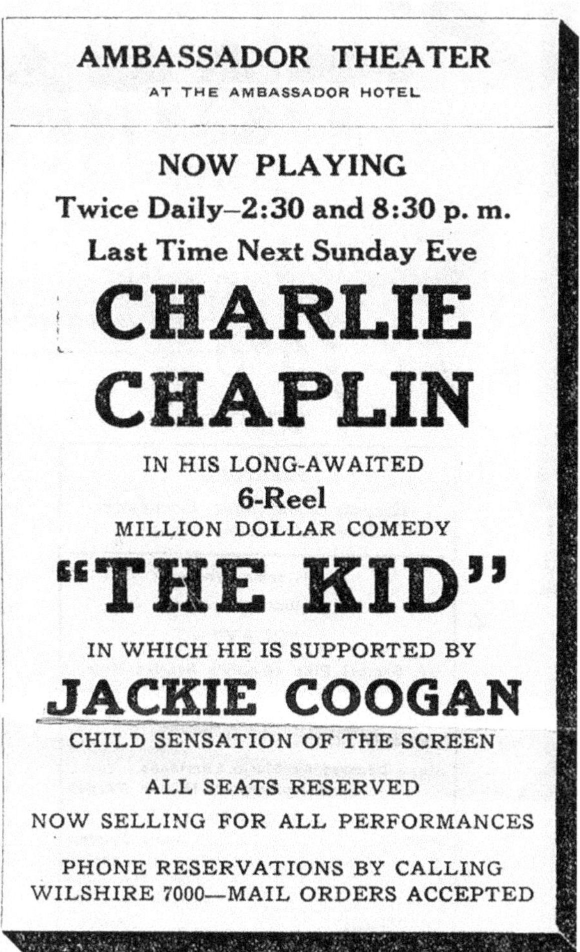

An Ambassador Theater advertisement for Charlie Chaplin's The Kid. Los Angeles, 1921. (Courtesy of Marc Wanamaker/Bison Archives)

The interior of the Ambassador Hotel Theater. Los Angeles, circa 1921.
(Los Angeles Public Library Collection)

I saw my first Mickey Mouse cartoon, *The Mad Doctor*, in the hotel theater when I was twelve. My little sister, just five years old, was with me. It gave her terrible nightmares. She was so distraught my mother wrote a terse letter to Mr. Walt Disney and saved a copy. Here is a transcription:

August 1, 1933

Dear Mr. Disney,

This note is in the nature of a protest against the continually repeated theme of your Mickey Mouse pictures. It has gotten to a point where I have to avoid picture theaters where the Mickey Mouse pictures are shown, as they have the effect of making my perfectly normal children nervous and giving them nightmares.

Last night we saw "The Mad Doctor" and I spent the rest of the night trying to quiet an hysterical child. I can scarcely find anything humorous about graveyards, coffins, and skeletons, and anything pertaining to death.

I can't believe that your sense of humor is so morbid that you can't find any other outlet for it other than unpleasant thoughts. Mickey Mouse could be marvelous entertainment, but I'm afraid "Looney Tunes" will usurp you if you don't watch out.

This letter is the result of conversation with many of my friends, mothers of children, so please consider it.

Mrs. Ben Frank

Ambassador Hotel

Mr. Disney replied to my mother in a letter dated, August 5, 1933, noting that her, "frank criticism," of *The Mad Doctor*, was "greatly appreciated." He shared with my mother that the cartoon was originally designed as a "burlesque on the cycle of horror pictures" playing around the country. Appropriately, he said he realized his mistake seeing a humorous moment played out in "grotesque subjects." He went on to say, "it has never been my intention to make pictures that would frighten children." He closed by adding that he hoped in the future his cartoons would be more to my mother's liking of "good clean fun."

The Elevators

Let's head back to the Casino floor and my next stop. By way of the lobby, past the curved grand staircase, I would arrive at the main bank of elevators. The elevator men were some of my favorite hotel staff. Instead of running up the stairs with the wide brass banister (actually more appealing for sliding down to reach the lobby), I usually rang for the elevator. If there were no guests, the elevator man allowed me to take over the controls. Over each elevator door there was a brass half circle with an arrow indicating the six floor numbers associated with the guest rooms, an "L" for lobby, and a "C" for Casino. When it finally arrived and emptied out either at the Casino or Lobby level, it was my turn.

The elevators ran the old-fashioned way. The brass doors would open and shut by pulling or pushing an iron bar that folded across the door. Going up or down was easy. On the right side of the door was a heavy brass circle with a slot halfway across the top that held a lever. Pulling the lever to the right I could take us up to any of the six floors and pulling the lever across to the left we could go down. I would practice opening and closing the door and then I'd have to practice bouncing until I'd come level with the floor. The trick was to steady the car even with the floor when the doors were opened. We always bounced up and down for quite a while until I could make a level landing. Each time I "soloed," it was always with a backup in uniform at my side. I had that wonderful feeling of being in control—something that has remained part of my character to this day. And for a kid, it was just a great sense of power.

I loved visiting the laundry room on the lowest floor, which was always steamy. In the linen room, thousands of towels and sheets were neatly pressed and folded, waiting for Housekeeping to stack them on the cleaning cart to change them out. I liked to visit Miss Lena Brooks, who was the head housekeeper, in her office. For someone who was in charge of keeping the guest rooms spotlessly clean—which she did with great aplomb—she was surprisingly unkempt, though always very friendly. There was also the staffing manager's office and the chief engineer's office; they were all part of my routine.

Post Office—Ambassador Station

Coming back up to the Casino floor, you could find a branch of the U.S. Post Office. The Ambassador Station was the official name, and every card or letter mailed from the hotel had the Ambassador postmark. Many people who came to Los Angeles from the east would rent apartments in the surrounding neighborhood to winter in the sunshine. They could rent a post office box from the Ambassador Station and buy stamps, mail letters, and purchase postcards picturing the hotel. They were hoping friends and family back in the snow country would see the Ambassador postmark and think they were vacationing at the hotel—never to discover their fantasy vacation residence.

Over the years, the Ambassador offered its guests a stunningly wide range of services. In addition to the above, these included:

Ambassador Barber Shop

Ambassador Candy Store

Ambassador Florist, Inc.

Ambassador Lido Club (health club for women)

Ambassador Ladies Shoe Shining Parlor

Ambassador Men's Clothing Shop

Ambassador Smoke Shop

Ask Mr. Foster (travel service)

Ye Betty Alden Shoppe

Belle Myers, Electrologist

Olva Carson, Psychic

Cooley Ambassador Studio, Photography

Del Monte Hotel Office

Dr. Harold P. Duey, Dentist

Dr. Louie Felger, Surgeon

E.F. Hutton, Stock Brokers

Honorable Dr. Josef de Sigall, portrait studio

Irma Hungerford, Piano Studio

Jackson Manufacturing Co., Custom Built Furniture

The Jeffreys' Bath and Massage

Olga Klarquist, Ballroom Dancing

Chas. Levy & Son, Men's & Ladies' Tailor

G.T. Marsh & Company, Oriental Art Goods

Dr. Morris Melnik, Physician

Old Santa Fe Indian Shop, Indian Art Crafts

Professor Migge, Hair Rejuvenator

Roy Randolph Dance Studio

Harriet Rosenstein, Public Stenographer & Notary

Tanner Motor Tours

Dr. Tirman, Chiropodist

Walton & Company, Jewelers

Weaver Jackson, Beauty Shop
Wetherby-Kayer Shoe Company
Western Union Telephone Company
Yellow Cab Company
Yvonne Shop, Costume Jewelry & Hand Bags

Dear Mom,

WOW! There were so many places along the Casino floor for shopping, coiffing, casual dining, and movie-viewing at the Ambassador, and they were yours 365 days a year. With everything in one place, it was like a modern-day cruise ship on land.

I love the story of the Bavarian plates. You inherited them from your mom and I inherited them from you, but I had completely forgotten I had them until I was working on your manuscript. When I read that you "asked Bob to show me the plates with the pink borders and the flowers in the middle. I liked them because on the back of the plate there was a crest and a crown and it said 'Bavaria,' which sounded so glamorous to me," I screamed in surprise and happiness and exclaimed out loud to myself, "Oh my God, I have those plates!" It was so exciting to make that instant connection after reading those two sentences. I use the Bavarian plates all the time for little cakes and cheese and crackers with my dear friend, Elizabeth, when we have our weekly tea at my house.

Although it seemed Mr. Disney recognized the error of his ways, I feel he still lacked a level of sensitivity as to how terrifying it would be for a child to see Mickey Mouse walking up a set of stairs as they turned into coffins with skeletons coming out! The fact he offered no apology is disappointing and telling. What a frightening experience for Aunt Jackie.

Love,
Lisa

10

ROSE, THE SULTAN, AND TODD

For several years, the hostess in the Fountain Room coffee shop was a beautiful young woman named Rose, who had wavy red-brown hair. She brought glamour to the coffee shop. More than a few businessmen, rather than dining upstairs in the elegant French Room, opted for a coffee-shop lunch instead—just to see Rose.

One day in the early 1930s an exotic guest with his retinue of attendants checked in for a lengthy stay. Ibrahim Al-Masyhur, the twenty-second Sultan of the state of Johor in Malaysia, who was considered to be fabulously wealthy, and his very British, blonde wife, the Sultana, arrived with tons of luggage and their private secretary. Many weeks later when they eventually departed, Rose was soon to follow and was away from the hotel for a long time. Rumors swirled. About a year later when Rose returned to resume her hostess job, it didn't go unnoticed that she had added quite an elegant look to her wardrobe. I remember her walking across the Casino floor wrapped in a mink coat, wearing beautiful jewelry and a feathered Eugénie hat, the "in" style that year. The Eugénie is a small hat, usually worn tilted forward over the face, or angled low over one eye. It was named in the mid-nineteenth century after the French empress Eugénie de Montijo, a fashion trendsetter.

The hotel staff was amazed by Rose's return, but there were a few who were somewhat resentful that she would come back from her sojourn in Malaysia or London (I was never able to find out the details), get rehired, and take up her position at the Fountain Room coffee shop doorway with her arm full of menus and that gorgeous smile. The Sultan may have changed Rose's financial situation, but something more appealing must have called her back to the coffee shop.

There were several return visits to the hotel by the Sultan, and between times, many letters and cables were sent to my father, keeping him up to date with the Sultan's travels. He continued to be very much interested in everything that went on in the Fountain Room and, oddly, he was especially concerned about Todd Jones's hair loss. The Sultan said that each time he came to the hotel for a stay it seemed that the Fountain Room manager was growing balder. The Sultan sent a recipe to my father to give to Todd with directions on how to regrow hair. It consisted of "Richfield tar oil and arsenic acid to be applied thrice daily, and a good shampoo with petroleum jelly." He also suggested that users would grow "beautiful curly hair and blond too. It would be most attractive to all the girls in the Fountain and then I shall be jealous." His letters usually ended with a PS sending his love to all the "girles (sic) and Rose." According to the Sultan's correspondence from abroad, it seems his fondest memories of his times at the Ambassador were those connected to the Fountain Room. I don't know if Todd ever tried the recipe, but I never saw him with any more hair than he had before the Sultan came into his life. I like to think that if Todd had had success with the recipe, it might have become the Rogaine of the 1930s.

One night, before the royal couple were going to head back to Malaysia, they gave a dinner party in the Cocoanut Grove for eighteen guests, including my parents. A special customized round table was constructed so everyone could be seated together. Dress attire was very formal; the ladies were all in evening gowns and bedazzled with exquisite jewelry. The gentlemen were all in tuxedos with tails, and the Sultan was in full dress uniform with ten very large gold medals, heavy gold-braided shoulder decorations, and a round-cut diamond cap for his upper middle tooth. The menu, set at each place, was engraved in blue with the royal crest, and indicated thirteen items, from Beluga caviar to chocolate mousse. What a swell party that was—not that I was invited, but I may have peeked in!

The Sultan of Johor, with an inscription to Ben Frank.
May 21, 1934. (Gilmour Family Collection)

Dear Mom,

It's a shame Rose didn't write her own memoir, so we could unravel the mystery of her leave of absence and subsequent gossip-inducing return. There'd likely have been some juicy bits you could have quoted in this chapter.

You got such a kick out of displaying the Sultan's signed and framed photograph on the antique wooden side table in our living room. You loved sharing his story with your guests. The Sultan's hair restoration recipe is hysterical. I wonder if he ever shared it with Professor Migge, the Hair Rejuvenator, who you said ran a hair restoration business on the Casino floor. And why would this fancy resort have a hair rejuvenator available to guests? Them were the days . . .

Love,
Lisa

11

DRESSES AND DANCES

Continuing down the Casino floor was the Ye Betty Alden Shoppe. Back in the day, any shop spelled with a double "p" and ending in "e" would be very pricey. My best clothes came from Ye Betty Alden, until Bullocks Wilshire opened its exquisite store in 1929, about seven blocks east of the hotel on Wilshire Boulevard just past Vermont. Although the store itself is no longer, surprisingly the building remains and is today still one of the most iconic examples of Art Deco architecture in Los Angeles.

Bullocks Wilshire

This feels like a good place to pause and really appreciate the incredible building that housed Bullocks Wilshire and its historic place in the development of Wilshire Boulevard and Los Angeles. John G. Bullock and P. G. Winnett were business partners, and both had very ambitious ideas about the final design for their upscale establishment. They both visited the Exposition of Decorative and Modern Arts in Paris in 1925—the birthplace of Art Deco, also known as "Moderne" style. After visiting the Exposition, the two men met with Los Angeles-based architect Donald Parkinson, and together all three men were so inspired by this new type of architecture that Bullocks Wilshire became one of the first Art Deco buildings constructed in the US.

The year was 1929 when this magnificent nearly 250-foot tall structure was built. It was covered in copper, tarnished green, with a display of dry frescos all along the outside of the building, featuring examples of the new era of transportation. It was something no one had ever seen before. Built in the shape of a grand church, the store was the first to cater to the automobile culture. Guests drove through a wrought iron gate into a painted porte cochere, where valets whisked their cars away to be parked. Or, in the case of Mae West, busy shop girls had to run to and fro with dresses and long minks draped over their arms as Miss West preferred to shop from the comfort of her limousine.

As a young girl, I spent so many fun afternoons with my mother in the stunning penthouse Tea Room, enjoying our very ladylike luncheons and watching the fashion shows. I vividly remember the food. There were little finger sandwiches with turkey and watercress, the chicken salad with strawberry dressing, and the pecan rolls. And the best part, their famous fluffy coconut cream pie and the French chocolate layer cake. Divine!

The Tea Room catered to movie stars and upscale residents within the surrounding communities of Hancock Park, Windsor Square, and Fremont Place. It is said that these loyal customers helped the store survive the Great Depression, which began a month after its opening. The store lasted for sixty years. However, for many reasons, it closed in 1993, when its current owner filed for bankruptcy, generating serious concern for the future of one of the city's most beautiful and beloved buildings. Fortunately, in 1969, local officials recognized the structure's unique place in architectural and civic history and named it a Los Angeles Historic-Cultural Monument, though there was still worry that it would meet its fate with a wrecking ball. But nine years later, the building took its well-deserved spot on the National Register of Historic Places.

In 1994, Southwestern Law School purchased the Bullocks Wilshire building in bankruptcy proceedings and relocated their burgeoning law library and other facilities there, where they reside today. The city owes Southwestern Law School a debt of gratitude not only for saving this incredible building, but for fully restoring it inside and out to its original splendor. It breaks my heart that the same saving grace did not come the way of the Ambassador.

Here's an interesting side note about Bullocks Wilshire and my mother: It was around 1942, four years after we had left the Ambassador. My mother's dear friend, Marion "Gerry" Fields, was hired by a perfume company to manage the representation of a new, elegant perfume called *De Toi Je Chante*, which means "Of Thee I Sing." (Marion was the wife of the well-known playwright Joe Fields, who wrote the comedy *My Sister Eileen* in 1938.) Bullocks Wilshire was one of Marion's accounts, so she asked my mother if she'd like to represent the perfume.

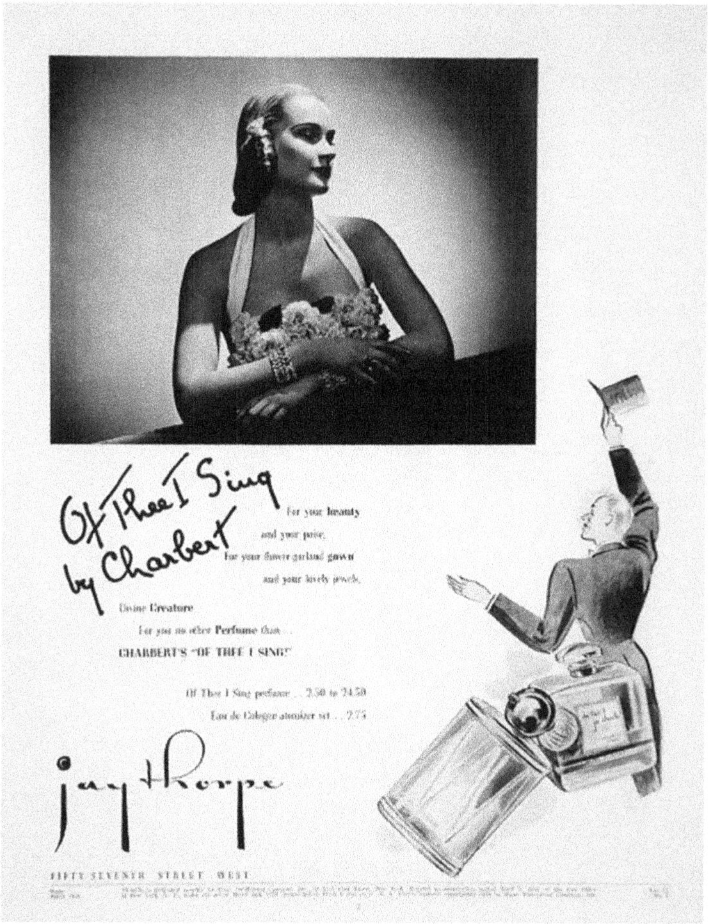

A Jay Thorpe advertisement for De Toi Je Chante [Of Thee I Sing] perfume.
(Stage Magazine, 1938)

The ad from 1938 promoted the perfume at Jay Thorpe, an exclusive store in New York City, offering custom-made clothing from Paris. My mother was such a striking blend of beauty and sophistication, the perfect combination to represent this expensive scent.

A photograph of Bea Frank. Los Angeles, 1935. (Los Angeles Times Photographic Collection, UCLA Library Special Collections)

To be successful, my mother needed to hire a part-time counter girl to sell the new fragrance in the famous Bullocks Wilshire Perfume Hall.

The perfume hall at Bullocks Wilshire department store. Los Angeles, 1934. (Courtesy of the California History Room, California State Library, Sacramento, California)

Within the first week, Mother happened to meet a young woman named Angela, who was working down in the stockroom where the perfume and cosmetics were inventoried. Mother was so taken by her looks and sophistication, she knew she'd be the perfect fit to sell the line—especially with the holiday season approaching. My mother convinced the young woman's manager to bring her up to work behind the *De Toi Je Chante* counter. However, Angela's perfume-selling days didn't last long because the head of cosmetics decided she wanted her to work in *her* department. This in-demand young woman went on to become a very famous actress—Angela Lansbury!

Now, back to shopping at Bullocks Wilshire with my mother. The Collegian Department on the third floor became the destination for all my school dresses. After selecting them, it was on to the shoe department. My shoes were properly fitted by standing with my feet under the fluoroscope X-ray machine. These machines were first installed in shoe stores in the 1920s. However, consumers had no idea of the radiation hazards they created. I remember the machine had a ledge to put my feet on with an opening at the top where my mother and I could look down at the X-ray view of my feet in the shoes to check the fit. The bones of my feet were clearly visible, as was the outline of the shoe, including the stitching around the edges. It was great fun to watch my toe bones wiggle around in the X-rays, but also kind of creepy. It did keep me entertained while mother waited for the saleslady to bring out more shoes for me to try on.

Typical advertisement, circa 1930, describing the benefit of X-ray shoe fitting for kids.

I learned about the damaging impact of cumulative X-rays as an adult when I volunteered with an organization called the National Committee for a Sane Nuclear Policy, better known as SANE. It was launched in 1957 by a group of prominent Americans to bring to light the dangers of above-ground nuclear weapons testing and the inherent danger of radiation.

Cotillion

As a teenager, the pastel taffeta "formals" I wore to the dances at Miss Klarquist's Cotillion, which were held at the Ambassador, came, of course, from Bullocks Wilshire. Several times a year we were required to wear long dresses. Because all my high school girlfriends bought their clothes at Bullocks Wilshire, it *had* to happen that one formal evening at the cotillion, *five* of us appeared in the same dress, three of us in different colors—sky blue, pastel pink, sunny yellow—and two others, both in mint green. We were mortified, as only thirteen- and fourteen-year-olds can be. The boys wore white gloves at these dressed-up events, so their hands wouldn't sweat on our taffeta-covered backs, and the girls—most of us—wore flat heels or little low-heeled Capezio dance shoes, so as not to be taller than our partners.

The evening's dance cards were attached to ribbons or shiny satin-like cords that were tied around our wrists. The cards were made from heavy paper stock. Your card had to be filled up early in the evening, or you were humiliated by having to sit on a chair against the wall and wait for the next name on the card to ask for the dance. The cards were designed to have ten or so rows showing the number of dances for the evening. Boys would sign their name on the line opposite the dance number using a small pencil attached to the ribbon or cord. You felt like such a wallflower if you had to stroll to the ladies' room to avoid having anyone see how terrible you felt being momentarily unpopular.

My grandfather's suite of offices opened off the same hallway as the cotillion, so if I was desperate, I could go in there and wait out the empty space or spaces on my dance card in the comfort of his reception room. I longed to dance with George—the tall blond, handsome boy all the girls wanted—and I *did* occasionally, but short, pudgy Raymond—who only came up to my chin—was the one who not only asked me to dance but invited me to leave the cotillion and go to the Fountain Room coffee shop for a Coke. When I finally ran out of excuses, off we went, my elbow securely in the palm of his hand, propelled down the Casino floor to the

Fountain Room, where I had to face the grins on the faces of whoever was working behind the counter. My favorite waitress Vera, with wild curly dark hair and cheerful smile, had known me since birth and got quite a kick out of my uncomfortable situation with Raymond.

Cotillion classes were held in a large room that was converted into a dance studio on the Casino floor, off the foyer entrance to the movie theater. The studio had an interesting history. Before it became the dance studio, it was the Zinnia Grill, the first nightclub to open in the hotel and the first overall in Los Angeles. It was a small supper club that became a very popular gathering spot for the Hollywood crowd for jazz music, dancing, and—despite Prohibition—drinking. I would imagine cocktails were drunk from coffee cups, perhaps with liquor brought in by the guests. From what my parents told me, it was a stunning venue that patrons and staff nicknamed the Patent Leather Room. The chairs were lacquered in Chinese red, the chair seats upholstered in black patent leather, and the small round supper tables fitted with smokey dark glass. The shiny black walls were painted everywhere, floor to ceiling, with brilliant red zinnias. When the supper club became too small to support its popularity, a portion was converted to a special dining room where children of hotel guests who travelled with a governess or nursemaid ate, so their parents could have a quiet meal away from their noisy offspring. The rest of the floor space was for cotillion classes.

With the Zinnia Grill converted, my grandfather knew that a first-class, one-of-a-kind nightclub would be a huge draw for the Ambassador. On April 21, 1921, the Cocoanut Grove was born. It was my grandfather who came up with the concept and overall look and feel of the Cocoanut Grove. And the timing could not have been better, as the jazz age was really starting to heat up. (I will share much more about the Cocoanut Grove in Chapter 25.)

Although not on my regular circuit of shops and businesses to visit—mainly because I was forbidden to—the Field & Turf Club was a private club situated off the South Lobby, near the exit leading to the swimming pool, tennis courts, and golf course. The club was also near the Cocoanut Grove, which made it a popular spot for social gatherings among Hollywood elites and other prominent individuals who wanted privacy to drink and socialize. Although very exclusive, some of the guests—if my father or grandfather approved—could get a card to be a temporary member of the Field & Turf Club while staying at the hotel.

In the 1930s, Wava McCullough, an American artist known for her signature drawings and illustrations, covered the walls of the Field & Turf Club with whimsical caricatures of celebrities and other notable figures, including my father! A treasured souvenir, which my sister Jackie thankfully kept, was a gift to our father from Ms. McCullough.

A gift from artist Wava McCullough to Ben Frank, circa 1935.
(Jacqueline Schwartz Family Collection)

The palette included a silly poem she wrote to my father:

You don't have this and that like Mae.
Your mouth is not like Joe's.
Your eyes are not like Cantor's orbs.
Nor have you Jimmy's nose.
And so I am at a total loss when I start painting you
for personality and charm I can't do justice to.

The way Ms. McCullough painted our father made us laugh out loud due to his resemblance to Chairman Mao, who, in reality, our father looked nothing like! In this photo of one wall of the club, the gentleman leaning on top of the door is my father, as is the caricature of the pilot above him. You can see the Marx Brothers to the right of my father, and Fred Astaire to his left.

Artist Wava McCullough at the private Field & Turf Club at the Ambassador Hotel. Los Angeles, early 1930s. (Courtesy of Marc Wanamaker/Bison Archives)

And here is McCullough with her painting in progress.

Artist Wava McCullough painting a wall inside the private Field &
Turf Club at the Ambassador Hotel. Los Angeles, early 1930s.
(Courtesy of Marc Wanamaker/Bison Archives)

Around 1940, two years after we left the hotel, Ms. McCullough had put the finishing touches on the caricatures, as seen in this photo, which pretty much covered every inch of the walls!

The fully painted walls of the private Field & Turf Club at the Ambassador Hotel.
Los Angeles, early 1930s. (Courtesy of Marc Wanamaker/Bison Archives)

Tap Dancing

I took tap dancing lessons from Roy Randolph, a tall Latin dancer with hair as shiny as a jaguar's coat. Roy had a large following of pretty Los Angeles ladies eager to learn the time step and "shuffle off to Buffalo," probably wishing to do so with him. Gower Champion (who later in life went on to win eight Tony Awards) and his original dance partner Jeanne Tyler took classes from Roy when they were in their teens. My father gave them their first professional job as dancers in one of the floor shows featured in the Cocoanut Grove. This came after Gower and Jeanne won a dance contest with 150 professional competitors, held at the Grove, while both were still juniors at Fairfax High in Los Angeles. Gower and Jeanne were a huge hit and danced at the Cocoanut Grove for thirteen weeks. Soon after they finished their time there, this remarkable dancing duo went on to be known as "Gower and Jeanne, America's Youngest Dance Team."

Many years later, Gower married his new dance partner, Marjorie Belcher, had a family, and lived nearby to me and my own family. Marge and I became friends, and her son, Gregg Champion, a film director, was a friend of my son Jeff.

More Tap and a Little Jazz

Around the time I was in my mid-teens, my friends and I took a tap and jazz dance class each week from Elisa Ryan. Miss Ryan was the cotillion instructor for Shirley Temple, and for the children of celebrities such as Ray Milland and Rosalind Russell. Her studio was on the second floor of an elegant-looking office building on Wilshire Boulevard and Manhattan Place, where it still stands, occupied, after all these decades, by a Social Security branch office—an organization my old dance classmates and I find useful these days.

Miss Ryan required us to wear god-awful uniforms that nearly broke up the class before it even started. They consisted of a one-piece pink bloomer suit with a white Peter Pan collar and a large white "ER" monogram on the bosom. Since none of us possessed anything like a bosom, the monogram was not very outstanding. We hated the idea of the pink bloomers, as well as the mini-course in social graces Miss Ryan insisted on. The clunky black shiny leather tap shoes with the professional metal toe and heel taps, which made my time steps sound so neat, kept my interest in Miss Ryan's class—despite the dreaded bloomers and manners lessons. I always loved a tap dance or a soft shoe, and secretly longed to be a tap dancer, though I never pursued it.

Dear Mom,

I was recently transported back in time when I toured the historic Bullocks Wilshire building with my two dear friends, Elizabeth and Carla. After the docent-led tour, we spent two hours savoring their exquisite high tea service in the beautifully restored Art Deco tearoom.

When our tour stopped on the fifth floor for the Collegian Department, I actually remembered what the room looked like because you took me there many times to shop for clothes. Although the room is empty now, the architectural details are still preserved, as is the little raised platform to model oneself in the mirror while trying on dresses. When we'd go shopping at Bullocks Wilshire—or anywhere for that matter—I generally didn't like any of the dresses you picked out for me, and our shopping trip usually ended in a snit. You favored dresses that reminded you of what your mother would have wanted you to wear. That way of thinking utterly frustrated me, yet, somehow, we'd leave the store with "your" dress in hand, ready for me to wear.

I'll tell you right now, if you had made me go to tap lessons wearing a one-piece pink bloomer suit with a white Peter Pan collar and the initials of the teacher monogrammed on the chest, I would have run away from home. Thank you for not replicating that part of your youth with me.

Love,
Lisa

12

"HELLO, DARLING!"

Next to the front desk in the lobby was Juel Park's office window. Juel, a lovely young woman, was the hotel's head cashier. She sat behind a little cage-like window where guests would go to cash checks and get their safety deposit box set up so they could leave their valuables if they didn't want to keep such things in their room.

Every year, a middle-aged couple from Chicago (I don't know their last name, so I'll refer to them as Mr. and Mrs. Peters) arrived for their long winter stay. They were well acquainted with all the hotel staff, since they stayed for long periods of time each year. One day as they came up to Juel's window to cash a check, Juel greeted Mr. Peters with a big, "Hello, darling!" Mrs. Peters immediately grew furious and insisted on speaking with the highest authority of the hotel: my grandfather. When he and his long-time secretary, Florence (who, after she'd retired and we'd left the hotel, told Jackie and me the story), quickly arrived at Juel's window, Mrs. Peters angrily told my grandfather, "I want that woman fired for being so intimate with my husband!" Grandfather turned to Florence and said, under his breath, "Who does she think she is? I knew her in Chicago when she was a *madam*!" Though my grandfather tried to placate the woman, Mrs. Peters refused to back down.

She became so hostile that he finally caved in and said he would "take care of it." Unbeknownst to Mrs. Peters, he moved Juel—a valued employee—to a new position that was less visible.

Mrs. Peters must have had a network of spies in the hotel, for she soon found out that Juel was still working there and raised holy hell. Since the couple were longtime guests and had a lot of influence with people of wealth, Grandfather was worried they would badmouth the hotel to all their rich friends back East. But he still wanted to look out for Juel.

I learned many years later, again, from Florence, that my grandfather had found a solution to keep Juel employed, just not at the hotel. Turns out, she was a remarkable seamstress and had a quiet sideline business making exquisite lingerie for movie stars who were hotel guests. My kind and generous grandfather funded a little lingerie shop for Juel in Beverly Hills, which later became Juel Park Lingerie on Wilshire Boulevard at Beverly Drive. The year was 1929 and Juel was twenty-two years old; for decades the store was known as the most expensive and elegant shop for fine haute couture lingerie. Her boutique quickly became renowned for crafting stunning, custom-made lingerie pieces that attracted numerous Hollywood stars and members of high society. Park's creations were celebrated for their exceptional quality and meticulous attention to detail. Each piece was uniquely designed, ensuring that no two items were identical. She utilized the finest silks and laces, embodying the elegance and glamour of the Golden Age of Hollywood. I often wondered if my grandfather and Juel had remained friends, and if he provided any business advice to her over the years.

Juel's clients included Joan Crawford, Marlene Dietrich, Elizabeth Taylor, Ava Gardner, Rita Hayworth, Lucille Ball, Katherine Hepburn, Mae West, Zsa Zsa Gabor, and Lauren Bacall. Only Juel—and their lovers—knew what they were wearing underneath their dresses. And to think it all started with "Hello, darling!"

Seamstress Juel Park sewing a gown in a window display. Beverly Hills, 1929.

Just off the foyer was the entrance to my grandfather's office. It was purposefully hidden away from the activities of the hotel. Florence had her desk in the large, elegant reception room, which was paneled in oak with red carpeting throughout. Grandfather's office was through a door to the right of Florence's station. He had a huge walnut desk with a large window on either side looking out across the hotel grounds. This setup was consciously designed to impress all who entered. Florence had been my grandfather's secretary when he was managing the Hotel Alexandria, and when he permanently moved to the Ambassador, Florence came along with him.

Many years after she had left the hotel, Florence told us that "A. Frank," the name she always used when speaking about my grandfather, kept several scratch pads in the drawer of his desk and she had better be sure he never ran out! "He always carried one in his pocket," she explained, "whenever he left his office for other parts of the hotel." Florence gave us examples of some of his notes: "The light in the front of the art gallery has been out since January 21." "The rug on the third floor between room 347 and 348 has a tear in it." "There is a loose wire coming from the table lamp in the lobby by the south door." Florence went on to say that my grandfather would keep all these memos for two weeks, and if the problems hadn't been taken care of by then, he would have Florence call the responsible staff member and summon them to his office right away, whereby my grandfather would give the staffer hell for not resolving the issue. Florence remembered overhearing staff members say, as they walked past her desk on their way out, "Who's been feeding the old man red meat today?" But she reassured us that all the employees loved him. And although he gave the appearance of being unemotional, he was really anything but. My father captured this quality perfectly when he gave my grandfather a silver cigarette case inscribed, "To our hardboiled egg, who is all soft on the inside."

Dear Mom,

Your grandfather sounds like a cast-iron cream puff—often harsh in his approach, but a real softie deep down inside. His solution to the problem with Juel was brilliant. I have to say his personality reminds me of you, Mom. You could be tough and demanding on people, just like your grandfather. There were times when I didn't care for the way you spoke to people you hired to do work around the house, such as the housekeeper, the painter, and the gardener. You could be bossy to those who worked for you if their output fell below your high standards. It was embarrassing for me to be around the less-than-kind version of you, even as an adult, but you also had a beautiful humanitarian side to your personality that was enviable. I loved you no matter which version showed up. Later in my life, I came to understand that it was insecurities resulting from your identity being stripped away after leaving the hotel that triggered the not-so-kind side of you.

Love,
Lisa

13

MY MOTHER'S PORTRAIT

Earl Stendahl was a pioneering American art collector who launched Stendahl Art Galleries at the Ambassador the year the hotel opened. The gallery was located just past the Ambassador Smoke Shop. At that time, Stendahl exhibited and sold works by California Impressionists of the early twentieth century, including Joseph Kleitsch, a Hungarian-born landscape artist who painted beautiful California plein air oil paintings, rich with vibrant colors. In addition, Stendahl featured works by Henri Matisse, Paul Klee, Wassily Kandinsky, Marc Chagall, Constantin Brâncuși, David Alfaro Siqueiros, and Diego Rivera. One of Stendahl's most significant collectors was William Randolph Hearst.

The gallery's high-profile location inside the hotel gave it a rare visibility, bridging the worlds of art, celebrity, and society. By showcasing European and Californian painters and championing bold new styles from Mexico and beyond, Stendahl's vision laid the groundwork for a serious art market in Los Angeles.

In 1925, Kleitsch painted *Mrs. Ben Frank*, a beautiful oil painting of my mother. It is a large, framed portrait of her dressed in a lovely silvery evening gown. He beautifully captured the elegance and grace that was my mother. She is shown wearing the white silk, flower-embroidered Spanish shawl that I described in Chapter 5—the very shawl placed on top of her baby grand piano. From the piano to my mother's back, the shawl made for a beautiful portrait and one of Kleitsch's few works of a person, rather than a countryside landscape.

The 1925 oil painting "Mrs. Ben Frank," by Joseph Kleitsch.
(Gilmour Family Collection)

We always joked with Mother that she had been "done" by a landscape artist. The portrait hangs in my living room today. A tag on the back indicates that it was shown at the Los Angeles County Museum—*the* art museum in Los Angeles—before the name changed to the Los Angeles County Museum of Art (LACMA).

A photograph of the portrait is included in Patricia Trenton's *Joseph Kleitsch: A Kaleidoscope of Color* (2007). Trenton asked me if my mother's portrait had been commissioned. I told her I didn't think so; I thought it was more likely in lieu of payment for a complimentary guest room and studio at the hotel. Other Kleitsch paintings were shown at the Stendahl gallery, two of which portrayed scenes specific to the Ambassador. *The Oriental Shop*, painted in 1922, features Mrs. Edna Kleitsch and her friend. *Saturday Afternoon at the Pool*, a painting of the Ambassador pool, was created while Kleitsch was in residence at the hotel. (It is uncommon to know exactly when his paintings were made, as they often went undated.)

Dear Mom,

Growing up, I can't remember a time when your mother's portrait didn't hang in our living room. I know ownership of the painting was always an issue between you and Aunt Jackie. It wasn't something you felt you wanted to share. So, after you passed in 2017, I decided to surprise Aunt Jackie and give her the painting on permanent loan. She was overwhelmed with emotion. The portrait now hangs in her living room, on the wall behind the piano your mother played Rachmaninoff on when you lived in the Rincon bungalow.

Love,
Lisa

14

CONTINUING ALONG THE CASINO FLOOR

Hotel Operators

A short hallway across from the Stendahl Gallery led to the telephone room. I never missed a chance to tap on the little window of the locked door to see if Goldie Palmer, the chief switchboard operator, would let me come in and watch her work. It was an exciting place to spend time observing all the communications coming in and going out! Goldie was one of my favorites of all the hotel employees. She monitored the operators—all women—sitting at a long wall of switchboards. Each operator wore a headset with earphones and a little microphone-like speaker to talk into. There were eight or so positions at the switchboard, and each operator had a section of the board to run. They sat on high-backed swivel chairs, and Goldie stood behind her troops with her own headset and speaker.

It was really exciting to listen to and observe all the communications coming and going. I loved to watch the ladies pull the long tan cords with the shiny brass tips out of the base of the board and plug them into the little holes when the lights flashed on as they answered, "Ambassador Hotel" or "Operator, number please." They worked rapidly because there were many hundreds of extensions in the enormous hotel building. I think Goldie was able to listen in on any call to make sure her operators were handling them properly. I always wanted to do that, too, as I was sure there would be juicy tidbits of gossip, but Goldie would never allow it. The operators must have been tempted to listen in themselves, and perhaps they did, but as far as I could tell, their lips were sealed.

Ambassador Barber Shop

Next stop was the barber shop, with its beautiful black-and-white tiled floor. I always looked in to see which gentlemen were getting a shave and a haircut. The shop had the best scent. The woodsy, spicy aroma of bay rum being slapped on the faces of clean-shaven men is forever embedded in my olfactory memory. It always smelled so manly to me, and I appreciated it even more when I was older, when my dates would use it before we went out. I also remember that every man usually had a pretty lady sitting by the side of his chair, manicuring his nails while the barber cut his hair. My father had regular manicures. His nails were always buffed and shiny.

Sache Knitting and Gift Shop

The tiny Sache (pronounced Saw Chee) Knitting and Gift Shop was either next door to, or possibly tucked into, the Oriental Shop inside G. T. Marsh and Company, which specialized in Asian textiles and gifts. It seems odd that the two businesses would be situated in that way, but it may be why Sache's shop was not included in any of the hotel directories from the late '20s that listed all the shops and non-retail businesses located on the Casino level—or "the Arcade," as it was sometimes called. Regardless, Sache and her shop hold special memories for my sister and me.

Knitting was very popular and ladies from around town came to buy yarns and ribbons from Sache, a tiny lady with frizzy blonde hair. She always had a lot of guests who wanted to partake in her private knitting and crocheting lessons. Knitting with silk ribbon was a new and very expensive "in" craft that Sache mastered. Her store had miles of yarns and ribbons in more colors than I thought even existed. Sometimes Sache would give me a job involving "yarn management." If my sister was tagging along, one of us would hold out our arms with the long lengths of yarn over our wrists, while the other one wound the yarn into neat balls to be picked up by Sache's customers. But the best part of "yarn management" was listening to Sache's stories of her life as a girl in Russia. My sister and I loved the time we spent in Sache's little shop.

The Doll Room

Down the west hallway, intersecting the telephone room and Sache's shop, was a door with a sign that said, "Doll Room." Most Mondays when I came home from school, I would end up there. It was the workroom where the ladies fashioned the beautiful wax dolls that decorated every table in the Cocoanut Grove on Tuesday nights—Star Night. The doll faces were made to look like the face of the movie star of the week. It was quite remarkable how accurately they resembled the humans they were modeled after.

The ladies made the dolls' clothes out of fabric, crepe paper, and ribbons. Only one lucky guest from each table got to take a doll home. But I seem to recall that extra dolls were made and sold in Bob Anstead's Remembrance Shop. Occasionally I was able to help by handing a dollmaker a piece of ribbon or a glue bottle. I was so excited when one day, one of the dollmakers made a mistake and I asked if I could have the doll just as she was about to toss it in the trash! Luckily the dollmaker agreed, but sadly, over the years I lost the doll. The following photo of Fay Wray with her wax doppelganger taking center table on Star Night in the Cocoanut Grove is a wonderful example of the realistic dolls.

*Fay Wray and Fredric March with Ms. Wray's wax doppelgänger
at the Cocoanut Grove's Star Night. Los Angeles, 1937.
(Courtesy of Marc Wanamaker/Bison Archives)*

The Pastry Kitchen

There was another connecting hallway at the west end of the Casino floor, which led to pantries and kitchens serving all the dining rooms, the Cocoanut Grove, the Fountain Room, and the Lido restaurant. This is also where all the room service orders and food for various meetings and convention luncheons and large banquets for hundreds and hundreds of guests were prepared. It was always really busy, bustling with so many bakers and decorators and the like. It was an interesting—and sweet smelling—place to watch the constant movement.

I loved to go through the swinging doors and down to the pastry kitchen. The pastry chefs had a kitchen all to themselves! It was like watching artists or magicians at work. I'd stare as they spun strands of sugar into fancy baskets and decorated them with candy flowers in all different colors. Sometimes, when the basket was finished, I was invited to taste some of the leftovers. The sugar baskets were filled with little cakes called *petits-fours*. They were topped with white and pink icing; some even had chocolate squiggles, and all of them had little sugar flowers. At least one night a week the baskets would get handed out, believe it or not, to *everyone* in the Cocoanut Grove. At other times, they would make their way to all the guests at fancy parties in the French Room or the Fiesta Room.

One of my father's fun ideas was to have cakes made in the shape of a telegram, with a message to the recipient about an upcoming event, meeting, party, or other gathering. He really was ahead of his time. Here's a photo of Stan Laurel with one of the telegram cakes:

Telegram cake for Stan Laurel from Ben Frank.
Los Angeles, February 16, 1936. (Gilmour Family Collection)

The Ambassador's famous executive chef, Henri Bassetti, created a thirty-two page promotional booklet entitled Recettes Ex Quises—De La CALIFORNIE PAR NORTRE CHEF, which means Exquisite Recipes From Our California Chef.

Apparently when you inquired about the hotel rates you could request the chef's recipe booklet at the same time!

*A 1937 Ambassador Hotel brochure with recipes and a "Chef's cookbook offer"
for guests. (Gilmour Family Collection)*

The first page includes a personal note from Chef Bassetti:

Most of the recipes which follow are not difficult to prepare, but should you have trouble, just send me a message when you arrive at the Ambassador, and I shall find it a pleasure to prepare them for you.

Wow, how about that for service?

There are whimsical drawings and photographs throughout the chef's booklet, showing people engaged in all sorts of activities around the hotel that have no relevance to the recipes. Oddly (and awfully), there are other drawings that include some racist cartoons about Japanese people—a terrible reflection of the times.

All the recipes in the booklet were written in paragraph form. Here are a few—exactly as they originally appeared. You will notice some important instructions missing:

Ambassador Coffee Shop Waffles

One egg, 2 tablespoons granulated sugar, two cups milk, 1 1/2 teaspoon baking powder, one tablespoonful melted butter, about 3 1/2 cups soft wheat flour. Beat up egg in large bowl and add sugar and sour milk. Mix soda and baking powder with a little flour and add to other mixture. Stir enough flour in so that your spoon will leave a track when you draw it through the mixture and then add to the melted butter. Have the iron hot and grease both sides. Put about 2 1/2 tablespoons of batter in the middle of iron and turn on immediately.

Milk-Fed Chicken, Cocoanut Grove

Unjoint a spring chicken. Have it well seasoned, fry in clarified butter. When almost cooked, add some chopped shallots and green onions, a little garlic, sliced mushrooms and 1/4 cup of chicken broth and smother it for another 5 minutes. To be served in a chafing dish with baby artichokes, green peas, olivettes, potatoes and in butter-fried chicken livers sprinkled over.

Pudding Diplomat

Take pudding molds, put some melted brown caramel sugar on the bottom. Fill the mold with small pieces of sponge cake or with lady fingers, add some sliced pineapple, raisins and chopped walnuts. Cover fully with custard, cream and bake. Add apricot sauce separately.

More than forty members of the Ambassador Hotel kitchen staff. Front row, in suits: Ben Frank, hotel manager, and his brother, Lester Frank, assistant manager; second row, in suit: Abe Frank, vice president. Los Angeles, July 1923. (Workman and Temple Family Homestead Museum, City of Industry, California)

I don't recall much about Chef Bassetti, so I did a little digging to see what I could find. First, he is not pictured, as he did not begin his employment at the Ambassador until the late '20s. Prior to coming to the Ambassador, he was the chef de cuisine at the Hotel Alexandria in Los Angeles. I also found a fun story about him by Ben Starr, a food critic. Chef Bassetti was famous for one of the Ambassador Hotel's signature—and somewhat decadent—desserts: black bottom pie. According to Mr. Starr, the black bottom pie was a lush, layered dessert that started with a rich chocolate base ("the black bottom") topped with a rum-infused meringue custard and crowned with whipped cream, or sometimes a brûlée.

What made the pie so popular was that, despite Prohibition, rum was one of its star ingredients. Generously laced with liquor, black bottom pie was enjoyed by the Hollywood elite and political power players at the Ambassador. It was a wink-and-nod kind of dessert. People couldn't legally sip rum at their table, but they could imbibe it whipped into their custard and served under the watchful eyes of the maître d'. Black bottom pie was boozy, elegant, and indulgent—a perfect fit for the opulence of the Cocoanut Grove nightclub and the glamorous guests it served. Sadly, I don't recall ever eating it, but that was probably because of its "adults only" status.

Dear Mom,

How fitting the name Goldie was for the times, and for someone with the job of head hotel operator. If her team of switchboard ladies could talk today, imagine what they might say.

I can't remember if Dad ever wore any cologne or aftershave. What I do remember is that he always shaved Monday through Friday, but unless you had plans, there was always a self-imposed no-shave policy on weekends.

I'm pretty sure none of the pastry chef's talents rubbed off on you, as I can't recall you ever baking anything except Toll House cookies and maybe an occasional two-layer birthday cake. I also seem to remember that Jeff and I preferred the birthday cakes from Ralph's supermarket over yours!

I have never been tempted to try any of the recipes in Chef Bassetti's booklet. Not only are they unappetizing, at least to me, but the recipe instructions were written in such an unfamiliar style and with so little information that most don't mention measurements, cooking times, or even the oven temperature. I loved your anecdote about how the chef's famous black bottom pie managed to evade the Prohibition laws. Could he have been arrested for a booze-laced topping of whipped cream?

Love,
Lisa

15

HEROES AND VILLAINS

I was six years old on September 20, 1927, when I stood in the lobby at the entrance to the French Room, where a private reception had been prepared for the arrival of a very important person. I was patiently waiting to meet the

"hero of the world," Charles Lindbergh, upon his return from his famous flight to Paris. He had come to Los Angeles to be honored at a public banquet in the Fiesta Room, attended by nearly one thousand guests.

Under huge headlines, newspapers of the day mentioned that the hotel was sold out, and that the cost of the banquet dinner was ten dollars per person, an extravagant amount for that time. The guests surely got their money's worth; the menu was presented in an elegant four- page program printed on heavy-bond paper and featuring a gold bas-relief of Lindbergh's head.

The cover of the menu program for Charles Lindbergh's banquet reception at the Ambassador Hotel. Los Angeles, September 20, 1927. (Gilmour Family Collection)

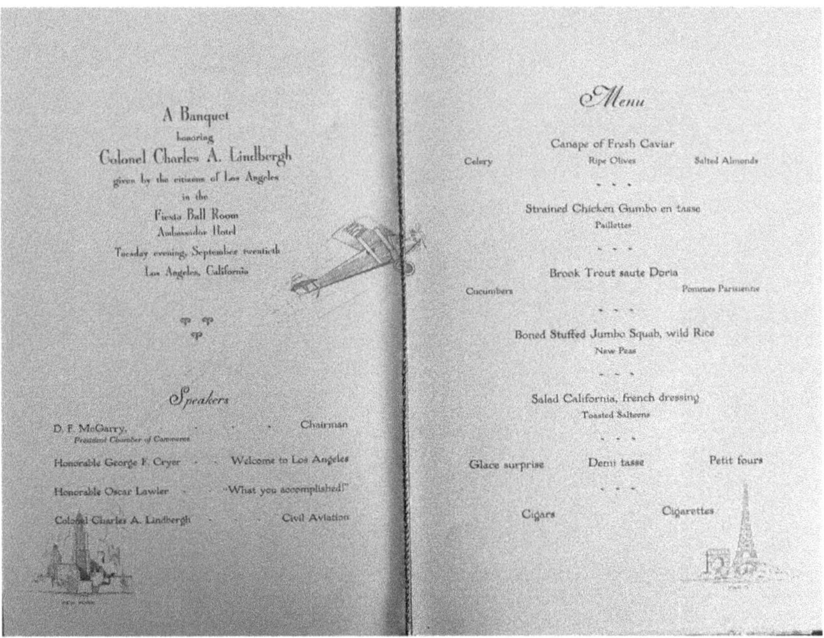

The menu prepared by the Ambassador Hotel's executive chef, Henri Bassetti, for a thousand guests attending the Lindbergh banquet. Los Angeles, September 20, 1927. (Gilmour Family Collection)

I was beyond excited to meet Lindbergh. Time seemed to slow down, and then suddenly he came walking across the lobby, escorted by a lot of important-looking men, and there I was, standing still, looking up at a very tall blond man. I was wearing my best dress and my white patent leather Mary Janes, with my father by my side. As Lindbergh approached, my starstruck eagerness got the better of me. I said hello to the hero before my father had a chance to introduce me, and Lindbergh, not missing a beat, bent down, smiled a big smile, and put out his hand to shake mine—like I was also an important person. I knew I would have a lot to tell the kids at school the next day. It was the most exciting and memorable moment in my whole six years!

Sadly, in March of 1932, the twenty-month-old son of Charles and Anne Lindbergh was abducted from their home in New Jersey. The infant's remains were found two months later, and this tragedy became known as the "crime of the century." The Lindbergh kidnapping was one of hundreds—some say thousands—of kidnappings with ransoms occurring across the country in the early 1930s, before kidnapping became a federal offense. Anxious parents everywhere were fearing for their children's safety. As a result, they were having their children fingerprinted. My sister Jackie and I both remember having our prints taken; I was eleven and she was five. A tall man in a dark suit and white shirt, smoking a cigarette, came to our bungalow, smudged our fingers with ink, and pushed them onto a piece of paper with our name on it, which he placed in his briefcase. I can't remember what our parents told us so we would not become frightened, but I remember the fingerprinting like it was yesterday. It wasn't until Jackie and I were older that our parents told us the man was from the local FBI office.

Much later in life, I learned about a terrifying, too-close-for-comfort kidnapping plot that, had it been executed, would have changed our family forever. A story in the *Los Angeles Evening Express* on November 30, 1931, four months before the Lindbergh kidnapping, reported that Ralph Sheldon, a former Al Capone gangster, and three other men had been arrested in conjunction with an elaborate kidnapping scheme. These arrests were said to have prevented at least seven high-profile kidnappings, one of which had targeted my grandfather, Abe Frank. The other men were Guy McAfee, a local gambling baron; Walter McGinley, a Santa Monica oilman; Sol Zemansky, a wealthy pawnbroker and politician; Wirt Bowman, a millionaire; and several others.

There's an unfortunate side note to my little-girl adoration of Charles Lindbergh. In the summer of 1941, there was an America First Committee rally at the Hollywood Bowl. Lindbergh was the keynote speaker. I was there as part of a protest group against Lindbergh and the isolationist position he and others were advocating. When he spoke, he said a lot of terrible things about Jews and the United States staying out of World War II. His rhetoric sickened me.

Another flying hero stayed at the hotel in July of 1932. Amelia Earhart was a guest after completing her solo flight, making her the first woman to cross the Atlantic by plane. I remember the excitement of her arrival, but unfortunately I was not able to meet her because I couldn't miss school.

Dear Mom,

Aunt Jackie told me she remembered the encounter with the FBI agent very well, and how weird and scary it was. Hearing about this firsthand really shocked me. I can't imagine how terrified you would be today if your grandchildren had to be fingerprinted for the same reason. Thank goodness the plot to kidnap your grandfather and others was thwarted! You told so many stories over and over again. How did I not hear about all this intrigue before reading your manuscript?

I love that you were a part of a protest group against Lindbergh and his awful politics and anti-Semitic rants. It is hard when our heroes fall from grace. You always fought for and raised awareness for things you believed in. I am proud you passed your advocacy mindset along to me, and I know how delighted you were that both your grandsons carried that same advocacy spirit forward.

Love,
Lisa

16

FROM A FIESTA TO AN EMBASSY

The Ambassador Hotel's original design featured a huge dining room that didn't have a distinct name upon Opening Day. But a few years later it was dubbed the Fiesta Room. Doing some research I found that the dining room was interchangeably called the Fiesta Room (this is my recollection) as well as the Fiesta Ballroom in the early '20s through the early '40s.

I vividly remember each year the Fiesta Room was transformed to accommodate a fancy costume ball for an all-staff party hosted by my father and grandfather. One year my father came as Henry VIII.

As you can see, he absolutely looked like the Tudor king. As he was getting

Ben Frank as Henry VIII at the Ambassador Hotel's annual staff costume ball. Los Angeles, 1935. (Gilmour Family Collection)

ready to leave the bungalow for the party, my sister Jackie noticed that "Henry" was missing his sword. It was nowhere to be found. Jackie ran around the bungalow looking for a suitable replacement and found mother's letter opener and voilà—costume completed. Whenever I come upon this photo of my father, I always wonder where on earth he got those crazy shoes.

One time, my father's secretary, Irma, and my grandfather's secretary, Florence, came as hod carriers, laborers who carried bricks to a bricklayer. The bricks were loaded into a "hod," which was a V-shaped trough mounted on top of a long pole. The two secretaries were dressed in overalls, carrying bricks in a hod. My grandfather saw the two of them wandering around the lobby and tried to throw them out. He didn't recognize Irma or his own secretary, Florence, who had donned their costumes early for the ball! This was a story told many times over by all the staff members, with much laughter.

Sometime after 1943, the Fiesta Room was remodeled and renamed by the famous architect Paul Williams. By changing the name to the Embassy Ballroom, the hotel could have been aiming to evoke a stronger sense of elegance or prestige.

The Fiesta Room ran the entire length of the hotel's east side with windows reaching all the way around. Back in the day, it was known to be the longest dining room in California. It could easily hold a thousand people for a sit-down banquet. From it, you could see all over the city, though there wasn't much out there in 1921. One of the hotel's many marketing brochures boasted, "You can see all the way to the sea from the dining room," which was not true. You couldn't possibly, but it sounded good. At the end of the room was an arch, and a beautiful mural of early California life that was very colorful. The Fiesta Room was the venue for six Academy Awards ceremonies, from 1930 to 1943.

Ben Frank in his Ambassador Hotel office with a portrait of his father,
Abe Frank, on the wall. Los Angeles, 1934. ("Dick" Whittington Photography
Collection, University of Southern California Digital Library)

The Ambassador Hotel's original dining room. Los Angeles, circa 1926.
(Eyre Powell Chamber of Commerce Collection,
Los Angeles Public Library Collection)

The Fiesta Ballroom at the Ambassador Hotel. Los Angeles, circa 1936.
(Courtesy of Marc Wanamaker/Bison Archives)

In 1934, my thirteenth birthday party was held in the front part of the Fiesta Room. (I don't know why my parents planned my party in this enormous room when there were many other smaller dining rooms.) It was a surprise party. My folks told me we were going out to dinner, but first my father needed to check something in the dining room. The doors were closed. He walked in ahead of me, and as soon as my friends, about twenty of them, saw me they all started screaming "Surprise, surprise!" It was really very thrilling.

Tragedy

The Embassy Ballroom is where Robert F. Kennedy gave his acceptance speech for winning the 1968 California and South Dakota presidential primaries on June 4, 1968. And as we all know, when he left the podium, he went through the kitchen pantry and was assassinated. It was a hideous act that, still to this day, makes me unbearably sad. It also pains me because, from that point on—and understandably so—his death was all anyone ever associated with the hotel. I loved Robert F. Kennedy. I volunteered to help him get elected. His assassination had a huge impact on me; I saw him as the future of our country, and he was murdered in a place I had called home.

Given the tragedy of 1968, there are many who disagree with my belief that the iconic status of the Ambassador Hotel should have allowed it to be preserved as a historical landmark. However, I hope you can embrace the remarkable history of this legendary hotel and the lasting impact it made on Los Angeles, and on the tens of thousands of guests who spent so many glorious times there. We should never forget the tragedy of the Kennedy assassination, but that horrific event should not define the history of the hotel.

Dear Mom,

When I tell people I am completing your memoir about your life growing up at the Ambassador Hotel, a certain age group will always say, "Oh, that's the hotel where Kennedy was assassinated." Sadly, for so many, that's the only connection they have with the hotel. Hopefully, your book and the memories you're sharing will open a window for them into the grandeur of the Ambassador and the outsized role it played in the history of early Los Angeles.

I was fourteen years old when Kennedy was killed. I remember feeling your anguish on that terrible day, and in the weeks that followed. You grieved first for the loss of such a bright light and great leader. But you and Dad were also distraught that such a violent and senseless act, against someone you both believed in so deeply, could have occurred in your childhood home. It is a memory I can never forget.

Love,
Lisa

17

THE SOUTH PORCH
AND SWIM LESSONS

The South Porch

At the south end of the Casino floor, a stairway led up to the south porch, the swimming pool, the gardens, and the huge auditorium adjacent to the pool and cabana beach. (More about this interesting "beach" later.) All kinds of wonderful wicker furniture was set up around the very large south porch. A "Polly wanna cracker?" kind of parrot was kept outside there during the day. He had a little stand near one of the many canvas swings placed around the outside edge of the porch. These swings, with their striped green and white awnings and cushions, were quite large, so both couples and families could enjoy the porch in comfort.

This was the place where hotel guests loved to linger and relax, but it was also where people who lived in the neighborhood would frequently come to sit and enjoy their paper bag lunches, taking up all the swings and chairs intended for hotel guests. My grandfather would go nuts when he'd see local residents sitting on the south porch. Grandfather was a very nice man, but he didn't want people who were not guests occupying all the comfortable spots. At times some of these neighborhood people tried to get a hotel room to enjoy a lovely long weekend away from their apartment. I feel bad revealing this about my grandfather, but he didn't want the "riffraff" staying in the hotel. I'm not sure why, as they would have been paying guests. There must have been something else that bothered him about these folks to take such action. Still, Grandfather didn't want to hurt their feelings, so their names were taken and placed on "Grandpa's List." He instructed the desk clerks to tell the neighborhood dwellers they were on the "preferred list" each time one of them inquired if there was going to be an opening at the hotel. The "preferred list," which was actually Grandfather's way of excluding them, was presented as a "waiting list." So as awful as this sounds, at least they felt like they were special.

Pool Time

Just over the south porch fence was the nearly Olympic-sized swimming pool, and everybody who went to the pool had to walk through the south porch to get to it. Guests wanting to enjoy the pool could only use the south elevator, because swimming attire was not allowed anywhere else inside the hotel. I had a lot of friends who told me they used to sneak into the swimming pool when they lived in the neighborhood. They would just come in and swim and nobody ever stopped them. There were never any guards back then. I'm not sure why my grandfather didn't notice, but I am glad he didn't.

In 1923, the hotel had a very intriguing guest who performed an incredible feat in the hotel pool. His name was Harry Houdini, and although I was too young to have seen his spectacular escape trick, my father and grandfather were poolside, along with many hotel guests and reporters. As the photograph shows, Mr. Houdini dove headfirst into the pool with chains around his ankles. On April 26, the *Los Angeles Evening Express* reported the following: "Houdini is planning a sensational escape. Manacled and bound by members of the Los Angeles Police Force, Houdini will be thrown into the deep end of the plunge escaping from his fetters while under water." Another article said he was tethered to a 25-pound weighted ball, which you can see he is holding. Along with his cuffs and chains, this was left at the bottom of the pool when he emerged, unfazed.

Harry Houdini diving into the Ambassador Hotel plunge for an underwater escape performance. Los Angeles, April 1923. (John Cox Collection)

I loved the pool at the Ambassador. My first swim teacher there never went into the water. Word got around that he didn't know how to swim! He was a heavyset man, darkly tanned, with a big chest and belly, and he gave instructions poolside. He used a contraption of his own invention that consisted of a bamboo fishing pole and a long length of rope attached to a brown leather belt, about twelve inches wide and about double that in length. I would be in the water at the shallow end, lying with my stomach on the belt while he held me on the line like a large fish and walked along the side of the pool as I paddled up and back, shallow to deep, deep to shallow, kicking my legs with my arms breaking the water as he called out encouragement from the sidelines. After a while I made such great progress that I never knew when he'd let go of the rope that held the belt and I would be swimming unhooked!

A child's swimming lesson at the Ambassador Hotel pool. Los Angeles, circa 1930. (Eyre Powell Chamber of Commerce Collection/ Los Angeles Public Library Collection)

One summer I was lucky enough to have Fred Cady, the Olympic swim coach, as my coach, and he told me I should be able to swim at least one hundred lengths by the end of the season. He made me do a few more laps each day until I finally did the one hundred lengths without stopping. Little did I know, I had swum nearly three miles! It was one of the great accomplishments of my young life, and gave me dreams about the Olympics, but it was just that—a dream, not something I really wanted to pursue. Nevertheless, having my swim coach push me outside my comfort zone and actually hitting my goal of one hundred lengths made a lasting impression on me about the importance of achieving goals, and how good it feels.

Fred was also the coach for the 1932 Olympic diving team that practiced at the hotel pool. Marjorie Gestring was Fred's star pupil, and at the 1936 Berlin Olympics, at the age of thirteen, she became the youngest person ever to win an Olympic gold medal. It was not easy. She practiced complicated back dives over and over, landing hard on her back many times until she perfected the dive. She had a faithful audience of pool regulars, including me, rooting for her at every practice session. Dorothy Poynton-Hill was also coached by Fred at the hotel and won the high-platform gold in the 1932 Olympics. Thirty years later she had a swim school on Little Santa Monica Boulevard in the Westwood area of Los Angeles and was, for my children, a very tough swimming teacher.

An Olympic athlete who became an actor, Buster Crabbe was another luminary who trained at the pool. He won a gold medal in 1932 for the 400-meter freestyle before beginning his acting career a year later. Johnny Weissmuller, the Olympic swimmer and actor, and Duke Kahanamoku, a Hawaiian Olympian who popularized surfing, also showed off their waterpower in the Ambassador pool, adding to the attraction for hotel guests.

Dear Mom,

Reading about your one hundred-length challenge took me right back to our home pool, when you challenged Jeff and me to swim one-hundred lengths one summer when we were kids. I was probably eleven and Jeff was sixteen—a pretty uneven challenge, I'd like to point out! I remember swimming for what felt like days. I don't remember if I made it to one-hundred laps or not, even though you always pushed Jeff and me to set goals and hit them. With that said, I want to think I did make it to one hundred. I'm sure Jeff did!

I wasn't familiar with Buster Crabbe, so I looked him up online. Wow, how handsome was he?! What a catch—athlete and movie star! Going to the Dorothy Poynton-Hill swim school was torture. She was the meanest person I had ever known at that point in my life. I'm surprised I survived and ended up loving to swim.

Love,
Lisa

18

THE AUD AND SPORTS

Exterior view of the auditorium on the grounds of the Ambassador Hotel. Los Angeles, circa 1921–29. (University of Southern California Libraries and California Historical Society. Digitally reproduced by the USC Digital Library.)

The Ambassador Auditorium was a building large enough to hold horse shows or a convention, such as the Radio Show in 1930, food exposition shows, dog shows and many other highly attended events. It could transition into tennis courts and badminton courts for rainy-day sports. The Aud (as we called it) was located behind the pool on the Eighth Street side of the grounds. One Saturday when I was eleven, my six-year-old sister and I were allowed to go alone to a food show exhibit in the Aud. Many foods were available to sample. There must have also been things for sale because before we set out for the day, I persuaded my sister to break open her piggy bank; after all, spending part of my own allowance seemed rather foolish to me. We took her whole allowance, which probably wasn't that much, and spent it all at the show. We got in big trouble from our mother for wasting Jackie's money in that way, and were both grounded for a week. Jackie reminds me of the crime and the punishment whenever we reminisce about our days at the hotel. She never forgets to mention that it was *my* idea to break open her piggy bank, and how unfair it was of Mother to ground her as well.

During the 1920s and probably the early 1930s, when the horse shows came to the auditorium, the hardwood floor that made indoor tennis and badminton a pleasure would be covered with a deep layer of what looked like little brown wood chips, similar to the bark chips used in gardens today. Boxes were constructed to seat six or eight spectators. White wooden fences were set up for the jumping competitions, some with water hazards to make the jumps more difficult. The horse shows were a big deal, and people really dressed the part: men wore tuxedos and women fancy gowns.

Playing tennis or badminton in the Aud on a rainy day was great fun. Every ball and shuttlecock came off my racquet sounding like it had been hit by a champion. The echo between the floor and the high ceiling turned what would have been just an ordinary plop or ping on the outdoor courts into something that sounded professional.

I took tennis lessons from pro Ben Gorchakoff, who also ran the tennis shop where racquets and various tennis accessories were available. I remember many famous tennis stars using the courts, either for friendly games or for the several tournaments held over the years. Movie stars and socialites came to sit in the bleachers and boxes that were set up on the lawn so spectators could sit and watch such tennis greats as Bill Tilden, always so elegant in his pressed white gabardine trousers, Fred Perry, Ellsworth Vines, Gene Mako, Helen Wills, May Sutton Bundy, a very young Bobby Riggs, probably fifteen or so and already accomplished, and Don Budge. I learned more about tennis watching those great players than I ever did taking lessons. Had I not been exposed to these legendary tennis players, I might not have developed such a strong interest in the game or spent so much time on the courts, where years later I met my husband.

Next to the tennis courts were the rifle and archery ranges. I became a good shot with the rifle, and black-and-blue from the bowstrings hitting my arm as I tried to hit the big hay-filled target with a bow and arrow. An eighteen-hole pitch-and-putt golf course wound through the hotel grounds, complete with little streams and sand traps, and was always busy with guests enjoying the California weather. In the golf pro shop next to the tennis courts, I could borrow a club and get a bucket of balls and hit them into a huge net strung across the end of the lawn. It was always great fun, even though I had a lousy swing.

Guests enjoying the pitch-and-putt 18-hole golf course on the grounds of the Ambassador Hotel. Los Angeles, circa 1935. (Gilmour Family Collection)

Dear Mom,

It must have taken a small army to convert the Aud from a sports arena to a space that could hold an equestrian event. How many tons of wood chips—or whatever they used—must it have taken to cover the enormous floor? And then, it all had to be cleared away—perhaps shoveled by hand into wheelbarrows?

I had quite a laugh that you convinced Aunt Jackie to bust open her piggy bank. But it seems par for the course given your bossy older sister ways. The lesson for you was obvious, but I guess the message for Aunt Jackie was that she should learn to stand up for herself.

Given your access to the hotel courts, coaches, and trainers whenever you wanted, it's no surprise you were an amazing tennis player. Just think, you would have never met Dad if you hadn't taken up tennis.

Love,
Lisa

19

MY FATHER'S ZOO

At the back of the tennis courts, my father built a small zoo. The Ambassador really did have everything. There is a crazy story about how the zoo came to be. Josef de Sigall, a renowned portrait artist and longtime guest at the hotel, kept a companion in his room. The newspaper account of how this "large female friend" was discovered at the hotel is different from my father's version (or my memory), but regardless, I know for sure the outcome was absolutely true. My father's version: Apparently, de Sigall snuck his friend in using the sixth-floor service elevator. How this large friend got onto the hotel property unnoticed by guests and staff is a mystery.

Unusual sounds and strange and unpleasant odors began wafting out of de Sigall's room into the hallway, catching the attention of the management staff. My father, who was very fond of de Sigall, was notified of the situation and came to speak with him. On entering de Sigall's room after the required preliminary knock, my father found him lying on the bed, casually reading the newspaper, with his big, furry, stinky friend right by his side—an African lioness sharing the suite with him! I would love to have seen the look on my father's face when he walked in. But this version is too crazy to be true. I bet my prankster father made it up! The incident was written up in the *Los Angeles Times*, December 12, 1934, confirming that de Sigall indeed brought a lioness to the hotel, while reporting that my father refused to allow de Sigall to reserve the Princess Suite for him and his companion. He instead scrambled hotel staff, and a makeshift cage was constructed on the spot. I like my father's story better.

I don't recall if having a zoo on the hotel property was an ongoing pipe dream of my father's or if it was just the easiest and least disruptive solution to the problem. Regardless, my father took care of things right away.

There was already a small, abandoned building on the extreme lower end of the property on the Eighth Street side. My father quickly had this building converted into a temporary cage to house this non-paying guest until a real cage could be built. This was the start of our zoo, which eventually resided on the property behind the tennis courts. Four-legged and two-legged guests were added throughout the years, making for an amazing attraction on the hotel grounds. Behind the zoo, a children's playground was connected to what seemed to be a nursery school or perhaps a kind of day care center. According to an old hotel brochure, it was where hotel guests could leave their kids (ages three to ten) for a few hours or the entire day, along with their nanny or nursemaid. It was a little Craftsman house and just outside of it were all kinds of swings, a big sand area, and a little merry-go-round. I could go any time I wanted to. It was fun to play with the little kids, who loved visiting the zoo while they were in day care.

Every so often when I'd get home from school, I would go down to the zoo to visit de Sigall and the lioness. He was always there, sitting in a small armchair in the cage reading a book. The lioness, Chiquita, was usually sleeping at his feet, as content as her owner. They were really quite a pair.

*Josef de Sigall wrestling a lion
(presumably his pet lioness, Chiquita) in a cage. Los Angeles, 1936.
(Los Angeles Times Photographic Archive, LSC, 1429, UCLA Library)*

Josef de Sigall was born in Poland and lived in South America before moving to Los Angeles in the 1920s. He was trained as a physician, and he worked as a portrait painter in California. He painted many high-profile people including President and Mrs. Calvin Coolidge and President Herbert Hoover.

Perhaps to reciprocate the management's kindness in the affair of the lioness, de Sigall asked my parents' permission to paint my portrait in oils. However, sitting very still for forty-five minutes on the first day was torture. There I was, in my best dress, sitting up very straight in a very big red velvet chair, with de Sigall constantly yelling at me, sometimes in Polish, not to move. I hated every minute of it.

Josef de Sigall's unfinished portrait of Carlyn Frank , age six, at the Ambassador Hotel. Los Angeles, 1927. (Gilmour Family Collection)

After the second sitting, he had a talk with my mother. "She is impossible. She refuses to sit still. How can I paint her if she keeps moving?" I guess it was easier for him to get along with a lion than a six-year-old. In truth, the lion did pretty much stay in one spot at his feet. I had forgotten that I kept the unfinished canvas of my portrait stored away for decades. It looks like I was naked, which of course I was not. I came upon it one day in a drawer, and the whole awful experience came back to me as I peeled away the layers of paper and bubble wrap. But I must say I found the painting utterly charming. I had it framed, and it hangs in my home.

Eventually de Sigall left the Ambassador and moved to the desert. He kindly left behind his beloved Chiquita to live in our zoo. As time went on, my father added two brown bears, three parrots, an anteater, two little fawns, two kangaroos, two white swans (for whom a pond was built), and a bobcat. There is quite a story about the bobcat.

Walter Winchell, the famous newspaper gossip columnist, and my father were best friends, and always tried to top each other's practical jokes, some of which got pretty wild. One time when Walter was back in New York, he shipped a bobcat—yes, a real, live bobcat—COD to the hotel. The bobcat was immediately put into the zoo. A few days later my father had the bobcat shipped back to New York, COD, to Walter. The following day in Walter's newspaper column he reported that "Ben Frank of the Cocoanut Grove in LA sent me a bobcat COD and the charges are $14.32 and the shipment is at the express office." Well, that was convenient for Walter because he told the express office that the poor bobcat had to be marked "return to sender." When the bobcat arrived back at the hotel, the animal was permanently placed in the zoo. Walter and my father told their story of the bobcat over and over, laughing hysterically each time. They found it funny, but what an awful thing to do to that beautiful animal. If animal rights groups had existed back then, I am quite certain they would have advocated for a boycott of the hotel.

Here is another story about the zoo: Frisco, the beloved head groundskeeper, had reported to my father that a guest at the hotel had helped a young boy who had gotten into trouble at the zoo. On May 24, 1935, the *Los Angeles Times* reported that a little boy had crawled under the guardrail intended to keep people from reaching the bear cage and poked his hand through the wire netting to touch the bear. One of the bears thought the boy was offering food and unfortunately clawed the child's hand and arm.

The bear cage at the Ambassador Hotel's zoo. Los Angeles, 1937.
("Dick" Whittington Photography Collection,
University of Southern California Digital Library)

My father was horrified about the accident and was concerned the bear might get more aggressive, so he decided to ship both bears off to the big new zoo in San Diego. Upon an agreement with that zoo's director, Belle Benchley, the zookeepers came up from San Diego to put the bears into shipping cages. My father said that getting the bears into their boxes was a job for more than two men, so he offered to help.

I didn't see what happened because I was at school, but Mother told me that the zoo men were having trouble collecting the bears, so my father showed off how he could get into the cage and handle them. I think he had had a couple of Scotch-and-sodas at lunch, and in his relaxed state figured it would be easy. According to an article about the incident in a local paper, headlined "Hotel Manager Badly Bitten by Zoo Bear," my father was bitten by Jim, the larger of the two bears. Jim bit his right leg and, in the commotion, knocked my father down. The bite required fourteen stitches! Who knew that being a hotel manager was such a dangerous job. There is a slight difference between how the story was reported in the newspaper and my father's retelling, but in both versions it was a very close call!

Two years to the day after the incident with the young boy and the bear, my father had a more serious episode—with an animal that *wasn't* in captivity. He and some of his men friends spent a weekend visiting the owner of the Morse Ranch—ten-thousand acres in the mountains above the Carmel Valley. The idea was to go wild boar hunting during the day and then spend the evenings drinking and cooking dinner on the barbecue. Two days after my father left for Carmel, on May 24, 1937, the *Los Angeles Evening Post* arrived at our bungalow door with the following headline: "Boar Hunting Bores Him Nearly Dead."

Up to that moment, my mother had known nothing about the trip other than where my father was going. According to the newspaper report, he was riding a horse when he shot and wounded a boar, and then promptly fell off the horse. Karma? The enraged animal ran my father up a tree and did not lose interest until he somehow managed to shoot it again. We all had to laugh at how my father, who weighed 225 pounds, was able to make it up a tree fast enough not to get seriously injured by such a dangerous animal—and to bring his rifle with him. Thankfully he was OK. I loved so many things about my father, but the act of hunting animals was something I detested.

Dear Mom,

Boy, to be a fly on the wall (I imagine there were plenty!) in that hotel room and see your father's reaction upon seeing the lioness on the bed with the hotel's resident artist. He sure was unflappable.

Your father had hospitality down to a fine science, which inspired him to create the most unique experiences to keep guests entertained and happy, the zoo being no exception. But I think it's lucky the hotel didn't get sued over the incident of the bear biting the hand of the little boy. You lived in kinder, gentler times.

The story about the boar and your father is totally crazy. And you're right, how on earth could your 225-pound father scurry up a tree while holding a shotgun? I guess when adrenaline is your ladder, you can do it!

Love,
Lisa

20

THE AMBASSADOR LIDO

In the fall of 1933, my father was certain that hotel and travel conditions in Southern California were on an upward trajectory, and he made plans for a substantial upgrade to modernize the hotel and its grounds, the latter being his central focus. It was my father who conceived of the idea to create what guests and hotel staff referred to as "the Lido."

My father wanted guests and other patrons of the hotel to bask in the sun and sand without having to leave the hotel for a long drive to the beach or go out to eat and be entertained. He said he planned the Lido so smart people could spend the greater part of an enjoyable and lazy day in shorts, slacks, or bathing suits on the beach, in the cabanas, and at the plunge pool, and have luncheon in the open-air restaurant without changing their clothes or getting in a car. This strategy was a win-win, as it kept the guests happy and also kept all their spending within the hotel.

In May 1934, the *B'nai 'B'rith Messenger* reported the following:

The Ambassador Lido, conceived by Ben L. Frank, is unquestionably the most unique and comprehensive development yet created by him on the Ambassador Hotel grounds. Ready to open early in June, "The Ambassador Lido" will be all that its name implies. It brings all the charms of a smart social and exclusive beach life to the heart of the best residential section of Los Angeles. A beautiful al fresco restaurant now being established on the south grounds of the hotel where many newly planted, huge, royal palms and other trees and shrubs will surround the lawn and canopied dance floor. There were intimate booths and tables among the trees, gaily colored umbrellas will add to this colorful setting. An open-air barbecue pit for hotel specialties such as charcoal broiled steaks and chops and refrigerated cases for cold service will ensure novel selections for luncheons and dinners. Directly adjoining this new improvement will be the completed remodeled Ambassador Plunge with an enormous new sand bathing beach.

I loved the sandy beach. What a treat to have soft, super clean sand to play in and soak up the sun. The Lido was a huge draw for guests, especially for those who'd never been to a beach. There was really nothing else like it.

The Ambassador Hotel's Lido beach and pool. Los Angeles, circa 1934. (Security Pacific National Bank Collection/Los Angeles Public Library)

When reading the description above, I got curious about what the reporter meant by "The Ambassador Lido will be all that its name implies." So, I looked up the word "Lido," and it seems likely my father named it after the famous Lido di Venezia, a glamorous beach resort in Venice, Italy, established back in the nineteenth century. After that, the word "Lido" became associated with luxury, leisure, and high-end entertainment. As they say, if the shoe fits—and Lido was the perfect name for a glamorous hotel pool and lounge area designed for those seeking luxury and relaxation.

Dining outside at the Royal Palm Restaurant among the palm trees and tropical landscaping seemed miles away from the busy automobile traffic on Wilshire Boulevard. A small exotic tent stood under a large palm in one corner of the dining area, where Julienne, apparently a Gypsy, read palms (of the human kind).

Carlyn Frank, age seventeen, at the Ambassador Hotel's Royal Palm Restaurant. Los Angeles, 1937. (Gilmour Family Collection)

There was also a "Feminine Conditioning" amenity that was part of The Lido. I don't recall much about it, and the original hotel brochures didn't go into much detail, except to say there were plenty of attendants to serve the ladies, who were offered baths, massages, and "physical conditioning." There was probably a men's offering of the same type of service.

When the Lido opened, songwriters and composers such as Jimmy McHugh and Ben Bernie planted themselves outside one of the many gaily striped cabanas that lined the plunge pool. Jimmy was a prolific songwriter from the 1920s to the 1950s, and Ben was a jazz violinist and composer. One of his biggest hits was "Sweet Georgia Brown." Many other musicians and big band leaders who played at the Cocoanut Grove were also frequent visitors to the Lido. To support their creative talents, and to produce a bit of entertainment for the sunbathers, my father had a small upright piano placed in one of the cabanas, and everyone around the pool enjoyed the music and nonsense that went on when they assembled at the "beach" and in the pool!

Room service was kept busy bringing food and drinks, and sometimes the crowd got pretty rowdy, but there was always lots of laughs and music. I remember Jimmy Durante was a frequent visitor and really added a huge flair to all the goings-on. I would have loved to have talked to him but I was too shy to even say hello to such a big celebrity. I could barely mumble good afternoon to Bing Crosby in the coffee shop.

Another element of entertainment introduced by my father when the Lido opened was the water carnival. This was a delightful experience for hotel guests that involved all kinds of swimming and diving contests, including something called "comedy diving"—people dressed in funny costumes doing cannonballs and other silly movements off the diving boards. It was one of my favorite forms of entertainment; my friends and I loved it when we were young. Our own cannonballs were nothing compared to the enormous splashes made by the comedy divers.

*Music and dancing by the pool: Cocoanut Grove musicians performing in the
Ambassador Hotel plunge for the entertainment of guests.
Los Angeles, circa 1935. (Eyre Powell Chamber of Commerce Collection/
Los Angeles Public Library Collection)*

Adding to the Lido's outdoor entertainment, the hotel often hosted lovely
fashion shows at lunchtime. Beautifully dressed and coiffed models would
come out of the I. Magnin store on the Casino level and stroll through the
gardens, modeling their clothes. As you were watching the models strut, you
could also see people diving from the twenty-five-foot diving board and the
ten-foot springboard. There were so many things to look at. Sometimes I
climbed up to the top of the twenty-five-footer but always ended up climbing
down to jump from the ten-foot board. Now that I think about it, walking
backwards down the ladder from the highest board was scarier than diving
off of it would have been.

On the opening day of the Lido, my mother hosted a luncheon for "Sixty-
five Mesdames and Misses" in the open-air dining area. The *Los Angeles*

Evening Examiner society page mentioned the names of the members of the Los Angeles social set and the Hollywood community. In attendance were the wives of director Mervyn LeRoy; Columbia Pictures studio head Ben Kahane; playwright Joe Fields; producer Hunt Stromberg; and director Archie Mayo. Also in attendance were June Winchell, the wife of columnist Walter; the Sultana of Johor; Mrs. Clyde Russell Burr, one of the founders of the Junior League of Los Angeles; Mrs. Dwight Hart, whose husband was a successful hotelier and prominent real estate developer; and Princess Conchita Pignatelli, daughter of a prominent Spanish family, who served thirty years as columnist for Hearst's *Los Angeles Examiner*. It was a commanding array of white-gloved, wide-brim-hatted ladies who gathered at several tables in the sunshine to launch what was to become a very popular al fresco dining and dancing place. I found the dance floor a perfect place to roller-skate in the early morning before guests would gather.

The goal for my father, and his father before him, was to staff the hotel with faithful employees and a management team determined to provide guests, many coming from foreign countries, as well as every part of the United States, the ultimate in service and entertainment—not to be found anywhere else in the world. My father's innovative hospitality, and the blending of luxury, entertainment, and exclusivity, made the Lido a glamorous extension of the Ambassador Hotel's legacy.

Dear Mom,

Your dad was a bold visionary and intrepid entrepreneur, and he seemed to have carte blanche to implement his ideas. The Lido was such a grand concept and a brilliant way to attract guests who longed for and could afford both luxury and fun during the Great Depression.

I did some digging about the Ambassador's "Feminine Conditioning" amenity, as it sounded like an "interesting" marketing message. It seems the term may have implied that as a female guest of the hotel, simply being immersed in such a glamorous environment would inspire women to cultivate what society, at the time, considered "the ideal version of womanhood"— aided by services designed to "enhance a woman's appearance, poise, and overall well-being." I don't think that overtly sexist message would fly very far in today's environment.

If I had been a guest at the Ambassador back in the day, I think I would have passed on the Feminine Conditioning. Instead, I would have loved plopping down on the sandy beach with my morning coffee, the *Los Angeles Times* newspaper laying open across my knees, with the thought of a midmorning swim, a round of golf, and maybe some tennis. Then after all that exertion, I'd enjoy a lovely lunch at the Royal Palm Restaurant while sipping a cosmopolitan or two. What I would give to go back in time and observe you in your element, or even better, hang out with you!

Love,
Lisa

21

COCKTAILS FOR TWO

Bill was a handsome young man who sang with the Abe Lyman Orchestra—or possibly the Gus Arnheim Orchestra, I honestly am not sure. Both were regulars at the Cocoanut Grove. Bill's repertoire consisted of all the wonderful songs from the big band era, and as I became aware of him, I thought he was a most romantic fellow. He was tall and well-built, with wavy blond hair—an "older man" with a warm and, although I didn't think of the word at the time, "sexy" voice. When I was fourteen, he became a mad crush. Two years later, he seemed to have a semi-mild one on me, or quite possibly I imagined it. I loved to sit in the Grove after school and listen to his rehearsals. One of my favorites songs was "Cocktails for Two," and the way he sang those lyrics—my goodness, it was just *so* incredibly romantic:

> Oh what a delight to be given the right
> To be carefree and gay once again
> No longer slinking, respectfully drinking
> Like civilized ladies and men

No longer need we miss
A charming scene like this…

In some secluded rendezvous
That overlooks the avenue
With someone sharing a delightful chat
Of this and that and cocktails for two

As we enjoy a cigarette
To some exquisite chansonnette
Two hands are sure to slyly meet beneath
The serviette with cocktails for two

My head may go reeling
But my heart will be obedient
With intoxicating kisses
For the principal ingredient

Most any afternoon at five
We'll be so glad we're both alive
Then maybe fortune will complete her plan
That all began with cocktails for two.

Although that song was hardly written for young teenagers, I felt at the time it was written just for Bill and me. We never got to the "principal ingredient" stage, but our hands did slyly meet on one or more occasions. But it was more like a dusting, and probably very unintentional on Bill's part. Never in an atmosphere as romantic as under a "serviette" in the kind of rendezvous that the song suggested. And cigarettes, as glamorous as they sounded when Bill sang, didn't enter my life until I was fifteen and had to keep up with my friends, who were already "professional" inhalers.

During Bill's time singing with the Abe Lyman Orchestra, my father wanted to help him with his career and generously offered him a small room in the hotel without charge. It was on the lower first floor off the Casino level, one of the rooms usually assigned to the personal maids and chauffeurs of hotel guests. There was no private bath, just a corner wash basin and a communal bathroom down the hall, one for women and one for men, with tubs and showers and toilet stalls. The rooms did have large windows that overlooked the east gardens and the eighteen-hole pitch-and-putt golf course. I always found it absolutely necessary to walk from any point on the grounds to Rincon bungalow on the path that led past Bill's window, hoping he just might be looking out as I strolled by. If I walked slowly enough and stopped long enough to look up at the sky as though something interesting was grabbing my attention or practice the old tie-my-shoe trick, sometimes I'd hear "hello" and we would have a delightful chat of this and that.

My version of a secluded rendezvous was to go to the movies with Bill, along with hundreds of hotel guests and neighborhood apartment dwellers. I sat in my usual seat on the left aisle in the seventh row and Bill sat to my right, and sometimes, and I am sure quite by accident on his part, our hands would meet between the seats.

As I look back now, I wonder if he was, in some way, attracted to me, even though he was about five or six years older. Did he really like me, or was the "intoxicating ingredient" the fact that I might have some influence with management to move his career along? I hope that wasn't the case. Oh, and we had another hand-holding encounter when I was probably sixteen or seventeen. You can read about it in Chapter 24. The timing and ages may have been a little off, but the situations all happened. Funny, all these years later, I wonder why any of this even matters now.

Dear Mom,

Learning about your school-girl crushes helps me realize why you were so willing to play along when I asked you to do "drive-bys" of the homes of my crushes when I was in junior high school. You could be so much fun that way. I still remember how mortified I was in seventh grade when Gary Joseph caught us driving past his house! I'll never forget the expression on his face as he hopped on his bike. He obviously knew what we were up to!

I wish I knew a lot more about "Cocktails for Two" Bill! This chapter is so sweet, so romantic, so teenage girlish. I grilled Aunt Jackie for details, but she was just eight years old when you were goo-goo eyed about Bill. Sadly, she couldn't provide any juicy info on this dashing singer. It would have been so fun to be one of your giggly girlfriends and hear you talk about Bill and how you went out of your way to run into him.

Do you remember when I had that mad crush on Dad's client Sandy Whitelaw? I was fourteen or fifteen, around the same age you were when you had your crush on Bill. Sandy was probably thirty-ish, considerably older than your Bill. He was prematurely gray and had the most delicious voice. The way he spoke was so continental, suave, and debonaire. I melted each time he visited us. Every time he came to our home, I told you I was going to marry him. You always smiled as if you believed me, but years later, I knew that was never going to happen. And you *always knew* it was never going to happen! Thank you for not bursting my heart with the truth.

Love,
Lisa

22

THE EAST PORCH

When I was ten years old and my sister was four, we had to move into the hotel and share a room above the East Porch because we both got terribly sick. Given our contagiousness, I don't really understand (or remember why) we didn't stay in our own rooms in Rincon. We had both been feeling fine when our parents went to Chicago on a business trip and left us with our Fräulein. However, shortly after they left, my sister and I were diagnosed with scarlet fever, a highly toxic disease that was an epidemic for two decades starting in the 1920s.

Quarantine signs had to be placed in the windows of homes of infected patients. They typically said: **QUARANTINE SCARLET FEVER**: ALL PERSONS ARE FORBIDDEN TO ENTER OR LEAVE WITHOUT PERMISSION FROM THE HEALTH OFFICER UNDER PENALTY OF LAW. Thankfully, we didn't have to put up one of those frightening signs in our hotel room window.

The worst part of having scarlet fever was that all our beautiful toys and dolls had to be burned, as those were the medical rules in those days. The whole ordeal was just dreadful. My parents were away, and my precious personal comforts taken from me. My only solace was looking out the window of our room and watching the people on the East Porch and the golf course and dreaming about my clubhouse and my friends. In the following photo, I am a lot younger than I was when I was sick with scarlet fever, but I am holding my favorite doll, which was later burned.

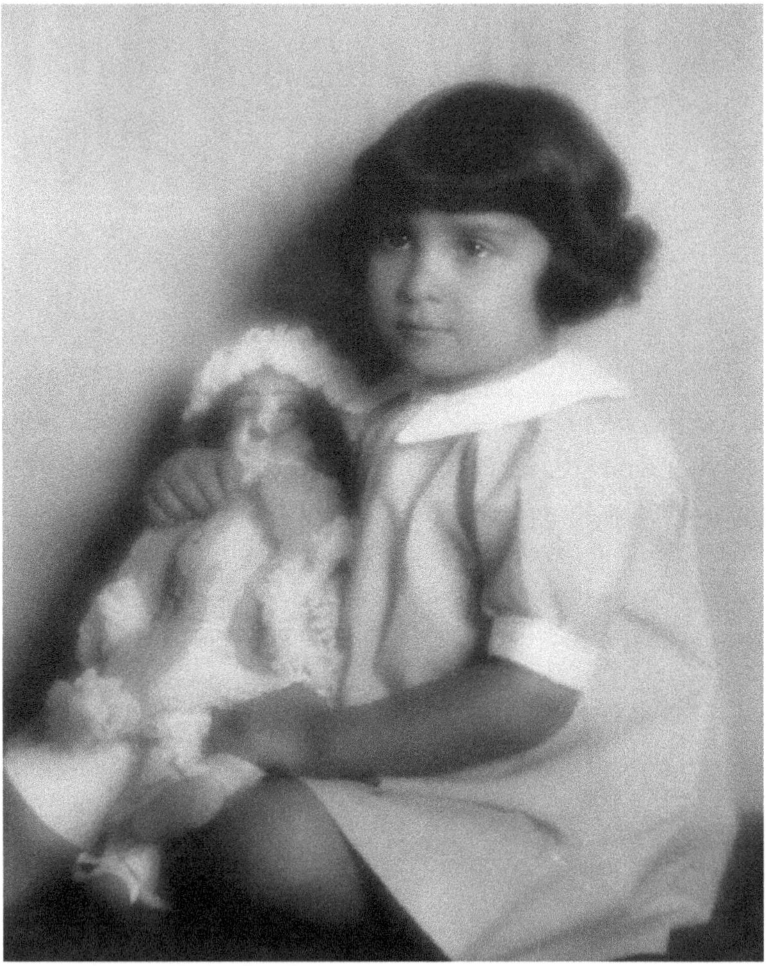

Carlyn Frank, with her beloved doll, Millie, at the Rincon Bungalow. Los Angeles, circa 1925. (Gilmour Family Collection)

Dear Mom,

How awful not having your mom with you when you and Jackie were so sick. I can't imagine as a child having my beloved Pinky bear, or all my Barbie dolls, burned. You always worried about Jeff and me getting sick when you and Dad would go away on vacation without us, even though modern antibiotics were available to treat whatever might come up. Now I understand why. When either of us did get sick, you were always so attentive, taking such good care to make sure whatever we had didn't get worse. I remember you bringing out the big black vaporizer and loading it up with Vicks VapoRub, which I can still smell to this day. And if you had ever been away when we were sick, I know you would have rushed back.

By the way, reading about both the East Porch and the South Porch made me think of the beautiful porch from my childhood home, and now I know why you loved having so much wicker furniture out there.

Love,
Lisa

23

SATURDAYS ON THE BUS

When I was old enough to leave the hotel grounds on my own, the best times were Saturdays when I would ride the double-decker Wilshire Boulevard bus. Eastbound, the bus stopped directly in front of the lawn of the hotel, just down from Rincon, and went directly to Sixth and Hill Streets. Westbound, the bus to Santa Monica would first stop across the street from the hotel in front of the elegant Gaylord Apartments, a neighbor of the original Brown Derby restaurant, which hung its hat on the corner of Wilshire and Alexandria, opposite the entrance to the hotel driveway.

Speaking of the Brown Derby, this feels like a good place to tell you a quick story about how the Brown Derby got its name, according to *my* family lore. The original Brown Derby opened in February 1926. The story in our family has always been that our father, along with Herb Somborn (film producer and Gloria Swanson's ex-husband), Jack Warner (president of Warner Brothers), and playwright and entrepreneur Wilson Mizner (all of whom would soon co-own the Derby) were all sitting in the Cocoanut Grove talking about having a restaurant across the street from the Ambassador. They talked about many things, including what to name this imagined place. Several ideas were tossed about, but it was my father who quipped, "You know,

155

if the food is good enough, people would eat it out of a hat." I know there are several other accounts of how the Brown Derby got its name—and who came up with the slogan that led to the naming—but my family stands by the story that it was our father's clever thinking and marketing brilliance that led Wilson Mizner to give the restaurant its famous name, tag line, and shape. Ever the smart businessman, my father didn't see an excellent restaurant across the street from the hotel as competition, but rather an added draw for the hotel guests.

Exterior view of the Brown Derby restaurant on Wilshire Boulevard. Los Angeles, 1920–29. (University of Southern California Libraries and California Historical Society. Digitally reproduced by the USC Digital Library.)

Now let's get back on the bus. When I hopped on, I heard the clink of the dime as it tumbled down the metal-and-glass coin box. Then I climbed the little curvy stairway to the open top deck with its rows of golden wicker benches—it was such a delightful treat for me. A center aisle divided the seats, and at the front, under the wide glass windshield, was a single long bench. I loved to sit up there with my shoes against the bulkhead watching Wilshire Boulevard disappear under my eyes and feet. I could ride all the way to the beach in Santa Moncia like that, through blocks and blocks of empty lots and long stretches of open landscape.

Even better than the ride to the beach, in my teen years, was spending a Saturday afternoon with my girlfriends at the Paramount Theatre, which was originally the Metropolitan Theatre, built in 1923 and located at Sixth and Hill Streets across from Pershing Square Park and the Biltmore Hotel. The Metropolitan was owned by Sid Grauman and was renamed the Paramount Theatre around the time the brother-and-sister act Fanchon and Marco began producing their live revues there. Sid Grauman owned several Los Angeles theaters and lived at the Ambassador as a permanent guest with his mother. He built the first "grand cinema palace" in Los Angeles in 1918, called the Million Dollar Theater. It is listed in the National Registry of Historic Places and is located at 307 South Broadway in downtown Los Angeles. Sid also owned the Egyptian Theatre at 6706 Hollywood Boulevard, which opened in 1922, and the famous Grauman's Chinese Theatre, which was located at 6925 Hollywood Boulevard and opened in 1927. All three theaters are still operating and attract thousands of moviegoers each year. It is said that the opening of the Chinese and Egyptian theaters was partly responsible for the entertainment district shifting from downtown Los Angeles to Hollywood in the mid-1920s.

Three or four of my pals would meet me around noon at Rincon bungalow and we'd jump on the bus going downtown. If we could get to the Paramount before one o'clock we could buy a ticket for fifty cents and see a double feature. Before any newsreel, short subject, cartoon, or feature film would play, there was a stage show, or "prologue," produced and choreographed by Fanchon and Marco, who became quite famous for their incredible live productions and their work in film. The live show was the main reason for the trip.

At the Paramount, a full orchestra in the pit would play an overture as the elaborate velvet curtains parted, and then it was "on with the show." There was always such excitement from the crowd as we knew the Fanchonettes would be coming on stage at any minute. They were a lovely group of young women performing in perfect unison, dancing, walking on large balls, riding unicycles, roller-skating, and the like. It was really one of the most remarkable live performances to see. Fanchon and Marco were very fond of my father and often performed at the Cocoanut Grove.

After the live performance was over, the curtain would close to reopen to a short subject, maybe a cartoon or a newsreel, and then the first feature. For the price of the bus ride and the early bird ticket, there was no better way to spend a Saturday afternoon. We always sat in the balcony, because smoking was allowed up there and some of my girlfriends were already lighting up when they were fourteen and fifteen. By the time I was fifteen I had to keep up with my peers and spent hours practicing smoking in my bathroom, standing in the bathtub under the open window, fanning the smoke out with a towel in fear of being caught in the act. By my sixteenth birthday I was openly smoking in public, even sneaking quick little puffs in front of my parents and others in the Cocoanut Grove where I typically hosted formal dress parties for twenty or so of my friends every Christmas Eve, and several smaller parties during the year. Of course, no one (except maybe the tobacco companies), knew how unhealthy cigarettes were. For us, they personified being grown up and glamorous.

Dear Mom,

I love the Brown Derby story. Given your dad's marketing chops, it makes sense he was the one to ignite the concept that led to the formal naming and the subsequent design of the restaurant.

Reading how you practiced smoking in your bathroom sent me right back to my own childhood bedroom closet, the one with the window. I remember coming home from college for winter break, already fully committed to my smoking habit. It was the middle of the night, and I woke up craving a cigarette because I had gone all day and night without one, as I kept my smoking habit a secret from you and dad. You both abhorred anything to do with smoking.

I had brought my boyfriend, PJ, home on that break, and in the morning I heard you grilling him, asking if he had been smoking during the night. You always had the nose of a bloodhound! I was mortified overhearing the inquisition. PJ knew it had been me because he didn't smoke. I denied it was me and told you that you must have been having an olfactory dream. That did not go over well, because sarcasm never went over well with you. Predictably, I generally fessed up each year over Thanksgiving dinner to something I'd never told you and Dad before. After a glass of wine or two, the truth always came out. It was during Thanksgiving the following year that I confessed I was a smoker, and you both were very upset with me, as I knew you would be. But you were a smoker at a much younger age than me, plus you smoked when you were pregnant with Jeff. I always felt it was a little like the pot calling the kettle black.

Your Saturday escapades on the bus with your girlfriends sounded like so much fun and reminded me of my carefree Saturdays with friends. I have such fond memories of grabbing lunch in Westwood Village near the UCLA campus. I loved that you let me stay there all day with my girlfriends when I was in junior high. We'd grab a donut from Stan's and an Orange Julius and catch a movie at the Bruin or the Fox Theater. Then we'd shop around the rest of the day at J. J. Newberry's or Bullocks Westwood. You'd pick us all up in front of Wherehouse Records in the afternoon. I was always so embarrassed getting in your car with the radio tuned to talk radio. I begged you to turn the station to KRLA or KHJ, the teenybopper stations of that era. But you refused. It made me so mad!

Love,
Lisa

24

SUNDAYS IN THE COUNTRY

There were many late Sunday morning departures when my family would pile into my grandparents' elegant Du Pont Roadster and take the long drive "way out in the country" to La Puente, a name we always pronounced "pee-went-tee," never associating it with the Spanish word for bridge. I don't remember ever seeing a bridge there, but there must have been one somewhere in the area. The drive, when freeways were just a twinkle in some engineer's eye, took at least an hour and a half from the hotel, over what we call "surface streets" today. The countryside was lovely, and we passed so many citrus orchards and groves of walnut trees that were so beautiful in the spring, heavy with white blossoms—the same type of terrain we traveled through when we went to spend time at our ranch in Riverside.

On this particular Sunday we were going to visit a family friend, Alfred E. Green, who had a beautiful ranch. Alfred was a motion picture director, and after a lengthy career in silent movies, he became even more well known for *The Jolson Story* and for directing Bette Davis in her 1935 Oscar-winning performance in *Dangerous.* Alfred and his family used the ranch as a second home. It was situated on acres of rolling hills and had a large old barn that held stalls for several horses we were allowed to ride. On one of our visits, my father had invited "Cocktails for Two" Bill to come along.

On this visit, Bill, Alfred's son Marshall, and I set off on our horses and headed for the hills. We went out for a long time and were far from the ranch, and I thought it was best to turn back before dark. As we started toward the barn, my horse moved from that wonderful comfortable rack gait to a gallop, I guess in anticipation of fresh hay. And there I was, just like in the movies, hanging on for dear life, unable to control my hungry steed, his pounding hooves competing with my pounding heart. Then came Bill, chasing after me and grabbing the reins. My hero! It was one of those "be still my heart" moments. We made it back safe and sound. The horses had their hay, and we had hot dogs and burgers.

On our evening drive back to the hotel, my father appointed Bill as our chauffeur, so he and I sat in the front seat, with my parents relaxing in the back. This time, we held hands—on purpose—all the way home. It was a secret thrill for me that my parents couldn't witness this sweet encounter. I can't really remember what happened after that drive home, except to say that Bill moved on to other gigs and I to my gaggle of friends and parties, with the hope of finding a boy closer to my age to start dating.

Dear Mom,

You seem to have experienced several "runaway horse" situations in your youth. When I was around ten years old, my one and only horse-riding encounter scared me for life, as I was assigned a very pregnant horse. She was so lopsided I was terrified I was going to fall off the entire time. I'm glad both our riding experiences were uneventful in the end.

What a lucky break your dad asked Bill to drive the family car back to the hotel. I have to wonder if your parents really had no clue about what was happening in the front seat. I bet they knew . . .

Your attitude toward my teenage dating adventures was not nearly as relaxed as that of your parents toward yours. You always knew, and you never ignored it. Your eagle eyes spotted the hickeys on my neck even though I tried to hide them with pigtails, and I remember you made me wear a turtleneck to school on a 90-degree day and being grounded for what seemed like forever for something I thought was innocent and fun.

Love,
Lisa

25

THE WORLD-FAMOUS COCOANUT GROVE

Advertisement announcing the May 25, 1921, formal opening of the Cocoanut Grove in the Los Angeles Times.

My grandfather was determined to create the most unique and grand nightclub at the hotel. On April 21, 1921, with the hotel only a few months old, my straightlaced grandfather's fantasy dream became a reality and the Cocoanut Grove opened with much fanfare. Then on May 25, the Grove had its formal opening for the general public. With lavish Moroccan-inspired décor, its unique atmosphere was a feast for the eyes, and the finest entertainment created a magical experience for all who attended.

On opening night, the most popular jazz band, led by drummer Art Hickman, was featured. My grandfather set a precedent with Hickman, and only hired the very best musicians, performers, and dancers to entertain hotel guests and local patrons. They had to be the very best or my grandfather would not sign them to play at the Grove.

The entrance to the Cocoanut Grove was from the north end of the lobby, past the grand staircase and elevators. Guests would walk through an arched corridor that led to the Cocoanut Grove by way of double doors exquisitely adorned with gold leaf and etched with palm trees.

Stars staying at the hotel could descend by elevator at just the right moment, minimizing their exposure to curious hotel guests camped out in the lobby hoping to catch a glimpse of their favorite celebrity. Elegantly dressed guests—men in dinner jackets or tuxedos, ladies in couture gowns— approached the Cocoanut Grove with grand excitement.

Before guests were escorted to their tables, they stopped at the hatcheck stand, which was really more like a huge room, to the right of the entrance. In those days, hats were a part of every gentleman's wardrobe. On nights other than Friday College Night (when the cover charge was lowered for the young crowd) the coatracks for women resembled a fur shop. There were racks and racks of furs safely hung while their owners dined, danced, and drank the night away.

For years, the "hatcheck girl" in charge was Peggy Harris, who worked with two assistants on busy evenings. Peggy was a pretty lady, with dark curly hair, and her husband George was an assistant manager. She also doubled as one of the cashiers in the Fountain Room coffee shop. Peggy knew all the gossip about who the stars came with to dance at the Grove, and all about the latest romances. When I was old enough to care about such juicy items, I would spend time chatting with her, usually at the tea dance on Saturday afternoons. The first thing I would ask her was "So, who's dating who?" and she would fill me in on all the latest romantic Hollywood twosomes.

In the photo that follows, the front table on the right side at the top of the stairway leading down to the main floor is visible. This table was reserved for our family. When there were no guests at ringside, either my father or grandfather would sit there, sometimes accompanied by my grandmother or mother. From there they would have a view of the entire room, allowing them to make sure the staff was doing a good job, and the guests were having a wonderful time.

Interior view of the Cocoanut Grove. Los Angeles, 1938. ("Dick" Whittington Photography Collection, University of Southern California Digital Library)

The Grove was quite something to behold, and there was nothing like it anywhere: The Moroccan décor with its arches, lanterns, rich fabrics, mosaic patterns, and palm motifs, created a sense of mystery, romance, and luxury. With a South Seas tropical mural that rose floor to ceiling, featuring a full bright moon and a flowing waterfall, guests enjoyed an almost immersive experience. The waterfall was made more realistic by special lighting and sound effects that gave guests seated at tables in front of the falls the impression they might be feeling a slight mist as they sipped their cocktails.

Interior view of the Cocoanut Grove, with the famous moon and waterfall mural. Los Angeles, 1938. (Photo courtesy of Marc Wanamaker/Bison Archives)

The ceiling of the Grove replicated the night sky with twinkling stars, a feature often seen in the ceilings of movie theaters in the 1920s. Life-sized monkeys with glowing amber eyes sat atop large coconuts attached to papier-mâché palm tree trunks. Though the trunks were manufactured, the fronds were real and treated with some kind of curing solution so they never dried up. It has been written that the thirty or so palm trees had been rescued from the beaches of Oxnard, California, where they had provided a tropical feel to the classic 1921 film *The Sheik,* starring Rudolph Valentino. The Grove provided a perfect new home for these majestic trees.

It has also been reported over and over again that actor John Barrymore brought his pet monkey with him when he came to the Grove one night for drinks with W. C. Fields. The monkey scrambled up one of the palm trees to get a closer look at one of the fake monkeys. It was said that the live monkey ended up living at the hotel in one of the palm trees. I have no personal knowledge of this.

Before Joan Crawford was Joan Crawford she was Lucille Fay LeSueur. My father gave her the opportunity to dance for her supper in the Charleston dance contests held in the Cocoanut Grove. This menu, from 1928, would have been similar to the one from which Joan had been able to select her meals.

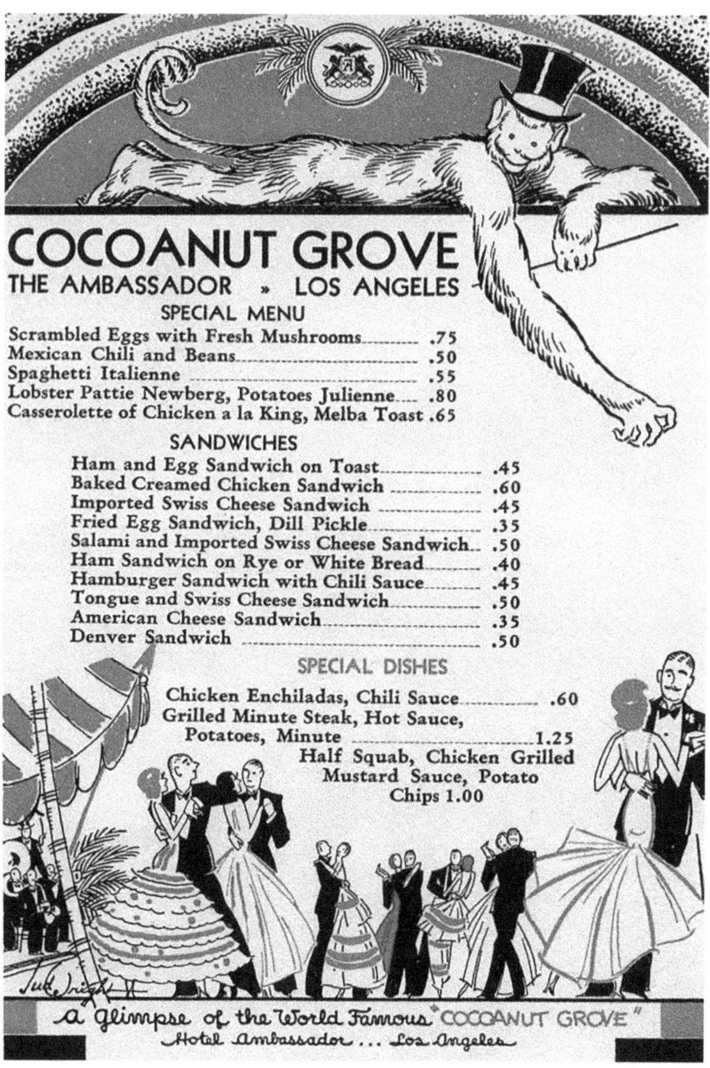

A dinner menu prepared for guests dining at the Cocoanut Grove. Los Angeles, 1928. (Featured in the Grolier Club's exhibition "A Century of Dining Out: The American Story in Menus, 1841–1941," from the collection of Henry Voigt, April 26–July 29, 2023)

By the middle of the twenties, Lucille had become Joan Crawford and was a frequent guest at the Grove with her husband, Douglas Fairbanks, Jr. A glamorous movie star by the mid-to-late 1930s, she was then on her second husband, Franchot Tone. Franchot was a very handsome American actor and a leading man in the 1930s and '40s, who came to dine and dance on Star Night with the Hollywood crowd. I have a vivid memory of an entrance Joan Crawford made one night, as I watched the party from the balcony with my friend Ronnie, the lighting engineer. It looked to me as if Joan was floating down the carpeted stairs leading to the main floor. She was dressed in a spectacular evening gown of flowing gray chiffon topped with a blood red velvet cape that brushed the floor. An eye-catching ensemble, made even more so by her famous star sapphire jewels at her throat, ears, and wrists. Mr. Tone, like a queen's consort, followed a respectful three feet behind. Joan and my father were great friends.

Here is a photo of my father and Joan Crawford, with her flirty inscription: "For Ben—Mrs. Frank is your best girl—Then I'm next. Joan"

Joan Crawford and Ben Frank at the Cocoanut Grove. Los Angeles, 1930s.
(Gilmour Family Collection)

As mentioned earlier, when I was in high school, I would wander into the Grove to see who was rehearsing before heading back to the bungalow to do homework. There was usually an agent or a manager of a dance act or a band sitting at one of the tables, so there was always someone interesting for me to have a conversation with. I spent many afternoons chatting with a young agent from the Music Corporation of America, who represented most, if not all the bands that played at the Grove. His name was Larry Barnett, which was my mother's maiden name, though no relation, and I had a huge crush on him. He represented several bands and was so attractive, with gorgeous black hair that had just the right amount of premature gray at the temples. Because of the gray hair he appeared to be older than the twenty-one he claimed, so he proved his age to me with his driver's license. When I came home from school, I couldn't wait to run up to the Grove to see if he might be watching a rehearsal. One of my girlfriends, Muffet, felt the same attraction and came home with me as often as she could so she could sit and chat with us. High school kids trying to act sophisticated with a Hollywood agent took some doing.

I have fond memories of a night in 1937, when, with my parents' permission, Larry took me with him to see Janet Gaynor and Fredric March in *A Star is Born*. It was playing at the Westlake Theatre on Alvarado Street across from Westlake Park. Although it wasn't a real date, I pretended it was more than just a nice gesture toward the manager's daughter. I couldn't wait to tell my friends I had gone out with an older man. I cried through most of the 111 minutes of the film. Larry gave me his handkerchief. I don't remember ever giving it back.

Jimmy Manos, a handsome Greek, was for eighteen years the Grove's head waiter and maître d' and was himself a sought-after celebrity. He was adored by all those who worked with him, as well as by all the Hollywood luminaries. He had a way of making everyone feel welcome and well taken care of. He was also the one I gave my precious autograph book to, so he could gather signatures for me, since I was too young to be in the Grove at night. I have forty-four signatures, thanks to him, including autographs from movie stars like Clark Gable, Myrna Loy, and Claudette Colbert, though he also secured autographs from some of the Olympic champions I mentioned earlier who trained at the hotel pool, such as Buster Crabbe and Johnny Weissmuller. I still have the book.

Jimmy was the only one, other than Reuben, his second-in-command, or my father, who could order an extra table brought onto the dance floor for an important guest who might arrive on a sold-out night without a reservation. Heads would turn when waiters walked across the dance floor and set up tables and chairs. Everyone wanted to see who was important enough to have a table in front of those already at ringside.

Dear Mom,

How did I not know your grandfather was the creative force behind developing the Cocoanut Grove? And now, I have so many more questions! Why the Moroccan motif? Who helped design all the unique and gorgeous details in the room? How did your grandfather even know to ask for the palm trees on the beach in Oxnard? How did he transform the Rose Ballroom into the Cocoanut Grove within four months of the hotel opening? I mean, seriously. And the unusual spelling of "cocoanut" (versus the traditional "coconut")? All I could glean was that it was a stylistic choice made by your grandfather when establishing the club. Or perhaps the spelling added an exotic flair, distinguishing the club from others with similar names? It's also possible it was simply a common alternative spelling at the time.

I felt a little sad when I read through your autograph book, where many of the celebs wrote your name as "Carolyn" or "Caroline" instead of "Carlyn." Although impressive to see all the famous people Jimmy was able to wrangle to sign your autograph book, I know you hated it when people misspoke or misspelled your name. I can remember many, many times you tersely corrected people when they innocently and mistakenly called you Carolyn. But I guess that's why you and Dad decided not to name me Caren (Carlyn and Ben combined). You told me you thought I would spend my whole life correcting people who wrote or spoke my name as "Karen." Funny, I would have been OK correcting people in order to have a name that had a family connection.

Love,
Lisa

26

SATURDAY TEA DANCES

The Cocoanut Grove was not just a popular spot for dancing to wonderful big band orchestras seven evenings a week; the tea dances on Saturday afternoons were also a big favorite. The orchestra was the same one that played for the socialites and movie stars in the evenings, and because the Grove had no windows, the daytime room had the same lighting and ambience of the nightclub. For just $1.25, one could come to the Grove, have tea, finger sandwiches, a lovely dessert, and, with luck, meet a stranger from across the room for a dance or two. This ad promoted the Saturday Tea Dances and Evening Supper Dances.

The women came in groups, and the men would either bring a date or come stag. In a very refined manner, single men would walk among the tables and ask a young lady to dance.

A Los Angeles Times advertisement from October 8, 1921, promoting the Cocoanut Grove's Saturday Afternoon Tea Dances.

173

On many Saturdays, especially when the weather was not good for swimming or tennis, I would head up to the balcony where my friend Ronnie ran the spotlight, and hang out over the edge and watch the mating dance take place. My sister would sit at the table reserved in the evenings for my father and grandfather. She would sip sugar water thinking she was very fancy. Fancy or not, she would often nudge Jimmy Manos into dancing a rumba with her or engage with the assistant manager for a tango. She had a lot of chutzpah for a ten-year-old!

Every Saturday when the Grove doors opened, while I was perched in the lighting booth with Ronnie, I spied the man I thought of as a "regular," who was always the first to enter. Consistently wearing the same tan three-piece suit (it probably came with two pairs of pants, as the ads used to say), a nice tie, and never without a book under his arm, he was an ordinary-looking man, slim and elderly, with tan hair to match his suit. He never failed to sit at the same table for two at the bottom of the stairs. Always alone, he would read his book between sets as he sipped his tea, which he poured from the heavy silverplate teapot. As soon as the music began, he was on his feet making the rounds of the room, searching among the palms for a dance partner. Sometimes I would see him turned away by three or four girls before he had success. When the music stopped, he would escort his partner to her table of friends and return to his book until the next set began. Then the process would start over again. I remember even at my young age how sorry I felt for him, because he looked lonely and was brushed off by so many.

Tea dancers didn't consist only of working girls on their days off, in their little hats and white gloves, or lonely single men looking for female companionship; lots of the younger Hollywood crowd, including aspiring actors and actresses, came, as well as groups of men and women whose names you might read in the newspaper society columns.

One of the areas of the Grove I enjoyed a lot was the ladies lounge, located a few steps from the side of the entry corridor. I loved to drop by during tea dance time, plop myself down on a velvety pink chair, and watch the ladies sitting at the long dressing table with the lighted mirrors, as they redid their makeup and hair and gossiped about their dates or the men they had met that afternoon. The carpeted lounge with its sofas and comfortable armchairs in soft tones of pink and beige opened into the black-and-white-tiled bathroom: the six private lavatory stalls and rows of wash basins supervised by a maid, always impeccable in a black uniform and white apron. The maid handed out towels and any needed cosmetics for emergency repairs. A small dish on a table by her chair held some change from tips. I don't know if she worked only for her tips, but in those days tips were *really* small change, and I saw many women walk out without leaving the customary dime or quarter. The public ladies lounge off the Casino floor also provided the same service. I was very fond of the attendant in that area and visited her every time I walked past her domain.

The men's lounge in the Grove on the opposite side of the corridor and up a flight of stairs was always a mystery and off-limits when I was a kid. When I finally got up the courage to investigate what the men's bathroom looked like, I thought it was okay in the lounge part, but the bathroom with its urinals was an education for me. I wasn't quite sure how they were used, but it was interesting to wonder.

Dear Mom,

I wonder if tan suit man ever found the love of his life at the Saturday Tea dance? Or did he remain solitary?

No surprise Jackie talked the maître d' into dancing with her. She has always been a pistol—so funny and adventurous. By all accounts you were more serious and loved to engage with people conversationally, but Jackie was silly and more fun and enjoyed the simple things in life, even among all the privileges.

While you were spying on the tea dance crowd, my Saturday afternoons growing up were occupied by shopping trips, hanging out with girlfriends, Girl Scouts, and meetings of our exclusive Beatles Club with four of my best friends. Still fun, but certainly less intriguing.

Your reaction to the men's urinals is priceless. I remember cringing the first time I saw urinals, especially the weird sponge or netting thingy in the bottom of the bowl.

Ugh . . . what on earth, and why?

Love,
Lisa

27

BIG BANDS AND
THE BING FALLOUT

For many years, Gus Arnheim led the Grove's house band and played the music that helped bring the Rhythm Boys and Bing Crosby fame—and later, for Bing, a fortune. The Rhythm Boys were an American singing trio featuring Bing Crosby, Harry Barris, and Al Rinker. Crosby and Rinker began performing together in 1925. Bing Crosby and the Rhythm Boys had their first performance at the Cocoanut Grove in July 1930, as part of the Gus Arnheim Orchestra.

When Crosby sang solos, he began to steal the show, and my grandfather quickly realized Bing was a huge draw. When my grandfather decided Bing should permanently solo with the orchestra, it broke the Rhythm Boys up. Grove patrons were enchanted by the style of the laid-back singer with the "new sound." That new sound was what music historians called an "intimate" voice. Bing's "crooning" style was amplified with the use of a new technology—the microphone. He incorporated the "warble," or trill, that is a traditional form of singing performed by Irish tenors. That sound was something Bing perfected in the early years of his career, and it attracted droves of followers to his performances at the Grove.

177

My grandfather went on to sign Bing as a single act. Although he was aware of his widely known reputation for drinking, he had faith in his talent. Harry Barris had composed several popular songs when he was with the Arnheim Orchestra, and Bing recorded "I Surrender Dear," "Wrap Your Troubles in Dreams (and Dream Your Troubles Away)," and "It Must Be True." He became so popular, especially with the college kids on Friday nights and the Hollywood crowd on Tuesday Star Night, that it was standing room only. When it was Bing's turn to come to the front of the band, dancers on the crowded floor would push their way up to the bandstand and forget to dance as they swayed back and forth in front of him. His singing tone back then was bright, and agile—not yet the rich baritone he later mastered, which became his signature sound.

One of my grandfather's genius ideas was to set up a small radio station in the Grove, allowing the orchestras to be enjoyed by millions who either couldn't afford to attend or lived too far away. These novel, live, nightly broadcasts helped establish and maintain the Grove as *the* destination for the best entertainment on the west coast, while also elevating Bing Crosby's talent for the masses.

Because of his drinking, Bing started to miss performances, spending time in Tijuana or Caliente in Baja, California. It became my father's task to see that he was picked up and returned to the hotel in time for the live, nightly, ten o'clock-to-midnight remote broadcast over local radio station KNX. My father, a licensed pilot, would fly down to Baja and bring the wandering, inebriated crooner back to the hotel.

Naturally, there was tension between Bing Crosby and my grandfather, who expected people to honor their commitments. Crosby wrote about it in his 1953 memoir, *Call Me Lucky*. Crosby admitted that, toward the end of his engagement at the Cocoanut Grove, his responsibilities were not taken seriously enough to please my grandfather. Crosby went on to say that my grandfather was an "elderly, serious sort who disliked anything that disrupted the even tenor of the nightly routine at the Grove." My grandfather was very punctual, and he expected others to abide by the same courtesy, especially those on his payroll! Crosby admitted that he had missed one too many

Tuesday night shows, and my grandfather docked his pay as a result. Although Crosby could not disagree with my grandfather's actions, he thought it was rather petty, and he up and quit.

Crosby's actions crossed the line and, according to his memoir, "Abe Frank plastered a union ban on me for failure to fulfill the standard musician's contract, after that, union musicians weren't allowed to work with me." Crosby walking out on his contract with my grandfather was really a terrible thing to do because my grandfather gave him his start by recognizing his star power and letting him perform solo. After Bing walked out, he and my grandfather never spoke again. For my grandfather, who followed everything by the book, it was a situation he could neither forgive nor forget.

Dear Mom,

Your grandfather was a brilliant and imaginative businessman. The idea to set up a radio station inside the Grove was not only smart but incredibly generous—what a forward-thinking way to share the magic beyond those walls.

That story about Bing Crosby calling out your grandfather in his memoir—what a moment! That was quite a surprise. I still remember you telling me how your father had to fly to Tijuana on more than one occasion to retrieve an inebriated Bing. More often than not, he'd sober up just in time during the flight back and still make it to the stage. Your grandfather's expectations for professionalism and honorable behavior, especially from someone he was paying, were more than reasonable. Now I understand where you got your high expectations from. It's clear Mr. Crosby didn't fully recognize just how much your grandfather did to boost his career.

Love,
Lisa

28

DANCERS, MORE BIG BANDS, AND A WHOLE LOTTA FUN

Of the many dancers to perform at the Grove, Yolanda Casazza and Frank Veloz were the most exciting and beautiful team. They were a self-taught American ballroom dance team, husband and wife, who became stars in the 1930s and 1940s and were among the highest-paid dance acts during that era. Billed as Veloz and Yolanda, they were not just superb dancers; they had the looks, too, and the audience was as much in love with them as they were with each other. They exuded it when they danced. Yolanda's gowns were exquisite, and her black hair, fashioned in a chignon, complemented Frank's white tie and tails and handsome Latin face. They were a most romantic act and always drew crowds when they were on the bill.

Another beautiful dance team, Tony and Renée de Marco, were always kind to me. They loved to go horseback riding on Sunday mornings in Griffith Park, situated in the eastern Santa Monica Mountain Range, where the famous Griffith Park Observatory is located. I also became friends with the elegant dance team Virginia Lee and the Lathrop Brothers. They were such a great-looking trio. The men were always in top hats and white ties

181

and tails, and Virginia dressed in beautiful evening gowns. They always reminded me of two Freds and a Ginger.

A crowd favorite at the Grove was Ted Lewis, when he stepped off the bandstand and performed "Me and My Shadow" in a darkened room, sliding across the dance floor under a spotlight. In 1929, Xavier Cugat brought in the new Latin dance craze, the rumba.

In the 1930s and 1940s, the *Major Bowes Amateur Hour* was an American radio talent show hosted by Edward Bowes. Selected performers from the show participated in touring the country to perform under the "Major Bowes" name. One night in 1935, a new group, the Hoboken Four, appeared on the show. The aspiring quartet (three of whom had previously sung under the name The 3 Flashes), consisted of three young Italian men, all from Hoboken, New Jersey, who had recently joined forces with a twenty-year-old singer named Frank Sinatra. They won one of the amateur contests and came out to Los Angeles to do a show. As far as my memory goes, they didn't perform at the Ambassador, but they did stay there while in town, as did the other *Amateur Hour* performers. When they left the hotel, all four signed a parchment to my father saying how nice he had been to them during their stay. Frank Sinatra's signature is third from the bottom.

One night in 1933, Guy Lombardo and his brothers Carmen, Lebert, and Victor opened at the Grove, and it caused a small riot. This was their first appearance in California,

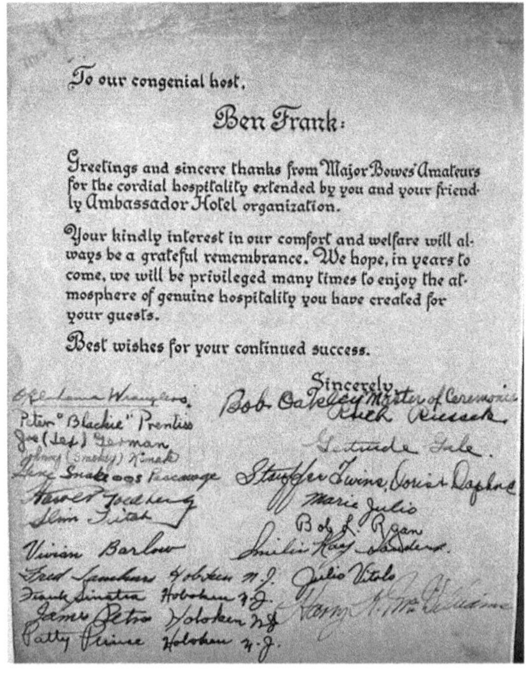

A thank-you message to Ben Frank, signed by Frank Sinatra and the Hoboken Quartet. Los Angeles, 1933. (Gilmour Family Collection)

and it was the hottest reservation in town. The Grove was completely sold out—in fact, it was oversold. Hoping to still find a table, a crowd formed a line in front of the doors to the Grove that stretched the entire length of the lobby. When the crowd became impatient and rowdy and started pushing and shoving, maître d' Jimmy Manos came out to try to calm them. The crowd was so enthusiastic that Jimmy was overrun and pushed to the floor and ended the evening in the hospital with a broken arm.

For the more elegant and well-mannered crowd, Eddy Duchin, the handsome society favorite from New York, would wow the room with his piano playing. Looking like he was born in a tuxedo, he was described as "the debutante's dream of romance come to life." And although I was far from being a debutante, I thought he was the bee's knees of all the bandleaders. One day he invited me to go with him to a Saturday afternoon USC football game at the Los Angeles Coliseum. But my parents objected to my going out, no matter how innocent, with a fellow twelve years older than me! I was crushed, but now as an adult, it is kind of creepy to think that he would have wanted to take out a twelve-year-old girl. I am glad my parents said no, but as a result, I had to settle for watching his rehearsals when I got home from school; it was still way more interesting than being at my desk suffering over math homework.

Later, when dates closer to my age asked me to go dancing, I would suggest the Grove and of course the boys always agreed. We knew that my father would probably pick up our check, and he did. Watching Eddy Duchin in the spotlight at the piano with the rest of the room in darkness was a wonderful way to spend an evening. Eddy had been part of a two-piano team with Leo Reisman's orchestra and took over the band in 1931, not long before he played the Grove. Sadly, he died of leukemia in 1951.

Two of my favorite entertainers were Ozzie and Harriet Nelson. They were the nicest couple, just as they portrayed themselves years later on their long-running television show. It was great fun for me to sit at the table in the Grove and talk with Ozzie in the afternoons while Harriet rehearsed her numbers. Then Ozzie and his band would rehearse with Harriet. They both spent a lot of time at the hotel.

The Cocoanut Grove marquee, featuring Ozzie Nelson and his orchestra. Los Angeles, 1936. (University of Southern California Libraries and California Historical Society. Digitally reproduced by the USC Digital Library.)

When I listened to the radio in bed at night after lights out, I discovered a group with the most unique sound. Hal Kemp and his band, and especially his singer Edgar Clyde "Skinnay" Ennis, immediately became my favorites. During their time together in college, Skinnay joined Kemp, initially as the drummer. After college they formed a professional band. Skinnay began singing and they became a huge draw. I listened to them every week for a long time and kept telling my father about them. I told him he really needed to bring them out to play the Grove. My grandfather had passed away by then, so I could only make my case to my father. I made him listen to their records. I kept after him. I was a pest. He was not as crazy about their unusual sound as I was, but he finally gave in to my pleas and agreed to bring them to Los Angeles from the east coast.

Skinnay, who looked like his name, had a soft, kind of whispering voice, and when he sang "Got a Date with an Angel" or "Foggy Day" it was magic.

My favorite tunes of theirs included "Long About Sundown," "It's Winter Again," "I've Got You Under My Skin," "Pennies From Heaven," "Serenade for a Wealthy Widow," and "You're the Top." The band had a wonderful unusual bouncy beat to dance to and they were a big hit, as I knew they would be. I reminded my father of this frequently.

During the time of their engagement at the Cocoanut Grove, I was probably in the tenth grade at Los Angeles High School (LA High). I don't know how I got up the nerve to talk Mr. Oliver, the principal, into letting the band come to play for a school assembly, but I did. To my surprise, Mr. Oliver said yes. Then I had to go to Hal and convince *him* to agree to do it. At the time, it never occurred to me what a big deal it was for the band members, who probably didn't get to bed until two in the morning, to rise so early, get on a bus bound for LA High, and play for the school assembly. Twice!

The student body at LA High was so large that two shows were required to accommodate the three thousand students. The morning of the first show I sat in the front row. After all, it was *my* production! I decided to ditch my next class and stay for the second show. When Skinnay got up to the mic to sing and saw me in the front row again he pointed at me and let it be known that I was at the first show and now I was there for the second one. I was sure I would be in trouble with Mr. Ault, the attendance vice principal, for cutting class, something I had never dared to do before. But grumpy Mr. Ault must have liked the show very much because he never summoned me to his office.

Dear Mom,

It's no surprise to me that you convinced your high school principal to bring the band and Skinnay in for not just one, but two, school assemblies, because in 1968 you persuaded a television producer to bring a group of former gang members out from Chicago to perform the song "Up, Up and

Away" on *The Smothers Brothers Comedy Show*. (I recount the details of this unusual event in Book III, Chapter 41.)

Your intuition about what a big hit Hal Kemp and Skinnay would be at the Grove was right on target. You instinctively knew what would be great—or not so great—in so many other instances as well.

Trivia tidbit: While doing some work on your manuscript I found out that "Skinny" changed the spelling of his name to "Skinnay" after it was misspelled on a record label early in his career.

Love,
Lisa

29

THIRD STREET SCHOOL

These next few chapters may feel a bit out of order since I'm stepping back in time, but I'm placing them here intentionally because I wanted to give you the full grand tour of the hotel first, before taking you into my kindergarten and grade-school years.

The day I entered kindergarten, my mother drove me to the Third Street School in Hancock Park. The beautiful red-brick two-story building and playgrounds covered the entire square block from Third to Second Streets and from June Street to Las Palmas Avenue. The playground stretched the length of Las Palmas, facing the Los Angeles version of a Tudor mansion that housed the Cumnock School of Expression, a private school for women established in 1894, which closed in 1946 (and, yes, I spelled the school's name correctly). It rounded the corner on Second Street, where the flower and vegetable gardens became an outdoor classroom.

The grammar school that served the Ambassador Hotel area, Hoover Street School, was located at 2726 Francis Street near Ninth and Hoover, only about a mile from the hotel. But my parents preferred the school in the Hancock Park neighborhood, where many of their friends lived. Mother obtained permission for me to attend Third Street. So there I was, a very nervous five-year-old, approaching the school's wide front steps between white stone columns supporting the second-story overhang. I knew we were late because not another child was in sight, a fact that only added to my unease.

Holding tight to Mother's hand, we walked down the long hallway to the kindergarten room. I could hear music. The sign on the oak door identified the teacher's names: Miss Brobst and Miss Ware. Thinking about this today, I can't believe we were late to my first day of kindergarten, and that we just walked into the classroom without checking in with a school administrator first.

When we entered the classroom all the children were already seated on little blue wooden chairs in a semicircle in front of one of the teachers, who smiled and warmly greeted me. Mother introduced me and said either she or Davis, the driver from the hotel garage, would be back to get me at noon. A phonograph was playing music in the background as all the children told me their names. I got settled as best I could, and then the teacher announced our first lesson. She handed each of us a square of pale blue chiffon fabric, changed the phonograph record to marching music, opened the four sets of French doors leading to the play yard, and instructed us on how to hold the scarves to float above our heads while running in and out of the doors, keeping time to the music. I remember thinking it was such a dumb thing to do.

Once marching to the music was over, boxes of crayons were handed out and my first school art lesson began. It must not have been memorable. After art, it was time to play in the sandbox (which really needed fresh white sand), slide down the slides (which seemed in need of some serious greasing), and monkey around on the jungle gym, followed by a welcome snack time. Our snacks consisted of Graham crackers and little individual glass bottles of milk that opened by pulling a small tab on a cardboard disc branded with the name of the dairy, Adohr. (You may wonder where that name came from. Mr. Adamson and his wife Rhoda Agatha Rindge Adamson established their dairy in Tarzana, California, in 1916. It was named Adohr, because Mr. Adamson thought it would be clever to use his wife's name spelled backwards.) After snack time, I gathered up my sweater and Crayola artwork and waited to be picked up. I hoped it wouldn't be Davis from the hotel garage. I really liked him a lot, but that day I needed my mom, and thankfully she arrived and I returned to my safe and familiar home. I can't recall anything remarkable happening in kindergarten, but once I settled in I made the best of it and started looking forward to first grade.

When I was six years old, Miss Cara Withington was my first-grade teacher. I remember her as a very sweet lady who provided a gentle atmosphere in Room Two. The highlight of first grade was the day we started to make a quilt. Each of us received a square of white cotton and a huge needle threaded with colorful yarn, which we were to use to stitch our name on the square. At the end of the term, after the squares had been taken away to be sewn together and quilted, the finished product was returned to our room and a drawing was held to see who would take it home. All the names were put in a bowl and the first name pulled out won the quilt. I didn't win. A major disappointment.

Up the hall, past principal Mrs. Dermody's office, was the third-grade room. Surprisingly, I can't recall the name of that teacher, but tales from other students about how mean she was had filtered down to me for two years and I was frightened when I was assigned to her class. All the children thought she was homely, and we knew that she was very, very old. As I look back, I realize she was probably in her thirties, and I remember her as a tough but very good teacher. After floating scarves and stitching quilts, I was finally beginning to learn something.

In fourth grade I was honored to be appointed bell monitor. That meant that just before recess and lunchtime, I would be excused from class to go down the hall to the office where I would stand at attention, watching the big schoolhouse clock on the wall over the doorway, with my hand on the switch, ready to ring the bells. Even better, in sixth grade, I was one of the chosen few to work at lunchtime alongside the cafeteria ladies at the steam table. I really loved dishing the mashed potatoes with real butter and all the other fresh vegetables served in those days. Sadly, I never got promoted to the ice cream counter, the highest status position in the sixth grade.

Several exciting events took place every semester. The paper drive was a contest to see which room could save the most newspapers during the spring. I never gave a thought as to why we saved the papers, I just wanted to win. My guess is the papers were sold to raise money for school supplies. On the day of the contest everybody came to school with their bundles of the *Herald Examiner* and *The Los Angeles Times*. They were stacked under the room number signs hung on the June Street fence. The room with the highest stack of papers won a prize. My room always won because the hotel saved newspapers for me for months *before* the contest. The morning of the drive, the big hotel stake truck arrived before nine o'clock with papers filled to the top. Tied with heavy string, the bundles would be stacked in three or four rows, to the top of the six-foot fence. Living in a hotel had its advantages.

When school got out for Christmas vacation, my parents invited all the sixth grade kids and their families to a Christmas party at the Grove. Even my teacher, Miss Greenwood, and the principal, Mrs. Dermody, came for the fete! In the morning before the party, I helped the housemen finish putting decorations on one of the many Christmas trees placed around the hotel. They let me have a box of pretty ornaments I could hang on the low branches. The tallest tree reached the ceiling, and the men had to use very tall ladders as the ceilings were probably thirty feet high. I put the place cards on tables that were already set up for that night. The plan was that after dinner, Santa Claus (I think it was Eddie, the assistant manager) would come in with his big red velvet bag of presents for all the children in the room. Then Phil Harris and his band would play "Jingle Bells" and "Deck the Halls" and songs like that, and all of us kids would march around the dance floor, while the grown-ups sat and watched.

Dear Mom,

The amount of detail you wrote about your first day of kindergarten was remarkable. The only things I can remember about my kindergarten class, taught by Mrs. Rice at Warner Avenue Elementary School in Westwood, are nap time, snack time, and a boy named Guy, who I liked a lot. Unlike your experience getting to school late with either your mother or Davis, you made sure I always arrived and was picked up on time.

I laughed out loud that, at the young age of five, you already had a critical eye for things that needed to be improved, such as the viscosity of the slide, the lack of fresh sand in the sand box, and the unnecessary flailing of the scarves you were required to fly while marching to the beat of the music. You must have really been a handful. If your father had been in charge of the school, you can bet the slide would have been well-greased, the sandbox pristine, and the music would have been performed by a popular live orchestra!

To say the least, the school paper drive seemed rather weighted to whichever class *you* happened to be in. There's no way any other class could compete with the number of papers left behind by guests in a 500-room hotel. I bet there were a lot of kids upset by your unfair advantage!

Love,
Lisa

30

THIRD STREET SCHOOL: FIFTH AND SIXTH GRADE

The Minstrel Show was the school's annual May event, produced by the sixth-grade children. I was in the show on May 11, the day I turned twelve, in 1933. We performed two shows each year, one for our school and one for the seventh-grade students at John Burroughs Junior High School, who each year were invited back to their old school to see the second performance. I am utterly ashamed and disgusted to share this, but we were a cast of seventy-five young white children in blackface. Back then I had no idea that performing in blackface went way beyond makeup, and was used predominantly by white actors to stereotype and caricature Black people. This appalling and hideous type of performance, considered normal at the time, contributed to the spread of racial stereotypes, and looking back on it makes my stomach turn. I was cast as Cuticle Highflooten in a skit titled "Black Clouds." My costar was my friend Miriam Patty, who played the part of Tacoma Washington. My costume was an ankle-length bright green satin dress with a big yellow sash and a yellow hat with a big brim. I was accompanied at the piano by Miss Roberta Vandergrift, the music teacher, and directed by Miss Elizabeth Tierney, the sixth-grade teacher we all loved.

The playwright's credit was not disclosed or noted on the four-page printed program.

As I waited in the wings to go on, I was terrified and forgot all my lines until I made my entrance. Then, suddenly, I felt like a "star" as I launched into my song: "If you care for something sweet in a gingham gown, give yourself a treat and meet Black-Eyed Susan Brown." The program lists twenty skits, dance numbers, and songs in two acts. The grand finale showcased nineteen "minstrels" singing "Deep River," "Up a Lazy River," "Alexander's Ragtime Band," and a rousing "When the Midnight Choo-Choo Leaves for Alabam'." Still in costume and black greasepaint, I came back to the hotel for an ice cream soda in the coffee shop. My "black face" may have been the only one seen in the coffee shop during the years we lived at the Ambassador. Another painful memory of that era.

In fifth grade we studied Egypt. We learned the whole process of making paper from papyrus plants (brought from backyards in the neighborhood), which was pioneered by the Egyptians. We learned a few hieroglyphic symbols to carve into the clay tablets we made. One of the teachers had a home kiln and fired them for our classroom. I loved my fifth-grade class, especially because my desk was next to Edgar's, a boy whose blond curly hair and blue eyes had all the girls competing for his attention. But he gave all his attention to me. Such a cute smile and always eager to loan me one of his slightly chewed-up pencils, which I secretly cherished.

I was among a group of best readers in my fifth-grade class who had a special reading hour every afternoon with Mrs. Tierney. I looked forward to that time each day because I loved books; every night after lights out, I would read in bed with my flashlight. I spent many nights under the covers with *The Wonderful Wizard of Oz*, *Heidi*, and Robert Louis Stevenson's *A Child's Garden of Verses*, a real favorite, first published in 1885. It remains on my library shelf today.

On the days we brought lunch from home, we'd quickly eat and then climb up on the old wooden tables in the lunch area under the vine-covered pergola and play all the parts in the movies we had seen. I always wanted us to "perform" from the movie *Rio Rita*, and because I always assigned myself the lead role (played by actress Bebe Daniels), all my friends had to settle for other roles from the movie. I was the producer, the director, and the star, and I am sure I was bossy and obnoxious about it.

When we weren't playacting, we played jacks until our hands were filthy from the concrete walkway, where we also chalked in hopscotch squares. Playing softball and jumping rope on the gravel-covered playground caused many a skinned knee. Knee scabs seemed to be a permanent part of my anatomy during my Third Street School years. Those crusty brown, ugly scabs barely healed before I would pick them off, only to have them reappear again.

Girls' softball and the traveling rings were after-school favorites. The bright blue paper-wrapped magnesia cubes used to keep hands from slipping on the heavy steel rings were an important possession. The overhead bar held a row of about eight rings hanging from chains. I never seemed to make it past the third or fourth ring, no matter how much "mag" I used or how hard I swung my legs back and forth while stretching out my hand for the elusive fifth ring. In elementary school, the phrase "going all the way" meant reaching the eighth ring. Later on I learned a much more interesting definition.

Birthdays always meant two parties, one at the hotel with my friends and another, if my birthday fell on a school day, for my classmates at school. The pastry chef at the hotel would bake a huge round chocolate cake, and beautifully and artistically decorate it to my utter delight. There were pink and red roses and blue and yellow flowers and green vines, and of course "Happy Birthday to Carlyn" and the correct number of candles, with one "to grow on." Somebody, probably my mother, would bring the cake to school after lunch recess and set it up in the cafeteria. When my class came into the room they found the tables set with the cake, ice cream, party favors, and funny hats. I think I was always more excited about the school party than the one at home. I loved the feeling of being so special.

By fifth grade I went to school by bus, rather than being chauffeured by Mother or Davis, though it wasn't like a real yellow school bus. The "bus" was, I think, a four-door Chevrolet sedan. I remember it being very big, dark, and ugly. There was a wooden bench across the back of the front seat to make room for more passengers. No one even thought about seat belts.

The driver, Mrs. Herod, would arrive each morning at the main entrance of the hotel and wait for me to walk across the lawn from our bungalow. I would have much preferred to be driven in my parents' Buick or, even better, my grandparents' beautiful dark green Du Pont Roadster. I think the truth is, I was embarrassed to be seen arriving at school in that strange-looking automobile. I know that sounds awful. I was so privileged in those days.

Carlyn Frank with her mother and the family's Buick in front of the home of a family friend. Hancock Park, California, 1927.
(Gilmour Family Collection)

I remember Mrs. Herod as being rather odd-looking and thinking that her appearance fit perfectly with the appearance of her vehicle. From someplace in my memory, I see her with wild red hair topped by unusual hats, and scruffy-looking clothes, and I can still smell her overpowering perfume, which flew into the back seat when she drove with her window down. Mrs. Herod's daughter, Charlotte, always rode along in the front seat. Lucky girl, she missed the perfume cloud. But then again, she was probably used to it.

I was the first pickup of the morning, and felt small and lost on that big, dark leather back seat. But at least I never had to sit on the funny old wooden bench, which became crowded as we continued our way to Hancock Park. After school, most of the time either Mother or Davis would come for me. Davis was always on time, but on the days when Mother said she'd be there, she was often late. All my friends gathered on the front lawn on June Street to wait for our rides to arrive. Sitting on the grass talking and laughing with my friends was fun for a while, but one by one they would go off with their mothers, and many times I would be left alone on the grass. Mother was usually not more than ten minutes late or so, but to me, it seemed like hours. I remember in the early years thinking that something terrible must have happened to her. Even today it is difficult to describe how physically ill I felt as I waited by myself, nervously picking blades of grass on the lawn, where a few minutes before I had been carefree in a crowd of laughing, happy children.

Those days of waiting must be the reason why, all my life, being on time has been so important. Even today I haven't overcome worrying when my adult children arrive much later than expected when they come to my house. Days when I have the fun of picking up a grandchild at school, I arrive at least ten or fifteen minutes ahead of time. Even though I know it would be no big deal for them if I were a little late, it is crucial to me that they will not be left waiting.

Dear Mom,

I recall you telling me about the annual sixth-grade Minstrel Show and how you had no idea how appearing in blackface was connected to racism. I don't understand how the adults in the school could ignore how offensive and demoralizing blackface performances were, and how they could think they would be appropriate for anyone, let alone children. Such a lack of cultural sensitivity, but so typical of the time. Then again, your parents—who as Jews understood discrimination, were open-minded, and accepted so many different types of people at the hotel—allowed you to perform in that manner, too. It all feels so wrong. Thankfully, at some point in your life you, and I'm guessing your parents, realized how demeaning and harmful these portrayals were.

Your sixth-grade performance was a far cry from how you conducted your adult life, supporting and uplifting people no matter their race. You did so much to help kids, primarily Black and brown kids, in underserved schools in Los Angeles, by giving away over 200,000 books through the nonprofit you founded in the mid-sixties, the Children's Booklift Fund. It was a herculean effort that helped hundreds and hundreds of kids ignite their love for reading. I was always so proud of you and the tireless work you did for many, many years. You always paid it forward.

Love,
Lisa

31

SUMMER AT RANCHO

We often spent time during the summer in a lovely cottage at the Rancho Golf Club off Motor Avenue. Now called Rancho Park, it's a public golf course adjacent to the Cheviot Hills Recreational Park in West Los Angeles, located across from the entrance to 20th Century Fox movie studios on Pico Boulevard. The Rancho golf course opened in July 1921. As previously mentioned, it was originally developed and owned by the Ambassador Hotel to provide a golfing experience more challenging than the eighteen-hole pitch-and-putt links available to all hotel guests at no charge.

Rancho Park was yet another distinctive perk my father and grandfather provided, offering the utmost in service and leisure for their guests. They even arranged transportation to and from the course. The lovely one-story California ranch-style clubhouse was considered way out in the country in those days.

Postcard of the Rancho Park Golf Club, which was originally created for Ambassador Hotel guests who wanted more than the hotel's pitch-and-putt course. (Courtesy Raphael Tuck & Sons, London, England)

The main lounge—part of the Rancho Park clubhouse, with its comfortable atmosphere and large open-hearth fireplace—led to the dining room, an informal space set up for casual family dining. On any day of the week, the men would spend the day playing golf and the rest of the family would arrive in the late afternoon for cocktails and an early dinner. The first summer that I had my playhouse, it came with us to the cottage. I just couldn't bear to leave it under the pepper tree back at the hotel, so after much begging it was decided that it could be put on the bed of the large hotel stake truck and moved right outside our cottage. The truck came rolling up the drive one afternoon and within an hour or two, my playhouse was unloaded. I seem to remember that the water and electricity were also hooked up—making it ready for tea parties with hot chocolate and cookies. It's hard to believe that all this effort was made, but then again, everything for me—and my sister—was always done on a grand scale.

The front windows of our cottage overlooked Motor Avenue. I remember that Mother spent much of her time in the "city." I also remember how I would stand at the window, watching for her car to turn up Motor Avenue in the late afternoons, when she was later than expected. As the time for her promised arrival passed, and the hour grew later and later, I would have this fear—just like when I was waiting for her at school—that she was not coming back. My stomach would ache with worry; it was a difficult time for me at the age of nine. It seemed we were so far away from home at the Ambassador. I could not imagine where she could be. But of course, she always returned. I wanted to ask her, "Where were you? What took you so long?" But I didn't feel like it was my place to question. She was probably shopping or lunching with her friends and just, as she would often say, "lost track of time."

Up the hill just past a big water tower, now occupied by the Hillcrest Country Club golf course, were acres of fields filled with stalks of sweet corn just beyond a roadside stand. People came from all over—women of wealth, young housewives, and families with children—and they would go out into the fields and pick the fresh corn off the stalks. Those who didn't want to walk in the dirt in their high heels could pick out ears from the stand at thirty-five cents a dozen. How delicious, to eat sweet corn on the cob, right out of the field.

Dear Mom,

Your childhood anxiety, which developed when people were late for whatever reason, stayed with you your entire life. Sadly, I too, developed this level of worry about my family. I wasn't brave enough to tell you about how your anxieties left their mark on me because I assumed you'd become defensive, no matter how kind my words would have been. In hindsight, I wish I hadn't made that assumption and had talked to you about it. I was only brave enough to tell my therapist. I continue to remind myself that every worry I've ever had about something awful happening to someone who was late, has, thankfully, never come true. I understand why you didn't talk to your mom about your anxiety over her lateness (and certainly didn't see a therapist back then) as that kind of child-parent communication on such matters wasn't acceptable in those days.

Love,
Lisa

32

MY FATHER'S FLYING MACHINE

According to family history, my father was one of the first private pilots issued a license in the United States. He obtained his aviator license in 1928, signed by no other than Orville Wright.

Ben Frank's original pilot's license, signed by Orville Wright in 1928.
(Gilmour Family Collection)

My father never owned an airplane, but he did have access to a rental, and he would fly down to our family's ranch in Riverside and land in a field that seemed to always need clearing before he could safely touch down. On the days he flew, my mother, my sister, and I would usually drive with my grandparents in their Roadster. Boy, did I love that car. How lavish it felt sitting on the soft gray plush seats, and on cold days covering up under the gray fur lap robe. The hotel kitchen packed a bountiful picnic basket that always came along for that sixty-mile drive to the country. Usually, before we got very far out of town, my grandfather decided we needed to picnic right there in the motorcar. Many weekends a busload of guests would arrive at my father's invitation to spend a day in the country with a wonderful picnic lunch provided.

There was an incident one day that nearly ended my father's plane flights to our ranch. He had called ahead to say he was flying in and instructed the ranch foreman to be sure to clear an area of deep ditches and holes he had noticed on his previous flight, so he could land safely. He landed easily but before he came to a stop one wheel hit a deep rut that had been overlooked, and the plane overturned. My father had to climb out of an upside down plane, which, given his size, was likely no easy task, all the while yelling at the ranch hand for being so careless. My mother, rightly so, was extremely upset. I know they had some big discussions about my father being able to continue to fly to the ranch, or anywhere for that matter. My father must have won out, because not long after that he took me to Mines Field on several occasions to go flying. Mines Field was a 650-acre field, filled with beans and barley—and even sheep—which would one day become the bustling Los Angeles International Airport.

My father would fly out of Mines Field in order to keep his flight hours up and maintain his license. I would often accompany him on these outings. My mother would tell him not to take me up with him, and that I was just to wait by the hangar and watch. But I did go up several times, in a little two-seater he borrowed from a friend and fellow pilot. We wore brown leather helmets and goggles, but no parachutes. My father sat in the front cockpit, and I was behind him as we flew north, following the coastline past

Santa Monica and then back, heading east flying over the hotel. My father would literally cut the motor three times, signaling to my mother that he was overhead. I thought going up with him was our little secret, but somehow, Mother always knew that I had not stayed on the ground. I have wonderful memories of the scary thrill of looking over the side of the plane with the wind blowing in my face, seeing, literally from a bird's eye view, the ocean and the beach from Santa Monica to Malibu pass beneath my eyes. More than occasionally, I would think about parachutes, especially when we did a loop the loop or some other fancy trick my father had learned to perform. He was a risk taker and a bit of a daredevil. Could my fear of flying come from those innocent days sitting in the cockpit watching my father's back? I'm pretty sure that would be a resounding yes.

My father also liked to fly a biplane from Clover Field, which today is the Santa Monica Airport. One of the oldest airports in the United States (it opened in 1922) and home of the Douglas Aircraft company, Clover Field was one of the world's foremost general aviation airports. It also held the Women's Air Derby in 1929, which was the first official women-only air race in the United States. Humorist Will Rogers referred to it as the "Powder Puff Derby." Clover Field also hosted the aircraft of pioneer aviators Amelia Earhart, Howard Hughes, Wallace Beery, and Wiley Post, among others. No matter which field we were flying from, I always felt an immense sense of relief when we landed.

Dear Mom,

Given your fear of flying, reading about your joy of flying with your dad in a little plane, open to the sky with no parachutes, is hard to imagine. Finding your father's aviation license, with Orville Wright's signature, in your Ambassador memorabilia box was a pretty exciting moment. Not many people can report such an experience! I didn't know the history of either Los Angeles International Airport or Santa Monica Airport before reading your manuscript. It made me laugh to know that back in the day sheep once roamed the fields of the now sprawling LAX. Although I am much, much more comfortable than I used to be, you did pass your fear of flying along to me.

Love,
Lisa

33

FROM CATALINA TO CORONADO

Catalina

During our years at the Ambassador, our family made many trips to other resorts in California, staying at hotels where all expenses were waived. One of the most beautiful resorts was the Hotel St. Catherine. The hotel opened in 1918 in the city of Avalon on Catalina Island. It was internationally known and attracted movie stars, athletes, and other famous and important people. It was very much like the Ambassador in terms of the kind of guests who stayed there, but also similar in architecture, which I imagine is why my parents loved it. It even had a dining room that could seat 1,200 guests, just like the Ambassador's Embassy Ballroom.

*The Hotel St. Catherine. Avalon, Catalina Island,
California, 1920. (Courtesy of the Santa Cruz Island Foundation and
the Chrisman California Islands Center)*

The Hotel St. Catherine was just a half mile from Avalon, with its own beach and private boat dock. It was a resort where boys, very cute ones I might add, would bring out our umbrellas and backrests. I loved going to Catalina because we took the Catalina Island steamship across the ocean. It left from San Pedro and the trip seemed to take forever. Following the Great Depression, thousands were directly employed in the fishing industry, with the San Pedro harbor being one of the largest employers. Fisherman working for canneries and fishing fleets could be seen throughout the harbor in the '30s. The ride over to Catalina Island was about twenty-six miles and took two and a half hours. The SS *Catalina*, also known as The Great White Steamer, was a huge white steamship built in 1924. It was over 300 feet long and could hold up to 2,000 passengers. I recall the ship had leather seats inside and gorgeous teak wood everywhere. I would always sit on the top deck on one of the long wooden benches.

Passengers on the deck of the SS Catalina, departing for Catalina Island. San Pedro, California, circa 1930. (Courtesy of the Santa Cruz Island Foundation and the Chrisman California Islands Center)

The SS Catalina steamship, circa 1930. (Courtesy of the Santa Cruz Island Foundation and the Chrisman California Islands Center)

Armed with a full supply of cellophane bags of oyster crackers, which were given to the passengers to help with seasickness, I shared mine with the seagulls who were busy swooping down to grab the crackers as I tossed them over the side. Big bands played to the delight of those who wanted to be entertained and dance. As we docked, little boats would circle the ship, and water skiers would speed by, waving and shouting hellos. I remember adults tossing coins overboard to the delight of kids who would swim out and dive for them.

The steamship's arrival at the Avalon pier was the event of the day in the little town. The whole population turned out to greet each ship that docked. The ship's band played as the gangplank lowered and residents of the island greeted us in song. I felt like a very important passenger. Everyone on board was dressed to the nines—men sporting suits and ties, women dolled up in fancy clothing, hats, and the completely wrong shoes for comfortably walking around the island.

What I loved most about visiting Catalina was the fact that kids could walk to the beach and wander freely all over town without a chaperone, and when the elegant new casino was built, we went to the movies in the Avalon Theater on its first floor under the ballroom. The Casino building, with its gorgeous Art Deco style, was built by chewing gum magnate William Wrigley Jr., and opened in May 1929. The theater accommodated 1,200 moviegoers and had a pipe organ similar to the one we had in the hotel's theater, but ours was smaller. A unique, yet appropriate feature given the styles of the day, was a hat shelf. These shelves were beneath every seat in the theater so that moviegoers could keep their hats and caps in a safe place and not block the view of other patrons.

When we were not guests at the St. Catherine, we stayed with Aunt Jane, one of my mother's four sisters. Aunt Jane and her second husband, who also happened to be her first cousin, Uncle Manny, owned a cottage on Catalina Island, a small brown wood bungalow a block up from the beachfront and just south of the center of Avalon town. It was one story, with a screened front porch and several small bedrooms. They had a goat that ate the garbage placed in the backyard.

Aunt Jane was an elegant lady, who when at home in Los Angeles, tended to have at least one "spell" a week, requiring a Christian Science Practitioner at her bedside. She had original Erté prints on her bedroom walls and a marvelous Tiffany wisteria lamp shade on a tree trunk base in her living room front window. Oh, how I wish I knew what happened to these treasures.

Aunt Jane was an entrepreneur when she arrived in Los Angeles from Chicago around 1910, before any other family members. She operated an "auto tour" company (which would be called a "sightseeing tour" today) that took visitors all over Los Angeles. She also had "property" on north La Brea Avenue. Whenever she was a passenger in my family car, we were required to drive by and "inspect the property," a small tan two-story storefront with a Chinese laundry on the first floor and apartments on the second. Family lore says she was considered the most beautiful woman in Los Angeles. Aunt Jane also built and ran a miniature golf course on Sunset Boulevard in Hollywood when that fad was at its height, and golf courses with their castles and waterfalls and funny little figures were constructed on lots all over the city. On hot summer nights if our parents weren't required to spend a black-tie evening at the Cocoanut Grove, it was great family fun to go play at Aunt Jane's miniature golf course for a few hours.

Hotel Del Coronado

The Del—as it was, and still is, affectionately called—was located in Coronado, off the coast near San Diego, and was my favorite of all the resorts we frequented. The hotel opened in 1888 with 399 rooms. Getting to the Del with my family meant a wonderful ride on the ferryboat from San Diego to Coronado. My sister and I always hoped to be the first car on the ferry.

It was exciting to park right behind the heavy chain that closed off the edge of the ship. Jackie and I would stand and watch the Navy boats and the gulls and know we would be the first car to come off the ramp. I can still smell the scent of the creosote pilings in my olfactory memory. This aroma would announce that we were ready to drive up Orange Avenue to the hotel.

Arriving at the main entrance of the Del, the doorman would take our luggage, and we would climb the rubber matted stairway up into the lobby. I still remember the warmth coming from the heat of the sun on the stairs and the floor of the veranda which ran across the entire front façade. There were rows of wicker rocking chairs where it seemed each time we arrived the same couples were stationed, sipping their afternoon cocktails. After registering at the front desk, we would walk across the interior patio to an oceanfront lanai suite. I always wanted to have our rooms on one of the upper floors so that I could use the beautiful brass grillwork elevator cage more often.

However, the lanai suites were the deluxe accommodations and nothing else would do for the manager of the Ambassador Hotel and his family. As I grew older, I was left to my own and could wander as I pleased all over the hotel—up and down the front and back elevators to the top floor towers, and downstairs to the bowling alley where all the pinball games were. I would also visit the gift shop, clothing boutique, and pharmacy.

Then there was the Crown Room, the hotel's elegant dining room. Dinner was always six or seven courses. Fortunately, because of my hotel background, the array of silverware to accommodate all the courses didn't intimidate me as it might other children who were not as experienced at the table.

Staying at the Hotel Del was always such an exciting vacation for us. Sometimes we would rent a speedboat and my father would go aquaplaning (water skiing) around Glorietta Bay while we all hung on for dear life watching him fly though the water. Picnics, music, bonfires, swimming, tennis . . . we did it all and it was such fun.

Dear Mom,

Wow, we have the exact same memories about the ferry to Coronado. I always wanted us to be the first car on so we could be the first car to drive off. I remember being quite a brat when that didn't happen. It wasn't a great way to start our vacation. I, too, loved the smell of the creosote pilings. I remember how weird and wonderful it was—both pungent and pleasant.

I have the very best memories of all our family vacations on Coronado Island, staying at the Hotel Del. You always wanted to stay in what you referred to as the "old part," because that was the section of the hotel where you and your family stayed. The Crown Room was so fanciful to my young eyes, with its "crown" of lights hanging so beautifully from the ceiling. I read somewhere that Frank Baum, author of *The Wonderful Wizard of Oz*, who was a frequent guest at the hotel, had designed the iconic crystal chandeliers.

Jeff and I loved the arcade downstairs, and every night after dinner we played endless rounds on the baseball-themed pinball machine. I remember feeling so independent because you let Jeff watch over me while you and Dad lingered in the dining room, you drinking your mainstay, Sanka, and Dad having his chocolate cake, both enjoying your alone time together.

What intrigued and fascinated me the most about the hotel was the fact that the enormous saltwater swimming pool was drained and cleaned every night. By morning the hotel had filtered out anything unsavory from the sea and the pool was refilled with clean salt water, ready for me to dive in!

Love,
Lisa

34

MALIBU SUMMER

In the summer of 1936, when I was fifteen, our family vacationed in a beautiful home at 23 Malibu Colony, in Malibu, California. The large two-story New England-style house, complete with tennis court and staff quarters over the garage, was owned by George Olsen and his wife Ethel Shutta. George was a big band leader who was very popular in the 1930s and 1940s and often played at the Cocoanut Grove. His wife, Ethel was a beautiful actress and singer. Their names are on the marquee in the photo below.

The Cocoanut Grove marquee, featuring George Olsen and Ethel Shutta. Los Angeles, circa 1925. (Courtesy of Marc Wanamaker/Bison Archives)

Malibu in the '30s was far different from the overcrowded, gridlocked Pacific Coast Highway of today, with its shopping centers, storefronts, movie theaters, restaurants, and the Pepperdine University campus on the hill. Back in the day, the famed Malibu Colony didn't have a guard kiosk or a fence preventing pesky celebrity seekers from catching a glimpse of their favorite star clad in a bathing suit. There were no traffic signals on the Roosevelt Highway, which was renamed Pacific Coast Highway in 1941. It was easy to dart from the house and cross the highway on foot to get to the Art Jones café, drugstore, cigar shop, liquor store, and the market.

The Malibu Beach Colony. Malibu, California, circa 1930.
(Ernest Marquez Collection, CL_555_06_2031, Huntington Library,
San Marino, California)

Creola and Goler Banks, a wonderful older married couple, lived in the guest quarters above the garage. They did all the chores around the house, plus the grocery shopping and cooking. They were the loveliest people and helped make our summer so special. Creola always wore a crisply pressed white apron, and Goler wasn't seen without his signature tweed cap. I don't know if they were the staff of the owners, or if my mother hired them through an agency, but they were like family and part of the ambience of the place. We had friends whose families owned year-round homes in the Colony (as it was called) so there was lots of visiting back and forth up and down the beach. Movie stars regularly walked along the shore and were a great added attraction for my girlfriends, who would come in pairs and stay with us for a few days or a week at a time. My sister also had her friends come and stay at the house, but they were too young to get giddy over spotting a Hollywood star.

Creola and Goler would do our food shopping across the street at the Art Jones Market. During that summer, on several occasions, my father had invited as many as 100 guests to Sunday barbeques on the sand in front of the house. and mother was shocked to see the food charges when she got the bills. Her idea of "paying" for food was signing a chit at the hotel. Playing housewife and not enjoying the convenience of room service was a new role for Mother. One weekend, my father invited all the members of the band that was currently playing at the Cocoanut Grove, including their wives and children and several other guests.

My father had heard that Jascha Heifetz, the Russian-born American violinist, was staying at a house just up the beach from us. As I remember, my father decided to walk up the beach to meet and greet Mr. Heifetz. Father, in his funny and persuasive style, told Mr. Heifetz to "bring your fiddle and come down to the barbeque." Unfortunately, I don't remember if he came— possibly because I was up the beach at a friend's house to avoid the mob of chatty grownups. Unless Mr. Heifetz was offended by my father's "fiddle" comment, he probably ended up coming to the barbecue, as it was hard to say no to Ben Frank. I can picture the guests, standing with their plates of chicken and ribs forgotten in their hands, mesmerized by the master's music.

Four houses up the beach was the home of Nacio Herb Brown, a famous motion picture and Broadway song writer from the 1920s through the 1950s. He was best known for his musical score for the 1952 film *Singin' in the Rain*. He was joined by his son, Nacio, Jr., who has been a friend of mine since the second grade and with whom I still talk on the phone on a regular basis. Every morning at seven o'clock, Nacio, Jr. and I would meet on the beach to swim in the early morning ocean. One day at the beginning of September when the tides were unusually high, the water came up to the

French doors of the living room that opened on to the sand. It took all of us—the houseguests, the Bankses, and the family, armed with brooms and mops—to keep the water from washing into the house.

Several neighbors in the Colony were in the motion picture business: Warner Baxter, an Academy Award-winning actor best known for his role as the Cisco Kid in the 1928 film *In Old Arizona*, and John Boles, best known for playing Victor Moritz in the 1931 film version of *Frankenstein*. There were the acting sisters, Constance and Joan Bennett; Neil Hamilton, a stage and film actor who often played opposite my favorite actress, Bebe Daniels; and agent Mike Levee, Sr. and family. Mike's son Michael and I have been friends since he was three and I was two.

There was also a young, handsome British figure skater and actor, Jack Dunn, whose lover and skating partner was Sonja Henie. My girlfriends, and even my sister, acted so goofy about him—he was *so* English and *so* handsome, it was often said he bore a strong resemblance to Rudolph Valentino. The girls and I would walk past his house several times a day trying to catch his attention until finally one day we were invited in for tea. It felt so sophisticated and English because we had tea with milk poured from a little china pitcher. It was the first time I had tried that combination and I loved it. Several times a week during the summer, tea with Jack became an afternoon pleasure. He treated us like grown-ups, and we were smitten. A year or two after those marvelous days, Jack went hunting with friends somewhere in Texas and after encountering a diseased rabbit, he developed a horrible infection in his eyes. After a long battle in the hospital, he died. It was a terrible blow to my friends, my sister, and me.

Other than the months at Malibu that summer, our beach days were spent at the Santa Monica Swimming Club, of which my parents and grandparents were founding members. In fact, my grandparents were founding members of the California Yacht Club, the Uplifters Club, the Hillcrest Country Club, and many more Los Angeles institutions, all of which are still in operation.

The Santa Monica Swimming Club was a large Tudor-style three-story building that was one of the first private clubs on Santa Monica beach. It was fenced off from the public State Beach to the north and the more conservative Beach Club next door. The Swimming Club, which allowed Jews, had a membership consisting of an interesting mix of movie stars, motion picture executives, businesspeople, and families. The Beach Club next door participated fully in discrimination, and did not admit Jews, actors, or African Americans—among others—into their club. In the Jim Crow era, the Santa Monica beaches were all white. In the twenties and thirties, banned from beach clubs and even public beach areas, African Americans were relegated to their own beach, derogatorily called the Inkwell. The Inkwell was a two-block section of sand just south of the Santa Monica Pier. There were so many terrible restrictions during that time. What disgraceful and vulgar thinking.

The Santa Monica Swimming Club overlooked the ocean and at the end of the day everyone would go upstairs to the locker rooms, shower, and change to have dinner in the main dining room. It was a milestone for me to reach the age of responsibility and have my own locker with a padlock. Attendants took care of towels and saw that bathing suits were rinsed out and placed on the bench in front of your locker. Beach boys, inevitably lean, tan, and attractive, provided backrests and umbrellas and manned a beach kiosk where one could sign for sandwiches and cold drinks during the day.

A wide verandah overlooking the private beach allowed parents who preferred not to dress for the sand to keep an eye on their children on the beach. Lots of movie stars used the club, especially on weekends, and that made it interesting for us kids. I remember handsome Buster Crabbe, the 1932 Olympic Gold medal winner, showing off his swimming prowess in the ocean. The younger kids were giddy over him because he was the star of the *Flash Gordon* and *Buck Rogers* movies. The beautiful actress Billie Dove—best known for her role in the 1926 film *The Black Pirate*, starring Douglas Fairbanks, Jr.—and her husband were there most weekends.

At the end of the summer, we headed back to the hotel. I was always sad that beach season was over and loved finding a little sand in my shoes or a shell in the pocket of my capris. The hotel had its own attractions, but Malibu would always have its magic.

Dear Mom,

"Bring your fiddle . . . " Your dad really said that to the most famous violin virtuoso, ever? Hopefully Mr. Heifetz had a sense of humor.

Spending the summer in Malibu sounds pretty great. You must have had a waiting list of friends ready to pack their beach bag and head up Pacific Coast Highway for a few days of fun in the sun. I wonder if Malibu is where you started your obsession with sunscreen? Was sunscreen even a thing in the thirties? All I know is I wish I had listened to all your crabbing about applying sunscreen because my teenage fad (a baby-oil-mixed-with-iodine suntan lotion concoction) came back to haunt me as a thankfully treatable form of skin cancer.

Did you flirt with the beach boys at the Santa Monica Swimming Club? If you were anything like me, I think I know the answer.

I loved reading about your weekly teatime with Jack Dunn. How gracious of him to entertain you and your friends, and what a sweet memory you kept. And what a sad ending for him. That really must have been hard for you to deal with back then. And speaking of dealing with things . . . the whole beach club/swim club/public beach segregation situation was upsetting to read about. I believe when my friends and I were teenagers, we may have hung out at what had probably been Inkwell Beach. I had no idea of its disgraceful history. I am so grateful that you and Dad raised us not to discriminate against anyone based on their race, religion, ethnicity, or gender. You taught us that if we were not going to like someone it should be because we don't agree with their sensibilities or values, not the color of their skin, who they love, or who they pray to.

Love,
Lisa

BOOK II

CARLYN'S POST-AMBASSADOR LIFE

35

JUST AN ORDINARY HIGH SCHOOL GIRL

"Girls, we are going to have to pack up and move out of Rincon. Your father's services are no longer needed here." I heard my mother's words but could not fully process them.

When I was a junior in the eleventh grade at Los Angeles High School, everything I'd ever known was taken away . . . and I became ordinary. It was a nearly impossible situation for me to handle with much grace, but I knew I couldn't let my friends see how utterly devastated I was that my family and I were forced to leave our home at the Ambassador Hotel. And even though my post-Ambassador life began with my identity and status lost, my friends still thought I was swell, and that was something. The hurt and shame I felt were powerful and didn't go away, but my high school days continued, and I kept busy as best I could with friends, tennis, and other activities. I wasn't particularly fond of school, but I was a good student nonetheless.

I dreaded the months leading up to graduation because my dream of hosting my class graduation party at the Cocoanut Grove had evaporated, along with so many other socially sophisticated events I had become so

223

accustomed to at the hotel with my high school friends. Compounding my lingering feelings of despair was the expanding anti-Semitism that was now rampant in Los Angeles and around the world. I remember there were Nazi death threats against popular Jewish actors and Nazis wanted to shoot Jews in the Boyle Heights area of Los Angeles. It was a very unsettling time.

Although I had noted in my senior yearbook that I wanted to continue my education at the University of Southern California, college wasn't in my future any longer because of money. My family couldn't afford the tuition after leaving the hotel. Instead, I went on to attend Woodbury Secretarial School on Wilshire Boulevard, near the Ambassador, to learn the secretarial ropes. This is not how I had imagined continuing my education—or my future.

I felt such shame after leaving the hotel. Not being able to attend college like most of my friends only added to a loss of self. My dreams had dissolved so quickly, and I knew my life would never be the same, but I hoped with all my heart that something would come my way to ease the pain.

Dear Mom,

Boy, did the word, "ordinary" hit me like a ton of bricks—I never knew *you* to be ordinary. This chapter really broke my heart. I felt the despair in your words. So many emotional charges coming at you with nowhere to hide in your suddenly broken world.

I started to wonder how I would feel in your situation. I grew up with abundance and privilege, as you did. I never took any of it for granted. Neither did you. But having to move from our beautiful home and losing my identity at such a pivotal age would have crushed me. To lose all of that overnight feels incomprehensible. I don't know how you managed it. And then, not long after your world fell apart in the late 1930s, the rest of the world did, too.

This chapter really helped me understand your pain. I am so sorry you had to experience all that you did at such a vulnerable age. But it shaped who you became, and there was so much goodness that was you—even with the challenging aspects of your personality. I always felt loved, seen, and understood.

Love,
Lisa

36

MY LIFE WITH COBINA

In 1940, two years after leaving the Ambassador and one year after I graduated from high school, I was hired as a switchboard operator at the Academy of Motion Picture Arts and Sciences. My starting salary was fifty cents an hour. The office was located in the Taft Building along the southwest corner of Hollywood Boulevard and Vine Street, across from the Pantages Theatre. Charlie Chaplin, Will Rogers, and other stars of the day also had their offices in the Taft.

In those days, during Academy Awards time, the office staff, including switchboard operators, oversaw organizing the mailing of both the nominations and the final ballots. They were all numbered by hand, addressed, and stamped by our group of twelve young women. We worked sometimes until two o'clock in the morning in the board-of-directors room, with a break for dinner. We received a seventy-five cent dinner allowance, but that didn't cover everything we ate, so we ended up digging into our own pockets to come up with enough to pay the check. The "generous" stipend for sending the girls home in a taxi at two in the morning was fifty cents.

At twenty-one years old, after a couple of years at the Academy, I needed a change. I went on an interview for a part-time position as a social secretary for Cobina Wright, Sr. Cobina was an opera singer, actress, and recent arrival from the social scene of New York City. She was known as an international "society hostess," a newspaper columnist, and a mother fiercely committed to having her daughter, Cobina Wright, Jr., become a movie star. Cobina Sr. had been married and divorced twice. Her second husband, William May Wright, a stockbroker, had lost his fortune in the 1929 stock market crash.

I was taken upstairs by the housemaid, Magdalene, for my interview with Cobina. We had a short—and for me, awkward—"interview," as Cobina was in the bathtub. I was hired on the spot and instructed to arrive early the following morning. Cobina's house was in Beverly Hills, above the Sunset Strip. It was a nicely furnished rental with three bedrooms upstairs and a living room, den, dining room, kitchen, and staff quarters below.

Magdalene ushered me back up to Cobina's bedroom for my first day of work, where thankfully she wasn't back in the tub. A handsome woman with wavy blond hair who dominated any space she was in, Cobina was sitting on the floor by the side of a large trunk overflowing with papers. There were twin beds, each dressed with fur throws, one in mink and the other in ermine, which gave me pause to wonder how I would fit in with this elegant household. Although a few years removed from living at the Ambassador, I was still used to elegance, but the fur coverlets even outclassed me.

Sitting there on the floor in her pale pink nightgown, wrapped in a rather tattered silk robe of the same color, her blondish hair in metal curlers and her face messily smeared with a thick layer of Elizabeth Arden cream, she was hardly the image of a New York socialite.

I joined Cobina on the floor, where we were surrounded by piles of bills, some of them months past due, and newspaper clippings about her actress daughter. There were personal letters and fan mail. Two telephones were constantly ringing. Cobina handed me her checkbook. "Darling, pick out a few bills, the ones that have been due the longest, and write some checks for me to sign." As I began to organize the scattered bills, she stood up. "I'm due at Romanoff's for lunch at one o'clock." Cobina proceeded to dress, with help from Magdalene and two very peppy Sealyham Terriers, and an occasional assist from me. She was stunning in a classic black-and-white silk print dress, red hat, red cape, black shoes, and a huge black alligator bag stuffed with what looked like enough to take away for a weekend. "Ta-ta," she said, as she strode out the door.

When Cobina returned home from lunch, I was working at a round, glass-top table in the breakfast room, continuing to sort notices and write checks. The breakfast room was lined with large double-hung windows that framed a well-cared-for sunny garden. It was a very pleasant room to be in if one must be paying bills. It was the end of my so-called half day, but I was asked to drive to 20th Century Fox where Cobina's daughter was under contract and needed a ride home. It was nice to have access to Cobina's car, as I wouldn't have my own for a number of years. Off I went. So much for working part-time.

When I arrived for work the next day, I found Cobina on the floor again, wearing her pale pink nightgown and a bed jacket, in bare feet and curlers, and with a breakfast tray beside her. She was talking on both phones, switching from one to the other. My task for the day? Answering her daughter's fan mail.

Once again, Cobina had a luncheon date that afternoon, and this time I was the designated chauffeur and dog sitter. All this service for ten dollars a week, part-time. We were driving down Santa Monica Boulevard in her beautiful black Cadillac coupe, with her two dogs in the back seat, when we ran out of gas. After much hand-waving and gesturing, we finally persuaded two nice young men in an old Ford to push us many blocks down the street to a Union 76 gas station. All the while, Cobina was complaining at the top of her voice. "I swear, Napoleon told me the car had more than enough gas to get us to lunch and back." Napoleon was the main household butler. By this time it was 2:10 p.m. and the service station attendant told us that her car, which was only two years old, was falling apart. "Sorry, lady, but you need new tires, an oil change, and a lube job, or this baby's not going anywhere." There was more, but the rest I could not hear as we tore out of the station and sped down Rodeo Drive to the now hour-late lunch date. While Cobina dined, I was given errands to run, plus I had her two dogs. I wondered how on earth my four-hour-a-day, ten-dollar-a-week contract covered all I was expected to do, as I was actually working eight hours a day!

The next afternoon I was asked to count all the Wright family sterling silver flatware that had been put away in an old trunk. I remember it was a really hot day and Cobina went upstairs to change into "something cooler," returning in her black corset and a pair of black bloomers.

We were sitting on the floor in her den surrounded by all her silver, bearing her family crest. The doorbell rang, and as I was buried under knives, forks, and spoons, Cobina went to answer it. I started to remind her of the outfit she was wearing, but I rethought that and just waited for an amusing situation to occur. She opened the door just a little, and a man stood in the doorway. He seemed to be introducing some kind of product to her. She explained that she could not really open the door any wider because "I'm only wearing my underthings." He replied that he understood her situation, but the look on his face was priceless. He could see Cobina's backside reflected in the mirror catty-corner to the front door.

It seemed as though every day I was sitting on the den floor counting and recounting the silver to be sure it had been counted correctly the day before. There were guests coming for lunch and Napoleon set out the everyday flatware on the table. I was invited to join, and as we started to eat Cobina realized we were using the everyday flatware and not the sterling with the family crest. "Napoleon! Bring out the good silver!" He hurried off to the den and returned, arms full, to replace all the guests' cutlery with the silver I'd been counting and recounting on the floor. Not only had it not been washed of the dirt it had gathered from lying in the trunk for two years, but it had been on the floor for two days while the dogs ran all over it. Realizing this, I excused myself from the table on the pretense I needed something from my handbag upstairs. I barely made it out of the room before I doubled over in laughter. It was just too much to take.

While working on the checkbook the following week, the back doorbell rang. It was someone from the butcher shop delivering a large leg of lamb for the dinner party that night. I asked him to leave the package on the kitchen table, but he refused. He wanted to be paid on the spot. I explained that we had a house account, but he said Cobina's credit had been changed to a cash-only basis and he would not leave until he was paid. I pleaded with him to leave it just one more time because there was going to be a party tonight. He took the package and started to leave, so I got my wallet and paid him with my own money. I knew I'd never see those seven dollars again—and I was right!

Upon my arrival the following morning, Cobina informed me that Hammonds, the butler who spelled Napoleon on his day off, had gotten drunk while serving her party the night before. She said his hands were shaking so badly that her important guests couldn't be served properly and Cobina had to leave her hostess chair and help him. Cobina heard Hammonds putting dishes away in the kitchen, so we went in and confronted him. "Why," Cobina asked him, "were you drinking whiskey last night?" He told her he hadn't been drinking whiskey, but Cobina reminded him that he'd been so drunk he could hardly stand up. He tried to convince her she'd not smelled alcohol on him—"It's just my shaving lotion"—but she was having none of it and stood her ground. He finally admitted that he'd been drinking, but it wasn't whiskey, it was gin. Cobina had had enough and instructed me to write out a check for the wages he was owed. I could only hope the check would clear.

Hammonds, wearing a beige gabardine suit, packed up to leave. His wife, Ester, came to pick him up. Ester, who spelled Magdalene on her days off, was in a camel-hair tailored suit, while the lady of the house had her hair in curlers and was wearing a tattered nightgown with shredded sleeves and her bed jacket. Both Hammonds and Ester looked devastated by the turn of events as they left.

One morning while I was answering fan mail, the phone rang. When I answered, a strong male voice on the other side asked for young Cobina. He said his name was Prince Philip of Greece and he was calling from New York and that he'd been trying for over a week to reach her. He was very charming and anxious to talk to her. I had no knowledge of Cobina Jr.'s love life, and figured this was probably a prank call. But after a few minutes of conversation, I realized it wasn't a joke, and I gave the prince another number to reach her. A biographical account about Cobina Sr. said that her daughter and the prince met in Venice in the summer of 1938 when they were both seventeen. The story said that her mother literally pushed Cobina

Jr. into his arms while they were all out at a bar, drinking. They dated while in Venice and he followed her to London for the rest of that summer, but the relationship didn't last when she came back to the States.

Had the prince finally made that connection and reached out to Cobina the day I spoke with him? It was nearly two decades later, after she'd married Palmer Beaudette, a member of a wealthy Detroit automotive family, that I learned (can't recall from who) that Prince Philip, who became the Duke of Edinburgh, had stayed in touch, or at least maintained occasional contact with the Wright family, sending royal Christmas cards for years. That early morning phone call I took from the Greek prince looking for the movie star still makes me wonder if he would have rather been standing next to Cobina, instead of behind the Queen of England.

Dear Mom,

This is one of my favorite chapters. It is certainly the one I laughed at the most. I remember when I was younger, you would be talk about your days working for Cobina. It seemed you had forgotten how overworked and underpaid you were, because when you reminisced about it, you couldn't help but smile and laugh out loud about how outrageous she was.

Reading about you counting the silver connected me to your obsession with counting your mother's beautiful Royal Danish silverware. You kept a paper record with a count of each fork, knife, spoon, and serving piece. You would count each piece after a dinner party to be sure no one had accidentally tossed a knife or fork into the trash. I still have the piece of paper with the counts for each piece of silverware you kept track of. This relic is tucked into the drawer of the buffet in my dining room, keeping the same silverware I inherited from you safe, sound, and accounted for.

Love,
Lisa

37

THE MEN'S ROOM

My time with Cobina lasted a little over a year. After I quit, I once again took a job with the Academy of Motion Picture Arts and Sciences. In March 1943, the Academy Awards were held at the Cocoanut Grove. It was surreal, emotional, and strange to be back at the hotel again, and even stranger to end up in the men's bathroom. Let me explain. There was a huge lounge in one of the men's bathrooms that had been converted to a press room with long tables with telephones for each reporter covering the Awards. Why another area wasn't designated I can't recall, but there we were, all night long in the men's lounge. There were tall two-piece black telephones set up on the tables. Ashtrays sat on every surface, overflowing with cigarette butts. Everyone smoked, including me.

Typewriters were positioned by each phone and a smaller table was installed for me with a telephone connected to the mic at the bandstand where the Oscars were handed to the winners.

My job was to listen to each acceptance speech and repeat it word for word to the reporters so they could call in to their copy desks or type on the noisy black typewriters. When Greer Garson won Best Actress for *Mrs. Miniver*, she started her speech in the usual gushing way, and I listened carefully and repeated each word for five-and-a-half minutes. According to the *Guinness Book of World Records*, hers was the longest thank-you speech in Academy history and remains as such today. It was an exhausting night in the men's room for me.

Little did I know that not too many years later, my husband, Ben Benjamin, an agent for those involved in motion pictures, and I would attend many Academy Award nights together, just not at the Cocoanut Grove. Do you remember that at the beginning of my story, I mentioned I was conceived in a tent near Butte, Montana, where my then future husband was ten years old and living with his family? Well, that was Ben. How we met, and how a life I never imagined came to be, begins in the next chapter.

Dear Mom,

How on earth did you repeat Greer Garson's five-and-a-half-minute acceptance speech word for word? I know you had a great memory, but that is unbelievable! I love how your time working at the Academy of Motion Picture Arts and Sciences came full circle many years later when you attended Academy Awards shows on the arm of Mr. Ben Benjamin. So much classier than sitting in a bathroom. And what a dashing couple you always were. If only I could have been your plus-one back in the day.

Love,
Lisa

38

TEN YEARS MY SENIOR

Over the years being coached by the tennis pros at the Ambassador, I had become a pretty good tennis player. A friend of the family, Bede Bensinger, knew I loved tennis and that I was single. She wanted to introduce me to a "very handsome gentleman" who was also a great tennis player. In January 1943, at twenty-two, I needed some excitement in my life so I agreed to meet this mystery man. We met at the tennis courts at the park on La Cienega and Wilshire Boulevard.

Ben Benjamin, ten years my senior, was truly the most handsome man I had ever met. It was a beautiful warm blue-sky day. Ben strode across the lawn of the park swinging his tennis racket, full of the confidence that so became him. He wore white tennis trousers and a cable-knit tennis sweater. I was playing mixed doubles at the time and hardly glanced at him because I was afraid I would not be able to stop staring. I remember hearing him laugh and say, "If I had known there were going to be so many attractive women here, I would have shaved this morning." Then Ben put his hand on his face, with his mischievous smile, moving his hand up and down his beard stubble in what became a very familiar Sunday morning gesture.

Looking back, I don't remember if my partner Esther and I won or lost. All I recall is that when the set was over, Ben took Esther's place and stood, racket ready, beside me. I don't think I spoke two words to him at the time. There was a snack stand and we got a Coke after our sets. We didn't stay long because I had to leave to go home to change and meet friends for dinner in Beverly Hills. I didn't dream of hearing from him again. I guess I thought he was too good to be true and just put him at the back of my mind, although he asked for my address and phone number and wrote it on a napkin, which he placed carefully in his pocket.

The following Saturday night, he called! He was at the Pirates' Den, a wild night spot on LaBrea Avenue in Hollywood where the waiters dressed in pirate costumes and the manager had a bullwhip to keep the employees in line. We talked on the phone for nearly an hour, despite all the noise in the background, while he occupied the only pay phone in the restaurant. I seem to remember Ben was working up to a couple of Alka-Seltzers because he said a lot of things he probably would not have under other circumstances.

When we played tennis the next day, he was a bit sluggish from the night before. After tennis we sat in the sun for the rest of the afternoon and talked and talked. We made a date for the following Friday to go to the Cocoanut Grove with Ben's friends, Steve and Marilyn, who were newly engaged. Steve drove to the Grove, and Ben and I sat in the back seat. On the way home he held my hand all the way to my house. He walked me to my door and we made a date to go to the movies the next weekend. We went to a theater on Hollywood Boulevard—either the Pantages or Grauman's Chinese—and saw *Yankee Doodle Dandy*, staring James Cagney. Afterward, we went out dancing and held hands again. When we got in the car, Ben leaned over and kissed me on the cheek. I liked it. So when he brought me to my door that night it seemed only natural that I kiss him goodnight. And that's when things started. We were pretty much inseparable from that moment on. We had so much fun.

We loved going to Olvera Street, the historic pedestrian street and Mexican marketplace located in one of the oldest parts of Los Angeles, filled with shops and restaurants. We would go and get our fortunes told there. The fortune tellers all seemed to agree there was something special between us. One even predicted we would live together in a tall apartment building. This could have been a lucky guess, but it did turn out to be true. We also loved going to the Cocoanut Grove. It was still hard for me to return to the hotel, but with Ben it was worth my pangs of anxiety to share those nights with him. We always got dressed up. One night before he picked me up, he sent me an oversized lei of red and white carnations. I might have looked like Seabiscuit, but I felt like a glamour girl—*his* girl. We loved going to football games, taking long walks, and attending the Santa Claus Lane parade along Hollywood Boulevard. We'd go dancing at LA's most famous clubs, make dinners together, and of course, play lots of tennis. We also wrote a ton of letters, and I still have many of them in an old shoebox. They are romantic and very innocent—written in his almost artistic, sweeping penmanship—and I swear some still carry the faint scent of his aftershave.

Ben was born on February 10, 1911, and raised in Butte, Montana. His father, of Russian decent, immigrated from Germany, and his mother from Romania, both via New York. His father was an accountant for a clothier in Butte and his mother—taught by her grandmother to read palms—used her psychic talents to tell fortunes during the war to raise money for the Red Cross.

Ben and his sister Rosalie both attended Berkeley and graduated one year apart. Money was tight, as Ben's father had passed away when Ben was only sixteen. One of Ben and Rosalie's relatives, Uncle John, paid for their tuition. Ben graduated from Berkeley in 1932, when I was just eleven years old. That just sounds crazy, putting it in writing! He was a business major and went to work at Roos Brothers in Berkeley, a San Francisco-based department store that opened in 1865. The downtown Berkeley Roos Brothers opened in 1926 and attracted customers with its public telephones, restrooms, beauty and hair-cutting parlors, and a golf fairway and putting green. I don't recall Ben ever mentioning all these amenities. He was probably too focused on selling clothes and earning commissions to be bothered with all the customer-capturing ploys. Then he was offered a job in the Los Angeles Roos Brothers store in 1940. And boy am I glad he came to LA.

Ben proposed to me one sunny Sunday afternoon after a rigorous doubles tennis match. Our friends, Julie and Bud, who knew what was to come after tennis, pretended they had to leave right after the game. As we walked off the court, Ben took my hand and we strolled over to a bench under a beautiful branching tree and there and then he proposed. When our friends knew the deed had been done (so to speak) they ran out and congratulated us. It was very exciting!

Ben and I were married in Los Angeles on September 24, 1944, in the rabbi's office at the Wilshire Boulevard Temple. Located at 3663 Wilshire Boulevard, the temple was founded in 1862 and is considered the oldest Jewish congregation in Los Angeles. I had my dear friend Muffet stand up with me. Ben's future brother-in-law, Nate, who would soon marry Ben's sister, Rosalie, stood up for him.

I didn't have a traditional wedding dress, as it was wartime and we had to watch our spending. I bought a beautiful blue-gray tailored two-piece suit, part of a collection of non-costume fashions designed by Metro-Goldwyn-Mayer (MGM) costume designer Adrian. My hat, surprisingly in the same fabric as my suit, was purchased from the "Moderne" department at I. Magnin.

Adrian (full name Gilbert Adrian) was an American costume designer whose most famous costumes were for *The Wizard of Oz*. In fact, he designed the iconic ruby slippers for Judy Garland to click her heels to get home. He also designed the overall look and costume concept for Dorothy, including her famous blue gingham dress. He designed hundreds of costumes for MGM between 1928 and 1941, when he had a falling out with the top brass. A few years later, he went on to establish his own line of retail fashions in Beverly Hills, on North Beverly Drive. American women responded to Adrian's clean-lined designs, and he exerted a strong influence on American fashion until the late 1940s. It was Adrian's Beverly Hills store where I bought my wedding suit.

Mr. and Mrs. Ben Benjamin, just married! Los Angeles, September 24, 1944.
(Gilmour Family Collection)

There was no money for a honeymoon, so we stayed our first night as a married couple in the Town House Hotel, where we had our wedding luncheon, on Wilshire Boulevard in the Westlake district, just a few blocks east of the Ambassador.

Ben had joined the Navy before we were married, so we lived in Long Beach during that time. We rented a one-bedroom apartment in the Villa

Riviera building, a registered historical building that opened in 1929. It was the fortune teller's tall apartment building. We had what in those days was called a "deluxe" apartment, featuring a pull-down Murphy bed. The rent was $75 a month. In the 1940s and early 1950s, the Villa Riviera was known as the "Home of Admirals," as many of the senior officers of the United States Pacific Fleet lived there. Ben wasn't an Admiral, but somehow we were lucky enough to get an apartment there.

When Ben completed his time in the Navy, Michael Levee, my childhood friend, asked Ben to join him in his father's agency. Michael's father was an agent for actors and writers, and Michael had been working there for about a year. Ben had zero expertise in the agency business, but he had a business degree from Berkeley, and he was incredibly kind, gracious, very intelligent, and the town's best-dressed man. Michael's invitation to Ben was the springboard for Ben's forty-year career in the entertainment agency business. He would go on to transform the careers and lives of many important actors, writers, directors, and producers.

Dear Mom,

I knew you and Dad met on the tennis courts at the park on La Cienega, but I don't think I knew that you were instantly so smitten with each other. You talk about Dad being so handsome, but Mom, you were stunningly gorgeous. I had found and read your "dating letters," and they were so innocent and tender it warmed my heart to know how in love you two were, since over the course of your forty-seven years of marriage, it got pretty bumpy at times. In fact, there were days I was sure you and Dad were headed for divorce, but thankfully that didn't happen because I would not have recovered from it. And maybe the two of you wouldn't have either.

I know you didn't get your fancy wedding, but I also know you had no regrets about the ceremony and celebration you did have. I love the fact that you kept your wedding suit. It really is an iconic and historic piece of fashion.

In fact, I met a woman who creates fashion events for the Wilshire Ebell Theatre, showcasing vintage clothing from women who lived and worked in Los Angeles in the 1920s and '30s. I told her about your wedding suit. She could not believe I was in possession of an original Adrian. I decided that your wedding suit should be part of a future fashion showcase, and I donated it for such an occasion. I know you would rather have people who appreciate Adrian's fashion be able to see your suit in person, instead of having it hang in my closet for the next several decades.

How crazy that Dad and your childhood friend Michael became friends and business associates. I know how close you and Dad were to the Levee family for so many years. It was a special and lasting friendship. Sadly all four of you are now gone, but your legacy of love remains.

Love,
Lisa

39

ON THE MOVE

It was around 1946, a year or so after the war ended, that we moved from Long Beach to live with my parents until we could find an apartment on the west side of Los Angeles. After a few months we got very lucky and found a place on Rexford Drive in Beverly Hills. I remember bursting into tears when the landlord said "yes," but also told us we had to pay him $1,000 under the table to get the apartment, which was something landlords were doing because of the lack of housing. We knew it was wrong, but we needed a place to live. We emptied our savings account, which we had worked so hard to build up, thinking we might put it toward the down payment on a future house.

After settling in and getting the lay of the land, I recall going to the laundromat every Monday morning with a neighbor who had a car. But what I really remember is the day when a grateful client of Ben's gave us a Westinghouse washer and dryer. It was a very exciting and life-changing event.

After a couple of years in Beverly Hills, we moved to a sweet little duplex rental on Rochester Avenue in Westwood—no bribe required. We spent a lot of time with family and friends in the early years—lots of backyard barbecues and picnics, my father manning the grill. The aroma of roasting hamburgers and hot dogs mingling with cigar smoke and laughter from my husband's stories heard on repeat, yet still as funny as ever. My Ben had a way of making everyone smile. My parents and sister adored him, and we were very happy.

I'm not sure how happy my parents were at that time, though, as my father was still trying to find his footing after being forced to leave the Ambassador a decade earlier. He kept the family afloat with a variety of hospitality jobs and other work, but being a businessman at heart, he wanted something bigger, something that would fan the flame of his entrepreneurial spirit. So around 1948, he took a leap and opened a restaurant—aptly named Ben Frank's—at 809 South Western Avenue. My father's idea was to open restaurants all over southern California that would be next to, or very near, a gas/service station. This way people could get their cars worked on and enjoy a meal at Ben Frank's while waiting for their car to be finished. The original Ben Frank's, located two doors down from a 76 gas station, was a big success. One unique aspect of Ben Frank's was a toaster on every table. I don't know how he came up with this idea, but it was a big customer draw. You could toast your own bread, just how you liked it.

Sadly, my father only lived long enough to open one restaurant, but he did get to see it flourish and his idea validated. Ben Frank's was sold after his death in 1953. The name changed to Mimmie's, or something like that. I don't know how long Mimmie's lasted, but where the restaurant once stood is now a busy block of Korean shops and cafes.

What very few people know is that Arthur Simms, who ran the MGM commissary after the war, and Bob Ehrman, a longtime associate of Simms, opened a Ben Frank's on Sunset in Hollywood in 1962. Bob worked for my father at the *original* Ben Frank's. As a tribute to my dad's influence and mentorship—showing Bob every aspect of the restaurant business—they named their restaurant Ben Frank's. This was such a lovely gesture, but it has always bothered me that any reference to the Ben Frank's restaurant on Sunset was deemed "the original," and it just isn't the case.

The postcard that follows is the only piece of Ben Frank's restaurant memorabilia I have. I never noticed until now that the signature on the postcard is John Q. Public! Once again, my father's brilliant marketing mind in action—driving customers to the restaurant by mailing postcards to local neighborhoods that read like a friend telling them to come enjoy Ben Frank's.

Postcard showing the front of Ben Frank's restaurant. Los Angeles, circa 1949–1950.
(Courtesy of Chris Nichols)

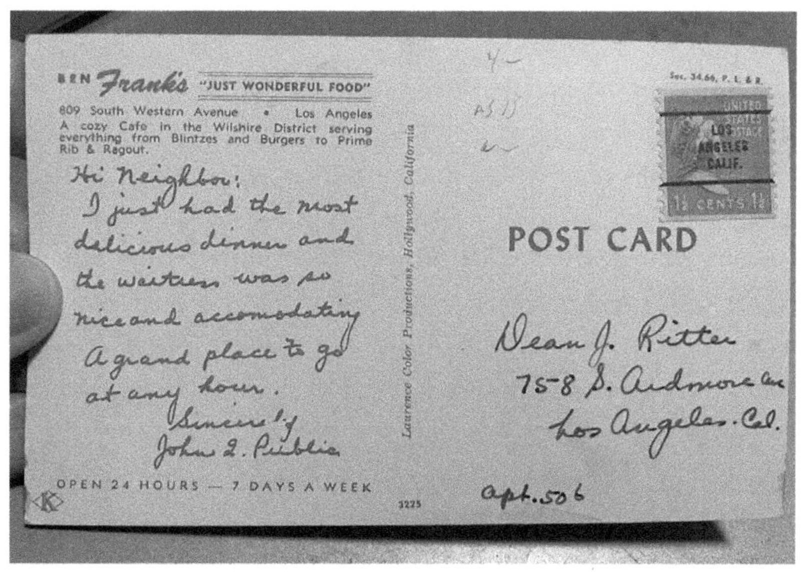

Ben Frank's postcards included a clever marketing message from "John Q. Public,"
drawing customers to the restaurant. Los Angeles, circa 1949–1950.
(Courtesy of Chris Nichols)

A few years before both of my parents passed, our son, Jeffrey, was born in 1949. What a joyous time. Looking back, I can't believe I smoked while pregnant, which horrifies me even more considering I lost both my parents to cancer, one year after the other—my father in 1953 from lung cancer, and my mother in 1955 from breast cancer. Those were very tough times, but our second child, Lisa, was born in 1954, and brought a lot of welcome distraction.

In 1956 we bought our first house, a few blocks from UCLA's botanical gardens, near Westwood Village. It was a marvelous thirties-style Spanish house on Manning Avenue—two stories, with polished black-and-white marble flooring lining the entry. As you walked in the house, the living room was to the right, two steps down and through an arched entry. The ceiling was high and there was a large picture window where we always placed our Christmas tree.

Downstairs we gathered in the cozy den on evenings to watch television or play games. There was a small sitting room upstairs along with three bedrooms and two baths. The kitchen had a GE dishwasher, which was worth the price of the house if you ask me. We had a built-in set of industrial-looking "ice boxes" with large metal handles and big chrome hinges that we soon replaced with a modern Frigidaire refrigerator, the kind with a big, refrigerated section and a small freezer on top for stocking up on all those "delicious" Swanson Turkey TV Dinners for the kids.

There was a big garage to fit my new 1955 Ford Country Squire station wagon and Ben's car. I don't remember the make or model, but it did have big fins in the back. We had a big backyard, and behind the garage was an incinerator to burn trash. This was a relic that was used before the invention of trash trucks and was outlawed when it was deemed to contribute to the horrendous smog developing in Los Angeles. In 1961, we wanted to move out of Westwood, as it was becoming very crowded with more and more traffic.

We found our dream home on North Carmelina Avenue in the Brentwood area of West Los Angeles. It was a John Byers-designed home. Byers was a well-known and highly respected architect who built homes in Brentwood, Santa Monica, and Pacific Palisades in the 1930s and '40s. Our home was built in 1931 and was called the Murray House, after the owner who commissioned the original build. The home was identified as Early American Colonial Revival architecture and had been featured in a 1931 edition of *Architectural Digest*. The use of brick-and-wood siding, brick chimneys, wood shutters, and double-hung windows all fit the design of that style. It was such a beautiful home. It was way more than we could afford at the time, but we really believed it would be our forever home. And it was.

We had a lot of art and very fragile items such as crystal and china that had belonged to my parents, which we were not comfortable having the movers pack up. We were also having the entire house painted, and the painters kept gallons of paint in the garage. We had moved all the precious items over to the new house on November 5, 1961. On November 6 a brush fire broke out in the Bel Air section of Los Angeles. At the time, it was to become one of the worst fire disasters in Los Angeles history, destroying nearly five hundred homes. Bel Air was to the east of us, but the wind was blowing everything west, toward Brentwood and the Kenter Canyon area. I was frantic. The winds were ferocious. Smoke was everywhere. Ben rushed home from the office and was on the roof with the garden hose watering it down to mitigate any flying embers. I filled up both cars with the valuables we had brought over the day before. Both my children were at school. I felt they were both safer there until I could pick them up and go back to the Westwood house, which, for the next few days, we still owned.

That afternoon, the fire jumped one of the canyons in Bel Air and was burning homes to the west in Kenter Canyon. We could see the hillside burning from our backyard. At one point, the fire jumped Kenter Canyon and ignited the backyard of the house belonging to actress Betty White and her husband, Allan Ludden, who lived four houses up from us. Thankfully, the Herculean efforts of the firefighters put the fire out before it could spread through our neighborhood. It was a horrific week, and we were so lucky to come out with nothing more than piles of soot and ash.

When we finally moved in and got settled, our home became the center of entertainment for both adults and kids. We seemed to always have a dinner party to give, or sleepovers and other fun kid activities. We eventually put a pool in the backyard, and that was summer entertainment. My strategy was to keep the best snacks and drinks for my kids and their friends so everyone would come to our house for fun. There was the pool, Ping-Pong, badminton, a bunch of board games, and many other distractions to keep their friends happy and to have them return often. It was, and still is, a lovely, comfortable, and really beautiful home. I feel very lucky to live here in my old age. I only wish Ben was still alive for us to share these years together.

Dear Mom,

I remember our house on Manning Avenue in Westwood, which we left when I was seven. It was such a great neighborhood. So many families and lots of kids. My goodness, remember the Mosbys who lived across the street from us? They must have had twelve kids, at least that's what it seemed like. There were kids everywhere in and outside of that house, all day, all night—a veritable circus.

When I was about five you fell at the gas station, tripping over the car jack someone had carelessly left out by one of the service bays. You broke your elbow. In my mind, that meant part of your arm that was connected to your elbow had been cut off from the rest of you. I was hysterically crying upstairs in our little sitting room, and Jeff tried to draw a picture for me of what your arm actually would look like when you got home from the ER, but I wouldn't have it. I was sure you'd be missing a large chunk of your arm.

By the way, I never told you how that rusty saw in the garage actually fell across my nose when I was six years old. I jostled the saw down from the peg board with a broom. I didn't trip and hit my head against the peg board as I swore up and down I did. Seven stitches later to stop what I remember as buckets of blood pouring down my face, we came home from the ER. I am pretty sure I had my favorite food that night—Swanson Turkey TV Dinner and rocky road ice cream. You and Dad felt so bad for me. I wonder how you would have felt if I had told you the truth that day? I'm pretty sure it would be a combination of anger and upset and definitely no ice cream!

I don't recall our actual move, in terms of packing up and leaving Westwood for the Brentwood house in 1961. What I do recall is the feeling of chaos surrounding the big fire, and feeling like you had forgotten me at school. I remember when my teacher told us about the fire, and I was so scared because I knew Bel Air was not that far from our new house. When you finally picked me up, you felt terrible about how scared I was, and you explained why you had stayed back at the house with Dad, but I still felt abandoned—just like you felt when your mom was late picking you up from school.

I've always considered the Brentwood house, not the Manning house, as my childhood home. That house holds so many beautiful memories. You and Dad built such an amazing life there for our family. I am so grateful you didn't sell the house after Dad passed in 1991. I know you considered it, saying it was too big for just you. You talked about buying a condo, but thankfully never went through with it. And given the circumstances of how things unfolded for you later in life, keeping the house was the best decision. It's funny how sometimes going with our emotions instead of practicality turns out to be the best decision after all.

Love,
Lisa

BOOK III

THE REST OF THE STORY

Dear Reader,

You've just finished the last chapter my mother wrote for *Life Without Reservations*. My guess is that between an aging mind and waning interest from publishers, she eventually set the manuscript aside.

The good news is that I know enough about my mom's life—and her voice—to finish the story with the same spirit and verve she brought to every page, which brings us to Book III. The following chapters reflect my memories, commingled with my mom's writings and musings and the connections she experienced in her post-Ambassador life that she didn't include in her manuscript. Gleaning information from letters to my father, transcriptions of video interviews of Mom walking the Ambassador Hotel's grounds before its demolition, and many conversations with my Aunt Jackie, I feel confident that by the time you finish *Life Without Reservations*, you will have the whole story.

Although my mother led a fairy-tale life at the Ambassador, we all know that, as far as fairy tales go, there is often an unsettling and unpredictable twist to the ending. I know she felt her life was essentially over after she and her family left the hotel, but I see her post-Ambassador life quite differently. I see a remarkable life from beginning to end.

I hope you enjoy the rest of her story.

Warmly,
Lisa

40

BURT, WARREN, JULIE, LARRY, INGRID, YUL, AND WILLIAM

Mom was a rare Los Angeles native. She was as fiercely loyal to her family as she was to her convictions. A passionate and determined political activist, children's advocate, fundraiser, and relentless fighter for the underdog, she was the one you wanted by your side in a crisis. Sharp as a tack, she lived by the adage, "pay it forward," and was undeniably a classic beauty.

My dad, Ben Benjamin, went from representing authors such as Ray Bradbury (who was a dear friend of both my parents) and other famous writers like Gordon Parks and William Faulkner, to becoming a legendary agent for A-list movie stars, producers, directors, and screenwriters. He joined Famous Artists Agency around 1950. It later became International Creative Management in Los Angeles, where he worked for nearly four decades. One of Dad's clients was Burt Lancaster. He and Burt had a remarkable and loving friendship; today you might call it a "bromance." I can't remember how many years my dad was Burt's agent, but I think it was from the mid-to-late sixties all the way through to Burt's last picture, *Field of Dreams*, released in 1989.

When checking dates for this part of the story, I read a funny entry in Wikipedia about Burt and *Field of Dreams*: "Burt had originally turned down the part of Moonlight Graham, but changed his mind after a friend, who was also a baseball fan, told him that he had to work on the film." That "friend" was my dad, an avid Dodgers fan and season-ticket holder. I clearly remember my dad insisting Burt take the role.

Burt was a frequent guest at our house. He was just as charming and handsome as you would imagine, and yet also such a normal guy. He had the most beautiful voice and a wonderful rich laugh. He adored my mom. She would always hit him up for donations to support political candidates she volunteered for, or for her passion project, the Children's Booklift Fund.

Dad's clients made up an impressive list, including Candice Bergen, Ingrid Bergman, Jacqueline Bisset, Yul Brenner, Julie Christie, Sir John Gielgud, Rex Harrison, Sir Laurence Olivier, Dame Vanessa Redgrave, Lee Remick, Ray Stark, Bob Radnitz, and many, many others. All of dad's clients were frequent guests in our home. Those who lived in Europe would always come by when in town visiting or working on a film, and many of the local clients would pop by on weekends for a swim in our sunny pool, a cocktail, dinner, and lively conversation.

I will never forget the day when Warren Beatty, clad in a very revealing Speedo, was swimming in our pool with my dad while my mom gave Julie Christie, Warren's then longtime girlfriend, a tour of our house. That tour included my room. There I was, sitting at my messy desk studying away as they walked in. I'm sure the first thing Julie Christie saw was a six-foot poster of her boyfriend plastered on my wall next to my bed! I turned five shades of purple from embarrassment, as I was probably around twelve years old at the time.

My mom was the consummate hostess and party giver, and everyone loved her gatherings. Her large dinner parties were always a catered affair with the most beautiful table set with formal place cards, 100-year-old sterling silver flatware, vintage Baccarat crystal candlesticks, and bone china from Europe. My mother loved these treasures, which originally were wedding gifts to her parents in 1920. Her signature touches included fresh flowers and candles everywhere. She had the most exquisite taste in everything she did. But then how could she not, given where she grew up and how she was raised. My mom's aesthetics definitely influenced me. I am a fresh flower hound, and they are always in my home, as are candles, lit to set a quiet atmosphere.

My dad was one of the most respected and loved people in the entertainment field. He was a unique blend of charisma, authenticity, integrity, and loyalty. His clients loved him and vice versa. This put my mom in a very enviable position. She was Mrs. Ben Benjamin, a role many women would have killed for. But I'm not sure she ever realized how envious others were of her "title." Here's why: Sharing the spotlight with my dad, who was so admired and loved, was often tricky for her. In a way, it was role reversal. Growing up at the hotel, Mom was adored and showered with attention from the groundskeeper to famous band leaders and everyone in between. But now, her husband received the lion's share of attention in every social situation. And Mom, despite her beauty, grace, and strong personality, often felt invisible. She was used to being the star of the show, but she was married to a supernova. In a note I found in one of the early versions of her manuscript, she mentioned her feelings of insecurity. It was like a gut punch when I read it.

What is confusing is that so many of my dad's clients adored my mom, and she had a great relationship with them. However, the insecurities my mom carried over from the shock of leaving her Ambassador life never really left her.

Dad was a member of the Motion Picture Academy of Arts and Sciences, and he and my mom attended many Academy Awards ceremonies together. One of my fondest father-daughter memories was when I attended the Academy Awards in 1971. I made my own dress in my home economics class at Palisades High School. It was so beautiful—long and black with geometric shapes and colors and a white Peter Pan collar with matching cuffs. Thankfully, my teacher helped me finish on time. When I stood in front of my bedroom mirror, I thought it looked perfect. We took a limo to the ceremony, and I could barely contain myself knowing that I would see Ali

McGraw and Ryan O'Neal in person. They were both nominated for best acting in one of my favorite movies at the time, *Love Story*. My dad knew everyone, and I felt like a celebrity princess just being with him. This must have been how my mom felt walking around with her dad at the Ambassador.

We spent many weekends and long family vacations at San Ysidro Ranch in Montecito, a beautiful enclave in the hills above Santa Barbara, back when "The Ranch," as we affectionately called it, wasn't fancy or elite as it is today—just homey and familiar. It was, and still is, a sentimental favorite. My brother and I gave our parents a surprise fortieth wedding anniversary party there, and Mom had her seventy-fifth and eightieth birthday celebrations with family and friends at The Ranch.

Dad's clients could always depend on my mom to help them with anything they needed when in town and called upon her often for hotel recommendations that could accommodate their often eccentric requests— she was their own private concierge. In 1981, she spent weeks working with a real estate agent to find a suitable apartment near UCLA on Veteran Avenue for Sir Laurence Olivier's son, Dickie, who would be attending school there. My mom advised Olivier to buy a townhouse rather than pay crazy rent for a well-used apartment. Mom and Olivier became great friends and often, when he was in Los Angeles working on a film, he would come to the house for a swim. He detested hotel pools, even at the swankiest of places, because the pool area lacked privacy. One late summer afternoon, he arrived by limousine wearing a suit and tie with his bathing suit in hand. I recall my mom telling a story about how she had directed him to the downstairs bedroom to change because he was having trouble walking up stairs. He said to Mom, "Oh no, darling, I'll just change out here on the terrace, not to bother." And there, according to Mom, was one of the most revered British actors of all time, stripped down, standing on our brick terrace, hands on hips, looking out at Kenter Canyon in all his naked glory!

Another client of Dad's was Ingrid Bergman. She and my mom were also good friends. In 1979, my parents arrived at the Beverly Wilshire Hotel to pick up Ingrid and take her to the American Film Institute event honoring Alfred Hitchcock. She was the evening's hostess. While Mom waited in the car in the courtyard driveway, my dad went into the hotel to escort Ms. Bergman back down to the car. A few minutes later, a bellman came to the car with a message for Mom, asking her to come upstairs to Ms. Bergman's suite. Mom was greeted at the door by Ms. Bergman wearing a beautiful bright sky-blue chiffon evening dress with long rows of matching colored beads dangling from her sleeves. However, there was a problem. Her arm was swollen, an ongoing condition resulting from her breast cancer surgery in 1977, and she was unable to button and zip the back of her dress on her own. She didn't feel right asking Dad to do it. So there was Mom, buttoning Ms. Bergman's gown and thinking about her own mother, who suffered from the same situation due to breast cancer. It was a very emotional moment.

While working on this manuscript, I found an old hard drive that had some of my mother's writings about other encounters with Dad's clients. In one story, she writes:

> I am watching *The King and I*, starring Yul Brynner, on the Turner Classic Movie channel, and I remember a day in September 1972 in the French countryside. Ben, Lisa, and I are in Lisieux, near Deauville out in the country where Yul Brynner and Jacqueline de Croisset, whom he had married the year before, had invited us for lunch. They lived in an historic fifteenth-century home in the middle of a pear orchard. They had modernized the kitchen and baths, but everything else was left undisturbed so as not to take away from the stunning ancient architecture. Sometime later, when we were back home in Brentwood, I was shopping at Vicente Foods Market, and I ran into Yul, who was in town filming a movie and had stopped off at the market to get some of his favorite snacks to take back to the hotel. The following week, I found myself back at the same market buying groceries to make dinner for Yul, whom we always invited over when he was in town. Anyway, I got a hug and a kiss from him in full view of the store manager, who, after that day, as never before, remembered my name and, for years, asked me about Yul.

Another memory involved the 1981 Thanksgiving holiday. Mom writes:

I'm in Malibu with Larry Olivier at the house I found for him to rent when it was requested he give up his suite at the elegant Hotel Bel-Air. He had checked into the Hotel Bel-Air in November 1981 for a week-long stay. When the end of the week came, the front desk called his room to inquire what time he would be checking out. Larry informed the clerk he'd be staying for another week. But his suite, and all the other suites and rooms for that matter, were booked, as it was Thanksgiving week, so Larry had to check out. My phone rang at 9:30 that morning. "Darling, it's Larry." As if that voice would never not be recognized! "I hate to ask you this, but I'm being thrown out of the Bel-Air. Do you suppose you could come and fetch me? Maybe we could find a rental in Malibu for a week or two. Perhaps you could be in touch with the real estate lady that helped you find the house for me when I was filming *The Betsy*?" Well, of course we couldn't have our client and friend stranded in front of the Hotel Bel-Air. I made a few calls and arrived at noon at the Bel-Air in my little Honda Accord to find Sir Laurence waiting for me. The arriving "ladies who lunch" openly took it all in and wondered with bewilderment at the sight of this very famous actor as he hopped into a little Honda Accord and sped off down the road.

We went to the agent's office and switched cars to something more suitable for such a luminary. With the real estate agent, we searched from Malibu to Topanga to the Ventura County line, finally ending up in the center of the Malibu Colony. We didn't have an appointment, but our agent thought there were a few houses available and wanted to at least show Larry the outside. In order to get past the guard gate you had to have your name on the guest list, and obviously we didn't. Larry remembered an actor friend and his wife whom he had stayed with a few times over the years, who had a house in the Colony. So, on a whim, Larry called his friend, and as luck would have it, the couple were in New York for several weeks extending their Thanksgiving holiday and they were delighted to have Larry stay in their home. His friend told us where the hidden key was, and he told the guard to let us in. Larry was so pleased with the house and the view he decided to stay for two more weeks.

As you can imagine, Larry was a very popular neighbor and had several invites for Thanksgiving dinner. It is now Sunday, November 29, of the long Thanksgiving weekend and I'm spending the day back at the beach house with Larry. The housekeeper is off, and Larry has asked me to prepare my famous veal marsala dinner for him, Ben, and me.

Late in the afternoon while cleaning up in the kitchen we had the radio on, and the news of Natalie Wood's body being found that morning in the water off Catalina Island sent a chill through all of us. Although neither were clients, Ben knew both Natalie Wood and Robert Wagner (RJ to his friends), and Larry knew them both well, too, especially Natalie, and he adored her. They had worked together in 1976 on a made-for-television version of *Cat on a Hot Tin Roof*. Larry talked for hours about his relationship with both Natalie and Robert. He was utterly devastated and sickened upon hearing the tragic news. It was an awful ending to such a lovely holiday week. One I have never forgotten.

I loved the relationship Mom had with Dad's clients. Mom was such a name-dropper, though. It used to drive me crazy. I'd give her a pass on using first names of clients, like Larry, but she'd do the same when speaking about famous people she'd never met. I don't know why it bothered me so much, but it did. I think it was her way of showing class and status that she once had when living at the Ambassador. It also may have been her way of leveling the playing field with my dad.

On another occasion, my mother writes:

William Faulkner, an American writer who won the Nobel Prize for Literature in 1949, was a client of Ben's. Ben invited William over for dinner shortly after we had moved to the duplex in Westwood on Rochester Ave. It is 1951. I am twenty-nine years old and I have a two-year old toddler, Jeffrey, and I'm worried about what I could cook for a Nobel laureate. Chicken and rice? It's so pedestrian, but it was my best, no-risk recipe. William arrives in a simple brown suit, and he calls me "Ma'am" in his soft Southern voice.

When he is seated comfortably in the wing chair in our den, my son toddles over to the coffee table, picks up the silver cigarette box, standard on every coffee table in those days, and hands William the box. William takes a cigarette and thanks Jeffrey, who looks very pleased with his hospitality. Although William was known to never sign any of his books, he does sign our copy of his *Collected Stories*, which was published in 1950 and won the National Book Award in 1951.

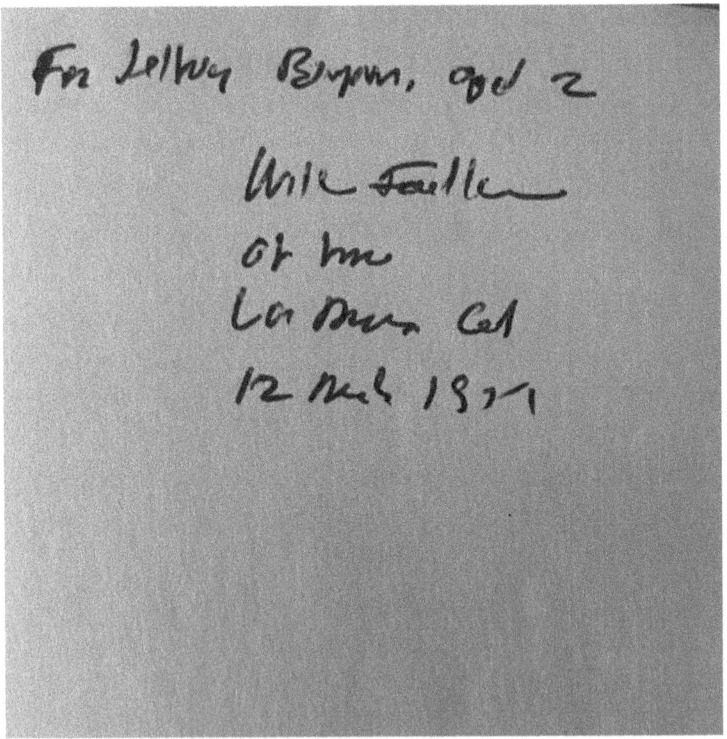

The inside cover page of Nobel Laureate William Faulkner's Collected Stories, inscribed to two-year-old Jeffrey Benjamin. Los Angeles, 1951. (Gilmour Family Collection)

For Jeffrey Benjamin, age 2

William Faulkner

At home

Los Angeles, Cal

12 March 1951

During dinner we asked about his Nobel acceptance speech, and he told us that as he was dressing for the presentation, he realized he had no paper with him, so he removed the cardboard insert from his freshly laundered shirt. And this, he tells us, is where he scribbled his speech. He was the most charming, understated, and brilliant man I'd ever met.

41

TWENTY-FIVE FORMER GANG MEMBERS AND MOM

One of the craziest acts of kindness, which really typifies my mother's heart, began with a surprising group of people. Mom became involved with former members of the Blackstone Rangers, who, between 1961 and 1963, were considered one of the most dangerous and powerful gangs on Chicago's South Side, according to the Chicago Police Department.

You're probably wondering how my mother, at the time a nearly fifty-year-old white woman from the posh Brentwood neighborhood of Los Angeles, got involved with a group of twenty-five former gang members. I found a story in which my mom documented her experience getting this group, who could all sing, on the *Smothers Brothers Comedy Hour*. (You can find the January 21, 1968, episode with the Blackstone Rangers on YouTube.)

As Mom writes:

The invitation to meet former members of a Chicago gang came from my friend Dr. Al Cannon, a psychiatrist on staff at the UCLA Medical Center. I was especially happy to meet this group because through Al, I had been able to contact many folks in the Black community who were helping me with my personal War on Poverty. In 1966, one year after the Watts riots, I founded the Children's Booklift Fund and launched a series of book fairs in Title 1 schools in Watts, East Los Angeles, and the San Fernando Valley. In the years that I ran my nonprofit, I raised enough money to give away over 200,000 new books to children in grades K–6. Although I only had the Children's Booklift Fund for seven years, it felt like my life's work. It meant the world to me, and I know I changed so many young people's lives by bringing the joy and adventure of reading to them.

In 1967, Al invited me to attend a private performance in West Hollywood to hear these twenty-five young people sing. It was exciting to learn of this group, whose members were working to shed their gang affiliation. With the help of a wealthy benefactor in Chicago, a theater workshop was established and each of the twenty-five attended the workshop to better themselves. This led to a collaboration with several other generous benefactors to create a musical revue called "Opportunity Please Knock."

Al was close friends with those who helped establish the workshop and wanted to pay it forward by arranging for the group to perform in Los Angeles. They had already been performing for about a year in the Chicago area. As they stood on the stage of this little theater on Sunset Boulevard, this group of twenty-five young men and women sang with such joy and spirit. When they burst forth for their finale with the song "Up, Up and Away," made popular by the 5th Dimension, I immediately thought they could do just that and rise above their former gang life. I would get them on national television, and all over the country, disadvantaged kids would see it was possible to reverse the hopelessness of their lives. So, during the coffee-and-cake hour after the performance, I promised the "balloonists" they would be back in Hollywood one day for a television appearance. I must have been nuts. I know my family thought so. But I was on a mission.

Ken Kragen, the producer of *The Smothers Brothers Comedy Hour*, was a friend of my husband's. Ken listened to my passionate speech about why he and CBS needed to give this group a break. It took a lot of explanation to convince him how important I thought it was for them to do this. At the time, the Smothers Brothers were considered very controversial for their outspoken stands on the Vietnam war, censorship, social and political issues such as civil rights, women's rights, and counterculture movements of the '60s. The show became a space for artists and performers to push the boundaries of what was acceptable on mainstream television, leading to both acclaim and controversy. It seemed like the perfect platform to give these young people a chance to change the course of their lives on a national stage.

Ken finally agreed, and negotiations for a show date began. Now that the hard part was done, the rest, I thought, would be easy. I only had to find a way to transport them all across the country. I told myself I could do this. I would find them a comfortable and affordable place to stay for a number of days. I thought there would be a few sleepless nights ahead of me, which I learned along the way was the understatement of the year. After weeks of telephoning and letter-writing to try to secure funding for this endeavor, an interesting mixture of benefactors came together. *Playboy*'s Hugh Hefner, *Chicago Sun-Times* columnist Irv Kupcinet, Chuck Kettering, one of the co-founders of the workshop in Chicago, and I formed the roster. Hefner and Kupcinet came on board to secure sponsors for airfare and clothing expenses. I pledged the lodging, and Chuck said he'd help with extra costs.

I made the arrangements for a bus, provided by Ted Watkins and his Watts Labor Community Action Committee, to pick up the group at the airport and drive them to a motel in downtown Los Angeles.

The week before the air date of January 18, 1968, the show was going to be taped. I sat in the car in the CBS parking lot on Beverly Boulevard and Fairfax waiting to meet my talented singers. Ted Watkins's bus pulled into the lot on time, and in my mind the twenty-five were on their way to fame and fortune. If they were as nervous as I was, they didn't show it as they climbed off the bus, looking very professionally dressed in perfect late '60s fashion of bright colors and vibrant prints. We got everyone into the studio on time and ready to perform. Dick Smothers took to the stage and made the following introduction to the television audience: "In 1957 a street gang was formed by a group of young boys living in and around Blackstone Ave. in Chicago. The Chicago Police Department named them Blackstone Raiders and they in turn renamed themselves the Blackstone Rangers. But the Blackstone Rangers are no longer a tough street gang. They are an example of what can be accomplished by the young people who live in the ghetto areas of our big cities and seem to have no opportunity to get ahead in life. But these kids got off the street and formed a musical revue company called Opportunity Please Knock. And they've been performing now for almost a year. I'm sure you're going to enjoy what they do. Ladies and gentlemen, meet the Blackstone Rangers."

The first song was "Wade in the Water," which they sang with so much feeling and pride. Next was "Up, Up and Away." They gave it their all and the audience loved them. I was beaming with pride and could finally breathe once it was over.

Now, for the after-show. I had promised everyone a party at Burt Lancaster's home in Bel Air. It was going to be a night of celebration and congratulations. Norma Lancaster, Burt's wife, as she always did for her guests, provided a lavish buffet. Everything on the table looked like the entire menu from the neighborhood standard, Junior's Delicatessen on Westwood Boulevard. Everyone ate and drank everything up. When the bus finally left, I thought, just one more promise to keep. The next morning, everyone arrived at a Sunset Boulevard recording studio, driven there in three lavender limos from a mortuary in Watts that Chuck arranged and paid for because Ted Watkins said there had been some kind of scuffle and he would not drive the group to the recording session. Ted never told me what happened. So, my final contribution was to have a recording session set up because I had been told that the group had never been to a recording studio. They sounded even better than they did on the *Smothers Brothers*! The session was a huge success. When we all listened to the playback they all shouted with glee how happy and thankful they were for all I had done for them. They left for the airport in a cloud of lavender exhaust. I left for home and cried all the way.

I never heard from them again.

42

CARLYN'S CRITIQUES

Mom did an enormous amount of volunteer work, from political campaigns to environmental causes and projects to lift the underserved. She did it all with great finesse. She was the first person organizations would call if they needed a volunteer leader because she was organized, experienced, and could motivate others to deliver under tight deadlines. My mom was relentless in her volunteer work, getting "her" candidates—who believed in civil rights—elected, banning the bomb, and many other very worthy causes. And, although she spent a great deal of time volunteering, my brother Jeff and I never felt like we were second fiddle. From lunch boxes to briefcases, she was always there for us.

Our parents taught us the values of fighting for what we believed in, paying it forward, and the gift of service. In 1969, my parents took Jeff and me to San Francisco to one of the largest protest marches in the country. Over 100,000 people marched to Golden Gate Park to protest the war in Vietnam. I remember how Mom insisted that she and Dad dress in business attire to show that "establishment" people, not just 'hippies," were against the war.

Years after my parents were empty-nesters, Mom decided she needed a "real" job, and although she continued to volunteer, in July 1978 she applied and was hired as the executive assistant to the president of the L'Ermitage Hotel, a very high-end hideaway on a palm-lined street in the heart of residential Beverly Hills, where her upbringing with extraordinary hoteliers manifested itself. She was to report to Mr. Severyn Ashkenazy. He and his brother developed and ran the hotel beginning in 1976.

I found my mother's L'Ermitage folder with many of her typed memos and notes, itemizing each and every problem that concerned her regarding the hotel. One memo in particular caught my eye, as it was about a guest named Andy Warhol. That memo, which follows, details Mom's efforts to save money and quickly provide guests with the amenities they requested.

Inter-Department Correspondence

To: Peter Shepherd

Date: September 25, 1978

From: Carlyn Benjamin

Subject: House Typewriter

We do get calls from some of guests for a typewriter, i.e. just this past week Andy Warhol needed one and we had to rent it for $30.00 which is the minimum. That is for two weeks and he only used it two days. If we purchased one and charged the guests the regular minimum that Beverly Hills typewriter charges, it would pay for itself in not too long a period. What do you think? An IBM small electric is $400. and Smith Corona is about $300 new.

✓ Go Ahead.
'Keep Records'   Over

Carlyn's memo regarding Andy Warhol's stay at L'Ermitage. Beverly Hills, 1978. (Gilmour Family Collection)

The hotel had seven floors. I found a single-spaced five-page memo with each room number listed, accompanied by very specific notes and observations for each. For example: "Room 210: carpet needs shampooing, only one hand towel is on the rack in the bathroom, plants need care, balcony needs swept, barstools need cleaning, and the bedroom wall needs paint."

Her observational acuity reminded me of her grandfather, Abe Frank, who always carried a notepad around with him and jotted down all the things he saw that needed fixing at the Ambassador. Apparently, the notepad does not fall far from the hotel!

As always, my mom was a strong advocate for herself. I found a memo dated November 1978, just four months after she started working at L'Ermitage. She wrote this to the hotel's managing director:

Dear Peter,

I Carlyn Benjamin am being paid at the rate of $3.4615 per hour, whereas my cleaning lady, who does not do windows, is being paid $3.7810 per hour. I request that you discuss at your convenience with Mr. Ashkenazy the fact that I wish my rate of pay to be revised to $200 per a four-day week, because I'm worth it and because I made a dumb deal for myself when I first came to work here on July 11, 1978.

Thank you.

PS: Please do not tell me you will raise me to what my cleaning lady makes.

Every memo she wrote was very direct, because she really cared about the quality of the guest experience and her role in creating the most comfortable and clean accommodations for their high-end clientele. And she knew a thing or two about how a high-end hotel should be run. I found another memo that speaks to her constant crusade to watch out for those she felt were being marginalized or discriminated against.

A memo to Mr. Ashkenazy, dated November 1978, reads:

To: Mr. Ashkenazy

From: Carlyn Benjamin

RE: Shoeshine cards

I cannot believe that in this year of 1978 we are actually putting cards in the shoes of our guests from the shoeshine "boy." I think we are not only degrading our employee who we hired to shine guest shoes, but that we are making our hotel appear like something out of the part of our history that any decent person does not like to remember. Also, if any of our minority guests should happen to leave their shoes out, they would be highly insulted to read that card. And if you don't want their business anymore, that is a very unkind way of telling them.

That was my mom through and through. It turned out Mr. Ashkenazy and his management team decided Mom was too much, and she felt underappreciated, so it was a mutual decision that she left her post nearly two years after she was hired.

43

CANCER TIMES THREE

In 1987, at age sixty-six, Mom was diagnosed with colon cancer. It was a terrifying time for our family. We rallied behind my dad and helped Mom through recovery. She was extremely lucky, as she had a surgical cure. No other treatment or special devices were required. Then, nearly six months to the day, my dad, who was seventy-six at the time, was also diagnosed with colon cancer. He waited too long to tell his doctor about symptoms he was experiencing, even though he knew what my mom had experienced before her diagnosis. I can't remember what treatment he had. I know they must have done something that worked, as he was able to get back to work—until cancer reared its ugly head again.

It was 1991, and Dad's eightieth birthday was in February. Mom gave him a huge celebration to honor his eighty years. I remember driving home with my parents after the party, and Dad looked so weary. Maybe it was just fatigue from being "on" for so many hours, but I was worried that his health was starting to decline again. I knew how important it was for him to reach his eightieth birthday, but I knew in my heart that that night he gave himself permission to begin to let go.

In April or May, he was back in the hospital, this time with stomach cancer, and it was incurable. After that episode, Dad didn't go back to the office, but he stayed connected with his clients. On the evening of June 19, 1991, I came over to my parents' house and sat on the bed with Dad. What I remember so clearly is how calm and peaceful he was. Real or imagined, there was this gorgeous golden glowing aura around him as he sat up in bed in his crisp white pajamas with navy piping outlining every edge—a moment I will never forget. Mom called me at 4:00 a.m. on June 20' to tell me my dad was gone. The pain of losing him was excruciating.

When my husband Mark and I pulled into the driveway of my parents' house, I let out the most piercing, guttural god-awful scream, as if Dad's passing was completely unexpected. I screamed and screamed until I almost passed out. How was I going to go on without Dad? How would Mom be? How would we all be? Going forward, the date would now be bittersweet, as June 20, 1991, marked my tenth wedding anniversary.

After Dad died, Mom was able to stay in her home, which was such a gift for her as she aged. During the ten years after Dad died, she stayed fairly active, lunching with friends, working on her memoir, advocating to save the Ambassador Hotel, and doing volunteer work. She picked up her grandkids from school when needed and attended all their events.

When things started heating up over the preservation of the hotel and it subsequent destruction, Mom was in demand. There were several lengthy articles in the *LA Times* and interviews in *LA Magazine* about her life growing up at the hotel. She also did radio interviews on KABC in Los Angeles and television interviews on local news stations, including a show on PBS about Los Angeles history. She loved every minute of all the attention given to her. I was so happy for her. I knew how much energy she derived from shining a light on the Ambassador and its history, including her own story of living at the hotel.

Mom was fortunate to have my brother's family and my family all within a fifteen-minute drive from her home. We spent many days and warm nights during the summer months swimming in the pool and just hanging out. We took her with us for long weekends in Santa Barbara and Cambria. She loved going back to San Ysidro Ranch on her own, and to the Simpson House in downtown Santa Barbara, where we often stayed with her. She loved staying in hotels and gently critiquing her stay, providing management with a very detailed list of "Carlyn's Critiques." Jim and Susie Lavenson, who owned San Ysidro Ranch for eleven years, and were great friends with my parents, had printed a pad of stationery with "Carlyn's Critiques" at the top of each page so she could put all her observations in one place after each stay.

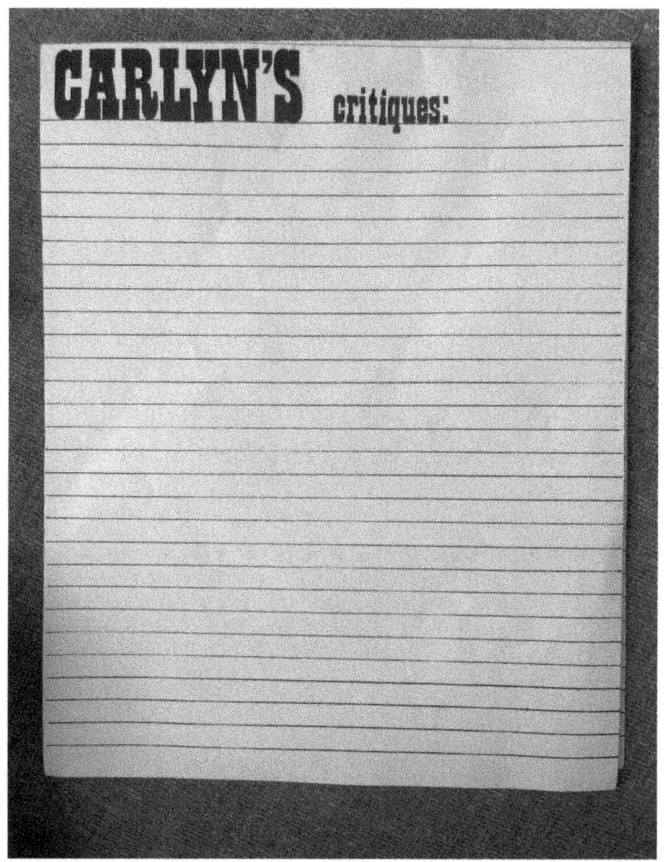

"Carlyn's critiques" memo paper. (Gilmour Family Collection)

Then, in the fall of 2000, my brother was diagnosed with pancreatic cancer at age fifty-two. Jeff lived for eighteen months with this brutal, unforgiving disease. It was a horrendous experience for all of us. The only time we'd ever heard of pancreatic cancer was back in 1991 when actor Michael Landon was diagnosed with it.

Decades later, the pain of losing Jeff is still there. Everyone loved him. He was like a human Google. He knew everything. He was handsome, hysterically funny, a brilliant writer, and a very devoted family man. He loved to travel. He was an amazing cook and was fluent in wine. We were very close, and I loved him so much.

I didn't think my mom would survive the loss of her son, but thankfully she did. We talked a lot about Jeff, keeping his memory alive. Mom bought a beautiful bonsai tree and placed it in her backyard along with a plaque with a quote from my brother that typified his philosophy: "The good life is, I think, one in which the elements are in balance and resonate to create satisfaction, fulfillment, and joy."

Mom had slowed down tremendously, but she took a few writing classes at UCLA and spent time with her beloved grandkids. She loved lunching at the Souplantation in Brentwood with her lady friends, but most of all she loved going there for dinner with her three grandchildren.

Even as she aged, she still talked about her days at the Ambassador to anyone who would listen. When Mom started to tell her story, it was amazing to watch the reaction of those who knew of the hotel and its history. I know it gave her energy and she felt seen and special—as she deserved to be.

42

WAKE ME WHEN IT'S OVER

On October 17, 2004, a meeting was held with the Los Angeles United School District (LAUSD) officials and concerned citizens and the Los Angeles Conservancy to try to save the Ambassador from the wrecking ball. And as often happens, the good guys lost the fight.

The LAUSD approved a $318 million plan to raze the Ambassador while preserving, or so they said, several historic structures on the site. This was all done to develop a 4,200-seat school campus for K-12 students. According to my mom, the evening was very contentious. It was impossible for her to wrap her head around the fact that so many people had fought for so many years to try to save this historic hotel, which had been her home of seventeen years. Although not a done deal, its demise seemed imminent. Mom was one of fifty citizens, including architectural photographer, Julius Shulman and civil rights leader, Dolores Huerta, who spoke in favor of saving the hotel. Here is Mom's speech.

"Good afternoon, my name is Carlyn Frank Benjamin and I speak for my younger sister and myself. The Ambassador and I came to life just four months apart and I lived there until I was seventeen; our grandfather and father were the general managers.

I stand with the Conservancy's plan. I believe if you have the courage to go with it, the public relations alone for LAUSD would put you in such a positive light for saving part of the history of Los Angeles, that you would be making your own history. I think of all the beautiful old buildings throughout the country that might be saved to become badly needed schools because of the example you set. You could become heroes to generations of Los Angeles children who would bring back inside those walls, a school unlike any other, the life and the music and the laughter that would echo the past.

Thank you."

Sadly, as we all know, the hotel was razed between October 2005 and January 2006. So many people and organizations were relentless in their epic pursuit to fight for the preservation of the Ambassador. According to the Los Angeles Conservancy's website, their preservation effort was the largest in the Conservancy's history, and the loss one of its greatest. The Conservancy worked for nearly two decades to halt the demolition of the hotel once it closed in 1989. But according to my mother, nothing could stop the blatant disregard for one of Los Angeles's most historic and important buildings.

The deed was done. On September 10, 2005, a final public auction was held for historians and those obsessed with the hotel. They all gathered in the hotel's parking lot to duke it out over the last remnants of a bygone era. Soon after the lot was emptied, the demolition began.

On January 16, 2006, the last section of the Ambassador Hotel fell. It took two years to build and only five months to destroy everything, except for a few famous sections, including the annex that housed the hotel's entrance, the shopping arcade along the Casino level, the Fountain Room coffee shop, and the Cocoanut Grove. These sections were promised to be preserved by the new owners and integrated into the high school. I think my mother hoped that the Cocoanut Grove would be returned to its original 1921 splendor, as she always referred to the 1970 remodel under the direction of Sammy Davis, Jr. as "tasteless and hideous." My mother was so furious that he turned the historic Cocoanut Grove into a tacky disco nightclub, installing chrome railings, disco balls, smoked glass mirrors, and a pink, purple, silver, red, and black color palette. Adding insult to injury, the remodeled room, renamed the "Now Grove," failed miserably and closed two years later.

The "Now Grove" at the Ambassador Hotel. Los Angeles, 2005. (Tom Zimmerman, Los Angeles County Building Survey Collection/Los Angeles Public Library)

A wake attended by hundreds of people was held for the Ambassador Hotel on February 2, 2006, at the Gaylord Apartments and the adjoining restaurant H.M.S. Bounty, both part of a historic 1924 building directly across the street from the Ambassador. The late actress Diane Keaton, one of many who fought and used their celebrity standing to bring more attention to the preservation of the hotel, was among the speakers at the ceremonial wake. My mother also spoke. Here are her brief and impassioned words:

> *"Until last March, the old girl across the street and I shared eighty-three years in this city. She was born January 1st, 1921, and four months later I came along—a close second.*
>
> *I always hoped if she could put on some new clothes, some comfy shoes, and a lot of rosy moisture lotion her bones could still hold up and she would have a new lease on life.*

Unfortunately, she couldn't afford a caretaker to put her together. We had a great time sharing living quarters for our first seventeen years and I will never forget those days.

And I'm still here, hoping the ghosts, both happy and sad, of those eighty-three years will stick around and find their way through the current mountains of debris and the new construction. Maybe they will slip into the minds of the new tenants and give them the gift to take in all the marvelous history surrounding them as they learn and play in classrooms and fields. Thank you."

The demolition of the Ambassador felt like the demolition of my mother's childhood. I remember she was depressed, hurt, and angry about how decisions were made and the promises that were broken. Mom wished she had done more, but she was honored to have fought the good fight alongside so many other Ambassador Hotel supporters. The fighting spirit to save the hotel wasn't just connected to preservationists and passionate Angelenos. The Ambassador's demolition was, and is, still seen by many as a tragic historical and architectural loss for Los Angeles.

Mourning a Lost L.A. Landmark

A February 2, 2006, Los Angeles Times article about the Ambassador Hotel's demise, featuring a photograph of Carlyn Frank Benjamin amid the rubble. (©2006 Los Angeles Times, reprinted with permission)

I want to be clear, my mother was a great supporter of public education and as described in earlier chapters, she founded a non-profit that provided free books to children in underserved neighborhood schools of Los Angeles. It wasn't that she objected to having a school built on the remains of the school grounds, it's that she believed certain iconic elements should have been preserved. Now here is where it gets tricky for me. The Robert F. Kennedy Community School opened in 2010, and Mom passed in 2017. I don't know the year in which she stopped working on her manuscript, which is why some important information about what was, and what was not preserved, was missing from her manuscript. Therefore, I felt it was important to understand and accurately convey where things landed in terms of what was and wasn't preserved. I wanted to see for myself whether what my mother reported was accurate, given the years between the school opening and her passing.

I reached out to the school, and one of the four principals (there are 4,000 students, so four principals makes sense!), Ms. Kwan, enthusiastically agreed to let my husband and me visit the Robert F. Kennedy Community School in November of 2025.

When the LAUSD was ready to build the new school, guarantees were made that a number of the hotel's most iconic elements would be preserved. The school would be built on the hotel's 24-acre footprint. The original design of the Ambassador was in the shape of an "H" and was six stories high. The school would retain one side of the "H" with its subtle curve, with six levels (true), for classrooms, study halls, student gathering, and other related facilities. The enormous port cochere, which made for a grand guest entrance to the Cocoanut Grove in the 1930s, would be kept, including the art deco clock (both were saved). The view from Wilshire Boulevard would evoke the original, familiar curve of the façade (it does).

The Cocoanut Grove would be returned to its original life (original, no, but in its spirit, yes). The ornate ceiling of the Embassy Ballroom would be saved and incorporated into the new campus (it was not saved but replicated). The former coffee shop, beautifully re-designed by Paul Williams, the renowned architect, would also be saved (design-wise, very close, but I know the coffee shop was not bathed in the color of a basket of tangerines!).

The LAUSD, citing structural integrity issues, had all but one wall of the Cocoanut Grove destroyed. Although the space was leveled, the former Cocoanut Grove now accommodates the school's auditorium and theater with 582 seats and is still nostalgically called the Cocoanut Grove. With a Moroccan-inspired motif, including a carpet with a whimsical palm tree print and a starry night ceiling, it captures the feeling of the original venue. Though it differs from the original Cocoanut Grove, I have to applaud the school for incorporating the Moroccan look and feel that was so intrinsic to the original design. It is a pleasant reimagining of a time long forgotten.

Interior of the Robert F. Kennedy "Cocoanut Grove" theater at the Robert F. Kennedy Community School. (Heliphoto. Architect: Practice (formerly Gonzalez Goodale Architects))

What just about took my breath away was walking up to the Cocoanut Grove Theater and seeing the legendary etched doors showcasing the famous palm trees and monkeys! Ms. Kwan said the doors were almost exact replicas of the originals. I'd say the architects pretty much nailed it.

The exterior doors to the Ambassador Hotel's original Cocoanut Grove. Los Angeles, 1930s. (Courtesy of Marc Wanamaker/Bison Archives)

The exterior doors to the Robert F. Kennedy Community School's Cocoanut Grove Theater. (Heliphoto. Architect: Practice (formerly Gonzalez Goodale Architects))

The Embassy Ballroom (the former Fiesta Room) became the school's library. Prior to demolition, LAUSD indicated that portions of the Ballroom would be saved and incorporated into the new campus. The architects replicated the high ceilings and the arched, recessed coves, creating a beautiful and welcoming library space. The back wall is arched and depicts Robert F. Kennedy with open arms greeting the outstretched arms of what I would imagine are students. It is an inspirational painting and lovely salute to the original Fiesta life mural that occupied the same spot back in the day. The remainder of the historic room was demolished. This was the room where Robert F. Kennedy gave his 1968 victory speech before he ventured out through the kitchen and was assassinated. Thus, its demise was welcomed by many, while others were upset that such a piece of profound, albeit tragic history, was not preserved.

The interior of the Robert F. Kennedy Community School library.
(Photo: Lisa Gilmour)

Interior view of the Ambassador Hotel's Fiesta Room. Los Angeles, circa 1930.
(Courtesy of Marc Wanamaker/Bison Archives)

The re-designed 1949 coffee shop became the teachers' lounge, thankfully retaining the iconic curved lunch counter and other interior elements from Williams's design. Just beyond the entrance to the teachers' lounge was a small portion of the original Casino Floor, with a number of empty shop windows that once enticed hotel guests to shop for just about anything they could want. I am grateful that I toured the school so I could see firsthand how the LAUSD interpreted the site's history. The issue of preservation was highly contentious, particularly given the expectations many had about what could and should have been saved. I know some people will disagree with me, including my mother, if she were still alive, but from what I observed, the school appears to have respected several important aspects of the hotel and made an effort to preserve some of the original architectural elements.

Because my mother never toured the campus after it opened in 2010, she never knew which elements of the Ambassador were incorporated into the school's design.

I should also mention that the school installed a set of glass display cases on either side of the walkway entrance to the library doors. These are dedicated to displaying a number of Ambassador artifacts, such as a bellman's uniform, branded dishes, menus, and other pieces of the past.

In my mind, what remains of the Ambassador Hotel is a thoughtful expression of design and architecture to honor its memory and to support the needs of the school.

Bird's-eye view of the Robert F. Kennedy Community School.
(Heliphoto. Architect: Practice (formerly Gonzalez Goodale Architects))

45

FULL CIRCLE

In 2013, Mom took a fall at home and badly broke her elbow. As she was unable to use the bannisters to walk up the stairs to her bedroom, we set up a bedroom in the den. Initially, it wasn't too bad. After all, this was everyone's favorite room in the house—cozy, with a wood- burning fireplace and the original gorgeous dark-stained pine paneling from 1931 with big, double-hung windows looking out at the front yard with its huge carrotwood tree shading one half of the house. Mom refused to let us put in a stair lift, because that was for "old people," she would say. Mom should have had surgery on her elbow, but the doctor felt it was too risky for a ninety-one-year-old.

The only good thing that came out of this event was my mom was no longer able to drive.

I had always insisted I should drive if we went to dinner or if she needed to run errands. She emphatically refused. She always would say that her response time was better than mine. It was useless for me to argue. I hated driving with her. The day I stashed her keys away was a huge relief to all family members—except, of course, Mom.

As a result of the broken elbow, her life became very sedentary; dementia took full advantage of that and boldly, without hesitation, stepped in.

Dementia is a thief that robs the mind of your loved ones. It lived in Mom's brain for four years. Although dementia significantly changed her personality, it never quieted her fear of dying. This fear was a persistent narrative that was hard to quell, because the fear was embedded and flowed from being unable to control the inevitable. She fought hard to stay with us.

On the morning of January 9, 2017, just four months shy of her ninety-sixth birthday, my mother passed away. Mark and I had been with her day and night for the two weeks leading up to her passing. She had two full-time caregivers who adored her and did everything to make her comfortable. I was in awe of their patience and resilience. Our son, Jamison, and his college roommate, Evan, stopped by a week or so before Mom passed. They played big band musical tunes on her CD player and read her poetry. It was incredibly touching and kind. Although her eyes were closed, I know she embraced the wonder of it.

Lying by her side the night before she passed, I knew she had already started to transition. Her eyes remained closed, and she was truly at peace. And then, the next morning, that dreaded moment arrived, and the stillness took hold. It is so profound. My mind was flooded with memories. It took me right back to being by my brother's side as he passed. That experience gave me the confidence to be with Mom as she took her last breath. I was grateful her passing was peaceful and quiet. Being with someone when they pass is extremely intimate.

I couldn't bear to see her taken from her home of fifty-three years. I went and laid down on the bed in my old room until I knew she was safely transported to the hearse. My husband told me that the kind people from the mortuary had placed a beautiful, dark green velvet blanket over Mom and gently carried her out of the house while a soft rain fell. When he told me, I gasped loudly, shocked, remembering she had been conceived in a green tent under a light rain nearly ninety-six years ago. It was such a full circle moment.

It has been a great honor and a gift for me to share my mother's remarkable life story with you. I hope the chapters about her life growing up at the Ambassador Hotel were interesting and painted a story of what Los Angeles was like in the 1920s and 1930s. I also hope you learned many things about the Ambassador you never knew before.

It was important for me to share my mom's post-Ambassador life with as much detail as I felt comfortable doing. It was always my hope that in the days before she passed, she would quietly let her heart and mind reflect upon how full, rich, and rewarding her entire life had been—not just those first seventeen years. I want to believe this is exactly what happened during her calm transition.

Carlyn Frank Benjamin touched the lives of so many people. I hope her story touched you.

I love you, Mom.

Mother and daughter Carlyn Frank Benjamin and Lisa Benjamin Gilmour, goofing around on their phones. Beverly Hills, California, circa 2001.
(Gilmour Family Collection)

Bea Frank and daughters Jackie and Carlyn at the Ambassador Hotel. Los Angeles, 1926. (Photo: Tycko, Gilmour Family Collection)

Carlyn Frank at John Burroughs Elementary School in 1931, age ten. (Gilmour Family Collection).

Carlyn Frank in 1939, age eighteen.
(Gilmour Family Collection)

Left to right, Carlyn Frank (age twenty-one), Jackie Frank (age fifteen),
Bea Frank, and Ben Frank, with the family dog, Lady. Los Angeles, 1942.
(Gilmour Family Collection)

Mr. and Mrs. Ben Benjamin dining at the Musso & Frank Grill. Hollywood, 1945.
(Gilmour Family Collection)

Carlyn Frank Benjamin. Los Angeles, 1946.
(Gilmour Family Collection)

Carlyn Frank Benjamin at the San Ysidro Ranch on her seventy-fifth birthday. Montecito, California, 1996. (Gilmour Family Collection)

www.ingramcontent.com/pod-product-compliance
Lightning Source LLC
Chambersburg PA
CBHW052354030726
47599CB00014B/1062